NEGOTIATING ARAB-ISRAELI PEACE

INDIANA SERIES IN ARAB AND ISLAMIC STUDIES

Salih J. Altoma, Iliya Harik, and Mark Tessler, *general editors*

NEGOTIATING **ARAB-ISRAELI** PEACE

PATTERNS, PROBLEMS, POSSIBILITIES

LAURA ZITTRAIN EISENBERG

AND

NEIL CAPLAN

INDIANA
UNIVERSITY
PRESS

Bloomington & Indianapolis

The paper used in this publication meets the minimum requirements of American National Standard for Information Sciences—Permanence of Paper for Printed Library Materials, ANSI Z39.48-1984.

Manufactured in the United States of America

Library of Congress Cataloging-in-Publication Data

Eisenberg, Laura Zittrain.
Negotiating Arab-Israeli peace : patterns, problems, possibilities / Laura Zittrain Eisenberg and Neil Caplan.
p. cm. — (Indiana series in Arab and Islamic studies)
Includes bibliographical references (p.) and index.
ISBN 0-253-33368-7 (cl : alk. paper). —
ISBN 0-253-21159-X (pbk. : alk. paper)
1. Israeli-Arab conflicts—Diplomatic history.
I. Caplan, Neil, date. II. Title. III. Series.
DS119.7.E353 1998
956.04—dc21 97-27408

1 2 3 4 5 03 02 01 00 99 98

CONTENTS

MAPS

PREFACE

This book seeks to provide a useful historical backdrop and paradigm for understanding the still unfinished business of the Arab-Israeli peace process. We have designed it with university courses in international relations, political science, and modern Middle Eastern history in mind.[1] At the same time, we hope that seasoned scholars of international relations and of the Arab-Israeli conflict will also find our premise and presentation cogent and convincing.

We write as historians who thrill to the exploration of past events via archival documents. We conceived of this book as an alternative to the flood of instant analysis and interpretation that has followed recent events in the often unpredictable Arab-Israeli drama. It represents our conviction that today's headlines follow naturally from the course of history, and that an understanding of current affairs is greatly enhanced by an appreciation of the past. Together, past and present events form a logical pattern with important implications for the future direction of this particular conflict and attempts to resolve it.

The basic structure of the book combines *case studies* with supporting primary documents. The case-study method allows us to apply our theory in a systematic way to successive episodes of Arab-Israeli negotiations. Each new peacemaking attempt is, after all, a new chapter in the same ongoing story. Our thesis is that there exists a historical pattern for failed Arab-Israeli negotiations, which contemporary diplomats must break if they are genuinely to advance the peace process. This pattern serves as the common thematic thread running through the case studies.

The reader will notice that within each chapter we have eschewed a strictly chronological narration of events in favor of seven subheadings characterizing traditional Arab-Israeli negotiating habits. Some students may have to work a little bit harder to pull together the storyline, but we believe they will be rewarded with a deeper and more analytical understanding of the processes at work. Mastery of the model will assist those readers who want to continue to follow unfolding events in the diplomatic roller-coaster ride we call the Arab-Israeli peace process.

The *documents* keyed to each case are critical to the relationship under review and should be read in tandem with the chapter text. Although we have tried to make our study as self-contained as possible, it is impossible to include every relevant document within the covers of a single volume.

We have therefore reproduced a selection of the most important documents in the Appendix, and give full references to others that are easily accessible in other published collections. There are a number of good documentary sourcebooks on the market, but we have chosen to refer regularly to three excellent anthologies for the majority of our documentary citations: *The Israeli-Palestinian Conflict: A Documentary Record, 1967–1990,* edited by Yehuda Lukacs,[2] *The Palestinian-Israeli Peace Agreement: A Documentary Record,* published by the Institute for Palestine Studies,[3] and the veteran *Israel-Arab Reader,* edited by Walter Laqueur and Barry Rubin.[4]

The stress on the importance of *primary documentation* reflects the authors' professional and pedagogical biases and preferences, which we share with readers from the outset. We firmly believe that maximum accuracy and authenticity demand a healthy respect for these primary sources, which are the building blocks of any balanced and comprehensive analysis. Here the disciplines of political science and history cannot function without each other.

All too often students are introduced to the raw material of diplomacy and policymaking through an interpreter's characterization only. Our classroom experience has taught us that students are perfectly capable of moving beyond an exclusive reliance upon second-hand analyses. We have watched them wrestle with the textual milestones of this conflict for themselves, read the protagonists' original language, and draw their own conclusions. Through this exercise they encounter firsthand the conflicting interpretations and experience the obstacles that peacemakers face in drafting mutually acceptable agreements. Original documentation, like no other source, reveals the true aims of the central characters, their psychology, and the often subtle tactical maneuvering at work. Secondary, after-the-fact interpretations—including ours presented here—should always be subjected to cross-referencing with authoritative primary sources as they become available. This is one way of keeping the study of international diplomacy honest, periodically weeding out partial or faulty explanations and replacing them with fuller and more convincing ones.

Another peculiar feature of our approach is a wish to share with our readers the richness and complexity of the *secondary sources and other authors* upon whom we must also draw in reaching our conclusions. The course of international conflict is intricate, but any presentation necessarily requires some measure of simplification and omission. To compensate, we include chapter endnotes perhaps longer and more generous than usual. Along with the standard brief citations for the sources of an idea or quotation, we also refer readers to other books and articles that deal with secondary aspects or conflicting analyses of issues treated in our main text. Students in search of paper topics will find our full notes an excellent starting point for further research. As such, we have emphasized English-language sources in this account, but we encourage serious students to develop the Arabic and Hebrew language skills required for more comprehensive research.

We have endeavored to impart to the reader our sensitivity to the historical depth of the Arab-Israeli conflict and the immensity of the challenge facing those who would resolve it. We write with sad certainty that more bloodshed and crises lie ahead. Whether bold leaders will persevere on the uncharted path to peace remains to be seen; the choice lies with them. As historians, we appreciate the constant pull of the past on the present, yet recognize that the future is not bound by any iron laws of historical determinism. We agree with a scholar who has written,

> Not all historical injustices can be eliminated and most will not be forgotten. But the past need not determine the future, just as the history and evolution of the conflict were not preordained. Israelis and [Arabs] can break with the past if they have the political will to do so. . . . [I]t is on the parties themselves, and not on history, that the future depends.[5]

Finally, we are happy to acknowledge the assistance of our colleagues who gave of their time and expertise in critiquing our model and analysis of Arab-Israeli negotiating efforts. Thanks are also due to students at the University of Pittsburgh and Carnegie Mellon University who took drafts of this volume on semester-long test drives. We are delighted with the contributions of the many cartoonists who gave so generously of their art and imagination, particularly Rob Rogers of the *Pittsburgh Post Gazette*. We also thank his associates nationwide: Steve Benson, Matt Davies, Chan Lowe, Jeff MacNelly, Jimmy Margulies, Tim Menees, Mike Peters, and Dwane Powell. We are especially grateful to Professor Mark Tessler for his encouragement, and to Janet Rabinowitch and Dee Mortensen of Indiana University Press for their kindly professionalism in handling this manuscript and its authors.

Any errors or inaccuracies, of course, are of our own devising alone.

NOTES

1. An instructor's guide to using *Negotiating Arab-Israeli Peace* in the college classroom is available from the publisher. Contact the text department at Indiana University Press, 601 North Morton Street, Bloomington, Indiana 47404-3797 or iupress@indiana.edu.

2. Yehuda Lukacs, ed., *The Israeli-Palestinian Conflict: A Documentary Record, 1967–1990*. Cambridge and New York: Cambridge University Press, 1992.

3. Institute for Palestine Studies, *The Palestinian-Israeli Peace Agreement: A Documentary Record*. 2nd edition, Washington, DC: Institute for Palestine Studies, 1994.

4. Walter Laqueur and Barry Rubin, eds., *The Israel-Arab Reader: A Documentary History of the Middle East Conflict*, 5th rev. and updated edition, New York: Penguin, 1995.

5. Mark Tessler, *A History of the Israeli-Palestinian Conflict*, Bloomington: Indiana University Press, 1994, xiv.

LIST OF ABBREVIATIONS

CMD	Command Paper
DOP	Declaration of Principles
IDF	Israel Defense Forces
ILMAC	Israel-Lebanon Mixed Armistice Commission
IPS	Institute for Palestine Studies
JA	Jewish Agency for Palestine
JAE	Jewish Agency Executive
JPI	*Jerusalem Post International Edition* (w/e = week ending)
JPS	*Journal of Palestine Studies*
JR	*Jerusalem Report*
MAC	Mixed Armistice Commission
MFA	Israeli Ministry of Foreign Affairs
NYT	*New York Times*
PA	Palestinian (National) Authority
PCC	United Nations Conciliation Commission on Palestine
PLO	Palestine Liberation Organization
PNC	Palestine National Council
UN	United Nations
UNEF	United Nations Emergency Force
UNGA	United Nations General Assembly
UNIFIL	United Nations Interim Force in Lebanon
UNSC	United Nations Security Council

NOTE ON SOURCES

The overwhelming majority of sources cited in the notes and bibliography are available at any university library. For access to an unpublished lecture, contact either the lecturer or the host institution and request a copy. Many of the individuals and institutions are on e-mail or the world wide web. Documents provided by the Israeli Ministry of Foreign Affairs, Information Division (MFA), are available from the Ministry's web sites, http://www.israel-mfa.gov.il or http://www.israel.org/peace, or by e-mail from ask@israel-info.gov.il. The Institute for Palestine Studies (http://www.cais.com/ipsjps) and the Palestinian National Authority (http://www.pna.org/mininfo) may soon offer documents at their web sites, under construction at the time of this writing.

Map 1, The Arab-Israeli Arena, reprinted with permission from the Brookings Institution. Source: William B. Quandt, *The Middle East Ten Years After Camp David* (Washington: Brookings, 1988).

Map 2, Palestine under the British Mandate, 1920, adapted with permission from Mark Tessler, *A History of the Israeli-Palestinian Conflict* (Bloomington: Indiana University Press, 1994).

Map 3, United Nations General Assembly Partition Plan, 1947; Map 4, Israeli Borders and Armistice Lines, 1949; and Map 5, Israel Occupied Territories, 1967, reprinted with permission from Mark Tessler, *A History of the Israeli-Palestinian Conflict* (Bloomington: Indiana University Press, 1994).

NEGOTIATING ARAB-ISRAELI PEACE

Introduction

HISTORICAL PATTERNS

There has been something surreal about Arab-Israeli negotiations in the 1990s and the rapid assimilation of ideas and images previously considered fantastical. It is unclear which is more stunning: that first public handshake in September 1993 between Israeli Prime Minister Yitzhak Rabin and Yasir Arafat, Chairman of the Palestine Liberation Organization (PLO), on the White House lawn—or the rapidity with which Israeli-PLO meetings have become routine. We have become accustomed to the juxtaposition of two contradictory scenes: regular meetings between Arab and Israeli leaders, and continuing confrontations among the protagonists on the ground.

In October 1991 a peace conference in Madrid brought all the parties together. That the mere presence of high-ranking Arab and Israeli politicians in the same room was cause for such celebration reflects how many steps backward from coexistence the adversaries had taken over the years. But, while most observers realize that these breakthroughs interrupt a century of intense conflict, many are relatively unaware that today's leaders are also heirs to a long history of Arab-Zionist negotiation attempts.

That history has been, of course, a dismal record of failures to achieve peace. The apparently successful conclusion of several Arab-Israeli agreements since 1978 is a happy departure from that tradition.[1] But difficulties in implementing those fragile accords persist, and other aspects of the Arab-Israeli and Palestinian-Israeli conflicts are proving resistant to negotiated solutions. Both proponents and opponents of various peace efforts have paid for their convictions with their lives. The cycle of hostility accompanying this many-layered and protracted dispute is not so easily broken.

One of the premises of this book is that the success or failure of contemporary negotiation attempts may be better understood (although not always predicted) by a reexamination of the historical patterns dating

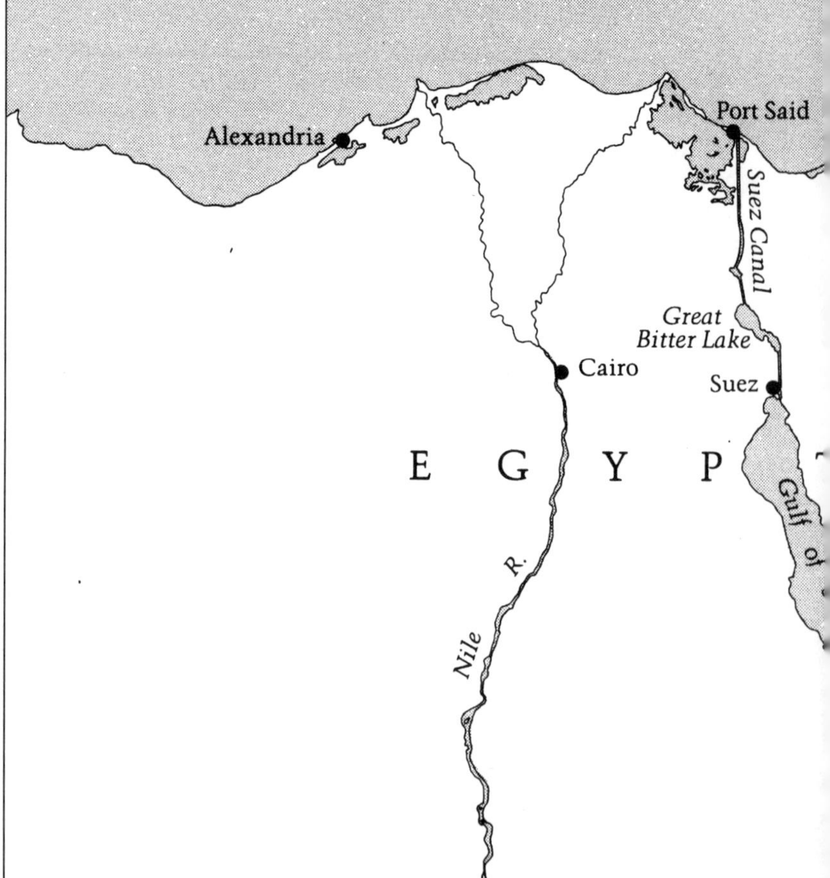
Map 1
The Arab-Israeli Arena
Mediterranean Sea
Alexandria
Port Said
Suez Canal
Great
Bitter Lake
Cairo
Suez
EGYPT
Gulf of
Nile R.

LEBANON
Beirut
Litani R.
Damascus
SYRIA
Tyre
GOLAN
HEIGHTS
Lake Tiberias
Haifa
Nazareth
Irbid
ISRAEL
Nablus
Jordan R.
WEST
BANK
Tel Aviv
Amman
Jerusalem
Hebron
GAZA
STRIP
Gaza
Dead Sea
Rafah
Beersheba
Al-Arish
JORDAN
INAI
Eilat
Taba
Aqaba
Gulf of Aqaba
Mt. Sinai
SAUDI ARABIA
Sharm
al-Sheikh
Red Sea

Courtesy of Rob Rogers, *Pittsburgh Post Gazette*

back to the end of World War I, and by carefully assessing the ways in which current episodes diverge from—or mirror—past negotiating experiences. We take as our point of departure Neil Caplan's article, "Negotiation and the Arab-Israeli Conflict,"[2] which was written on the eve of the 1977 Egyptian-Israeli breakthrough. Caplan examined the course of multiple failed Zionist-Arab efforts to negotiate a settlement before 1948 and identified characteristics common to all and largely responsible for their failure. In applying Caplan's analysis to the various Arab-Israeli peace processes since 1977, we measure six contemporary examples of negotiations, some apparently successful, against the historical patterns identified below, looking for both similarities and differences. The traditional obstacles to successful Arab-Zionist / Israeli diplomacy revealed seven recurring areas of diplomatic difficulty; accordingly, in the chapters following this introduction, we shall examine each case study under seven headings:

- previous experience negotiating together;
- variety of purposes and motives for entering into negotiation;
- questions of timing that affected decisions to enter into, or refrain from, negotiation;
- status of negotiating partners;
- effect of third-party involvement;
- proposed terms of agreement;
- psychological factors affecting both leaders and followers.

Our examination frequently refers to the three "p" words in the subtitle of this book. By *"patterns,"* we mean those behaviors, strategies, and outcomes common to most Arab-Jewish contacts since the Weizmann-Faisal talks of 1918–1919. *"Problems"* reflects the failure of those meetings to produce peace and suggests that, to the extent those patterns still hold true, contemporary negotiation efforts will similarly fail. "*Possibilities*" refers to the prospect that a genuine change in circumstances, purpose, aspirations, or leadership may break the historical pattern and lead to genuine peace.

Our hypothesis is that, the more closely negotiations follow the old patterns, the less likely they are to succeed. Hopes for resolution of this conflict rest on deviating from those patterns in very specific directions. Our paradigm is based on decades of failed negotiations, but can explain successful efforts as well. Whatever the fate of existing agreements and ongoing talks, we believe this model provides a valid tool of analysis.

AN OVERVIEW OF THE ARAB-ISRAELI CONFLICT, 1880–1977

The contemporary conflict between Jews and Arabs in the Middle East is really two separate but intertwined struggles. One is the battle between Jews and Arabs for control of the Land of Israel / Palestine. The other is the conflict between Israel and the Arab states over the establishment of a Jewish state in the heart of the Muslim Arab world, and over conventional issues like borders, resources, and territory lost and won in the cycle of wars between them.

The origins of the Israeli-Palestinian conflict lie in the clash of two fledgling nationalisms, Jewish and Arab. Zionism, the political expression of Jewish nationalism, developed in Europe in the 1880s.[3] Suffering harsh anti-Jewish persecution in the Russian Empire in the east and smoldering antisemitism in the supposedly enlightened countries of western Europe, Jewish intellectuals proposed to normalize Jewish existence within the international community by establishing a Jewish state. Drawn to Palestine by a 2,000-year-old dream of returning to the biblical land of their ancestors, small numbers of Jews began coming to Palestine at the end of the nineteenth century, intending to establish there a Jewish National Home and a haven from persecution.

At the same time, the peoples of the Middle East were beginning to consider their fate in light of the impending dissolution of the political order established under the Ottoman Empire. Arab nationalists espoused the idea of independence from both Turkish and western domination.[4] Their goal was the establishment of a vast Arab nation under Arab rule, although regional rivalries emerged over who should lead this new state and from what seat of power. In the area of Palestine, Arab inhabitants tended to identify themselves with a local family or clan, or looked to Damascus for leadership of and membership in this wider pan-Arab nation.

Zionism focused on Palestine but largely overlooked the Arabs already living there, seeing them as residents of the larger Ottoman Empire but not as a Palestinian national people. Indeed, in many respects, Zionism itself

Mediterranean Sea

SYRIA
(French Mandate)

Beirut
Damascus
Tyre
Haifa
Jordan R.
Tel Aviv
Jaffa
Amman
Jerusalem
Gaza
Rafah
Dead Sea
Beersheba

ARABIA

EGYPT
Aqaba

Red Sea

0 50 100
Miles

Map 2

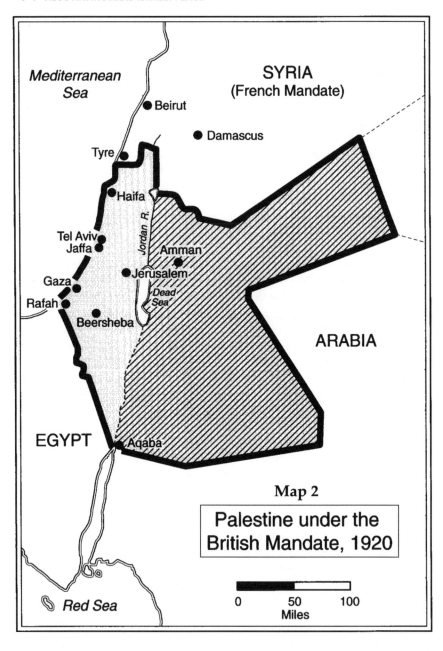

Palestine under the British Mandate, 1920

Area ceded by Great Britain to Amir Abdallah as the autonomous principality of Transjordan, 1921.

helped to create a distinctive Palestinian peoplehood, by confronting the local populace with a unique challenge not directly encountered by Arabs elsewhere.[5]

Between 1918 and 1948 the British controlled Palestine, for two years as a temporary military occupation force and thereafter under a Mandate from the League of Nations, the forerunner of today's United Nations (UN) (see Map 2). As Jewish immigration and settlement increased, so did Arab opposition. The willingness of many Arab landowners to sell property in Palestine to Jews persuaded many Zionists that the Arabs would eventually reconcile themselves to the establishment of a Jewish state, and led them to underestimate the seriousness of popular demonstrations against Jewish immigration and settlement.[6] For Zionists, the Holocaust proved the necessity and urgency for a Jewish refuge in Palestine; Arabs objected to a Middle Eastern solution to what they saw as a European problem.

For three decades, the British struggled to accommodate and then restrain the opposing Jewish and Arab national communities under their rule. In 1947 Great Britain turned its Palestine burden over to the UN, and in November of that year the General Assembly passed a resolution to partition Palestine into two states, one Jewish and one Arab (see Map 3).[7] Arab rejection of Jewish sovereignty in any part of Palestine was absolute, however, and Jewish-Arab fighting within Palestine erupted immediately. Following the departure of the British and the mid-May 1948 declaration of an independent Jewish state, the surrounding Arab states invaded Israel in support of their Palestinian brethren and with an eye toward territorial gain for themselves. The first Arab-Israeli war created hundreds of thousands of Palestinian-Arab refugees, and by the time the armistices of 1949 were signed, there was no longer an Arab Palestine.[8] As a result of the fighting, Israel's borders extended beyond what the UN partition plan had suggested, and the rest of what had been slated as a Palestinian-Arab state came under the control of Egypt (the Gaza Strip along the Mediterranean coast) and Transjordan (the West Bank of the Jordan river and the Old City of Jerusalem, which were quickly annexed to create the enlarged Hashemite Kingdom of Jordan) (see Map 4). For the last half century, the Palestinian-Israeli conflict has been a continuation of this struggle between Jews and Palestinian Arabs fighting for security and national self-determination in what both consider their ancestral homeland.

The Arab-Israeli conflict, superimposed on the original Zionist-Palestinian dispute, took shape as a battle between Zionists trying to maintain their Jewish state and the surrounding Arab states who vigorously opposed the very idea of Jewish sovereignty in their midst. After 1948, the struggle evolved into a more conventional interstate conflict between Israel and its Arab neighbors. Israel and Egypt fought a war in the Sinai Peninsula in 1956. During the June war of 1967, Israel captured large swaths of territory from its enemies, namely the Sinai Peninsula and the Gaza Strip from Egypt, the Golan Heights from Syria, and the West Bank

LEBANON
SYRIA
Safad
Acre
Haifa
Sea
of
Galilee
Nazareth
Mediterranean
Sea
Jordan R.
Nablus
Tel Aviv
Jaffa
Amman
Jerusalem
Dead Sea
Hebron
Gaza
Rafah
Beersheba
TRANSJORDAN
EGYPT
United Nations
General Assembly
Partition Plan, 1947
Jewish State
Arab State
Permanent Trusteeship
0
20
40
Miles
Aqaba

Map 3

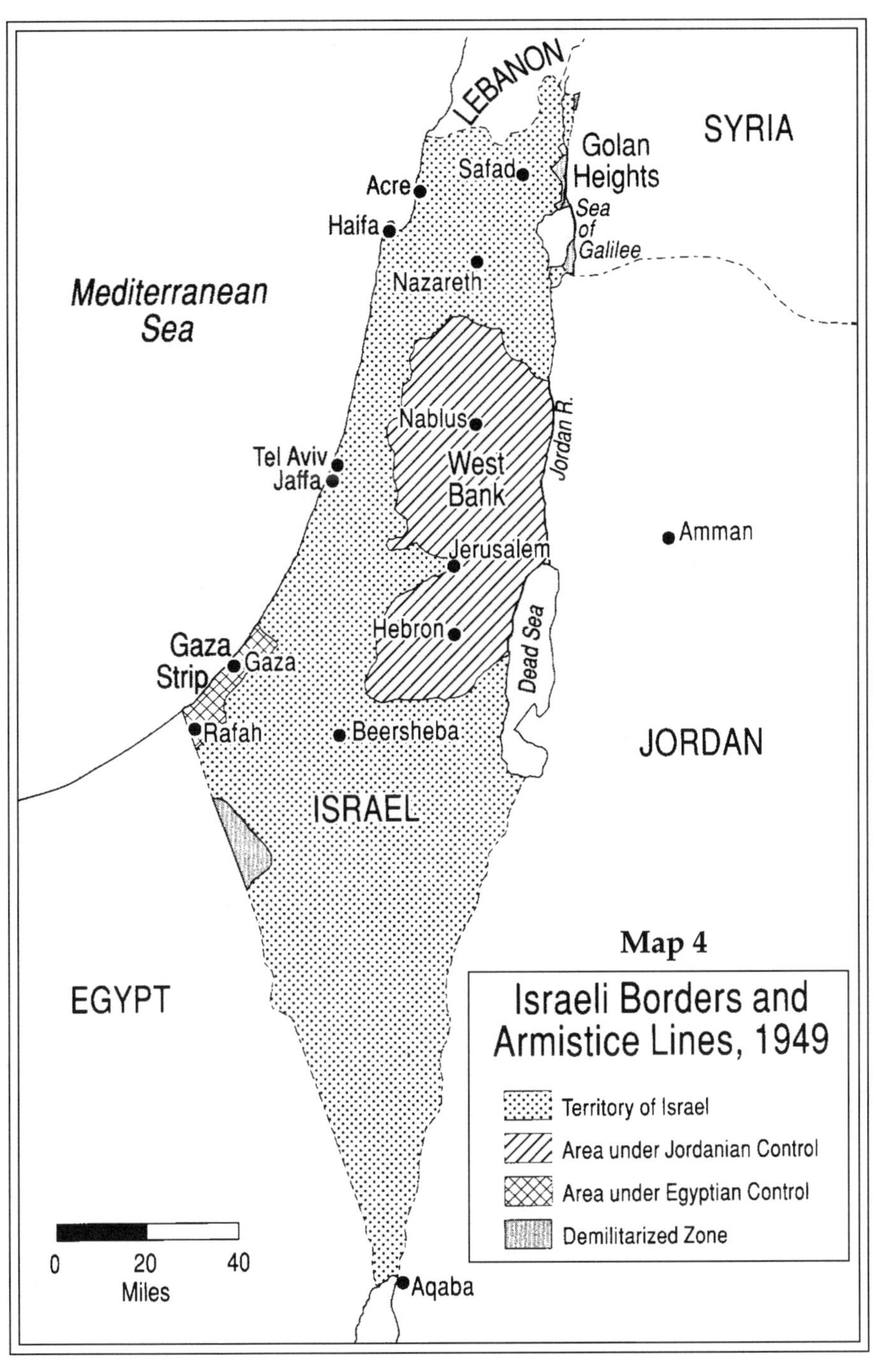
LEBANON
SYRIA
Golan Heights
Safad
Acre
Haifa
Sea of Galilee
Nazareth
Mediterranean Sea
Nablus
Jordan R.
Tel Aviv
Jaffa
West Bank
Amman
Jerusalem
Hebron
Dead Sea
Gaza Strip
Gaza
Rafah
Beersheba
JORDAN
ISRAEL
EGYPT
Israeli Borders and Armistice Lines, 1949
Territory of Israel
Area under Jordanian Control
Area under Egyptian Control
Demilitarized Zone
0
20
40
Miles
Aqaba

Map 4

Map 5
Israel and
Occupied Territories, 1967
Israel before 1967
Occupied Territory
Beirut
LEBANON
Damascus
SYRIA
Haifa
Golan
Heights
Nablus
West
Bank
Jordan R.
Tel Aviv
Amman
Jerusalem
Mediterranean
Sea
Gaza
Strip
Hebron
Gaza
Dead
Sea
Port Said
al-Arish
Beersheba
ISRAEL
Suez Canal
Ismailia
JORDAN
Cairo
Suez
Sinai
Eilat
Aqaba
EGYPT
Gulf of Suez
Gulf of Aqaba
SAUDI
ARABIA
Sharm al-Sheikh
0
50
100
Miles
Red Sea

and Old City of Jerusalem from Jordan (see Map 5). A new generation of Palestinians swelled the refugee camps in the Arab countries surrounding Israel. Those who remained in their homes in the West Bank and Gaza came under Israeli military occupation. Israel hoped to trade the captured land for peace treaties, but the Arab states would accept only an unconditional Israeli withdrawal.[9] Palestinian voices called variously for repatriation, compensation, and the establishment of a Palestinian state in place of the Israeli one.

In the wake of the 1967 war, relations deteriorated further between Israel and the Palestinians in the occupied territories and between Israel and its Arab neighbors. Another war in October of 1973 suggested that, barring some stunning diplomatic breakthrough, the Middle East was doomed to erupt into open warfare at least once every decade. No such breakthrough appeared imminent, however, and the Middle East remained one of the most volatile tinderboxes in the latter part of the twentieth century.

ARAB-ZIONIST CONTACTS AND NEGOTIATIONS, 1918–1948

The seeds of the modern Arab-Israeli conflict were primarily sown between the start of British rule in Palestine in December 1917 and Israeli independence in May 1948. The first half of the British Mandate period was marked by increasing Jewish immigration and settlement and recurring outbreaks of Arab violence, alternating with British commissions of inquiry and policy statements (known as White Papers). In 1936, a general strike and large-scale Arab revolt broke out against the British Mandate and Zionism, spreading to all parts of Palestine. The British finally suppressed the Arab rebellion in early 1939, but during the 1940s it was the turn of Jewish underground groups to revolt against British rule.

Against this background, and even while many observers recognized the inherent irreconcilability of Arab and Zionist aims, leading Zionists and Arabs met informally on dozens, if not hundreds, of occasions, during which they debated, and sometimes negotiated about, the conflict developing between them. Zionist emissaries traveled unimpeded throughout most of the Arab world and secured audiences with principal Arab politicians, editors, religious leaders, and businessmen, most of whom rejected the Zionist program in Palestine, but received their Zionist visitors hospitably, nonetheless. An Arab-Zionist accommodation over Palestine may have seemed as unlikely then as it did in the early 1990s, but direct contacts between Arabs and Zionists were in and of themselves not considered the breakthrough they seem today.

What were the major negotiation episodes and opportunities of the 1918–48 period? Who were the personalities, and what were the issues involved? The earliest, and perhaps the most famous, was the accord reached between Dr. Chaim Weizmann, president of the Zionist Organization and future president of Israel (1948–52), and Amir Faisal ibn Hussein, son of the British-backed sharif of Mecca, and future king of Iraq (1921–33). The British-inspired reconciliation aimed at harmonizing Arab and Zionist post–World War I aspirations and making them compatible with British and French plans to maintain direct and indirect control over much of the Middle East. By the terms of the Weizmann-Faisal "treaty" signed in January 1919, Weizmann recognized Faisal as the head of a proposed Arab Kingdom (outside of Palestine) while Faisal seemed to recognize Jewish claims to Palestine as outlined in the Balfour Declaration. The latter historic document, issued 2 November 1917, had announced Britain's conditional support for the creation of a "Jewish national home in Palestine."[10] Between the lines of their entente, Zionists expected Faisal to influence the Palestinians to moderate their demands for full independence in exchange for anticipated benefits to his future kingdom from Jewish capital, technical skills, and international political support. This "exchange-of-services" approach became the preferred Zionist model for accommodation with the Arabs. The Weizmann-Faisal agreement was never implemented, however, largely because of the main parties' respective inability—as minor actors on the world stage, dependent on the goodwill of England and France—to "deliver the goods" each expected from the other.[11]

A second source of Arab-Zionist pre-1948 negotiating experience was the sustained relationship between Zionists and Faisal's brother, Abdallah ibn Hussein, amir and later king of Transjordan. Secret good-neighborly relations between Abdallah and prominent Zionist officials began in the early 1920s and took on more serious political dimensions during the 1930s, when the Transjordanian ruler was wooed by factions both for and against the partition of Palestine.[12] When the fate of Palestine hung in the balance after 1945, Abdallah's and the Zionists' common interests drew them closer. Their efforts to divide the land on the West Bank of the Jordan River between Transjordan and a new Jewish state has led Uri Bar-Joseph to describe their relationship as "the best of enemies."[13]

Zionist leaders also attempted to build bridges with politicians in the other lands surrounding Palestine and established contacts with a number of prominent Iraqi, Egyptian, Syrian, and Lebanese personalities.[14] Some of these contacts were of only limited duration, while others developed into sustained and passably good relationships over the years. Zionists considered supporting plans for an Arab federation in exchange for Jewish sovereignty in a part of the country. Some hoped that Palestinian Arabs would replace their local attachments with a wider nationalism in a way that would have allowed for Jewish self-government in Palestine.

The Zionist search for agreeable negotiating partners outside of Palestine took another twist with the development of a "minority-alliance" approach to Middle East relations. Some Zionist strategists, skeptical of reaching a compromise with either the Palestinian Arabs or the Sunni Muslim majority in the region, focused their attentions on forging bonds with other non-Arab and non–Sunni Muslim communities in the Middle East. To their way of thinking, potential allies included the Druze, Shi'a, Copts, Kurds, and especially the politically powerful Maronite Catholics in Lebanon. The logic of "my enemy's enemy is my friend" sustained a decades-long relationship between the Jewish Agency for Palestine and one particular Maronite faction, both of which struggled against Muslim Arab opposition to their aspirations for Jewish and Christian national homes in Palestine and Lebanon, respectively.[15] Their shaky alliance against the anticolonial, anti-European thrust of the new Arab nationalism that swept through the region in the interwar years was essentially a reaffirmation of the classic "exchange-of-services" model for Zionist-Arab cooperation. In exchange for providing political, diplomatic, and material support for the cause of Christian Lebanon, the Zionists hoped for Christian Lebanese support in persuading the other Arab countries, and the Palestinian Arabs, to accept the establishment of a Jewish state in Palestine. But this relationship, as with all the other Zionist contacts with "outsiders," amounted to little when the recognized Arab leadership *inside* Palestine proved unresponsive to pressure to compromise its desire to maintain the existing Arab majority and Arab character of the country.[16]

The limited possibilities of a Zionist-Palestinian accord were explored, mostly during the early and middle 1930s, in less frequent talks inside Palestine itself. Many of the contacts involved senior Zionist policymakers, such as David Ben-Gurion (then Chairman of the Jewish Agency Executive [JAE] and later Prime Minister of Israel), Moshe Shertok (later Sharett, head of the JAE Political Department and later Foreign Minister of Israel), and their officials. The basic Zionist approach was to work for an arrangement under which the Palestinian Arab inhabitants of the future Jewish Palestine would be content to relinquish control over part of their homeland in exchange for being the first to share in the economic blessings that Zionist development would bring to the entire region. Even more frequent were unofficial overtures from controversial personalities from the *yishuv* (the Jewish community of Palestine), who championed a binational solution not in keeping with official Zionist policy.[17]

Only a few Palestinian spokesmen, such as Awni Abd al-Hadi, Omar Salih al-Barghuthi, and Musa Alami, were willing, on occasion, to enter into face-to-face dialogue with important *yishuv* and Zionist figures. The ranking leader of the factionalized Palestinian Arab community, the Mufti of Jerusalem, al-Haj Amin al-Husseini, wielded much greater influence than these individuals but was not inclined to negotiate. Leading notables of the rival Nashashibi family, on the other hand, were not averse to talks with the Zionists, but commanded considerably less popular support.

None of the "negotiations" that took place between Zionists and Palestinian Arabs aimed at achieving a mutually satisfactory solution to their conflict over the future of Mandatory Palestine. The political issues that dominated the discussions included immediate practical concerns such as the appropriate levels of Jewish immigration, communal representation in self-governing bodies, hardships caused by the Arab general strike, and proposals in the late 1930s for the future political status of the country.[18] Usually, contacts occurred when one party or another wanted to forestall some undesirable British action. Two examples of such motivation were (1) Zionist hopes to avoid schemes for setting up a legislative council in 1928–29 and 1933–36, which might have led to majority Arab self-government, and (2) Arab fears of the implementation of the Peel Commission's recommendations for partition during 1937–38.[19] The few alliances achieved between Zionists and Palestinian Arabs were tactical and temporary, based on only short-term advantage, such as electoral politics in mixed municipalities.[20]

Several times during the 1920s and 1930s, the British summoned Arab and Zionist leaders to London, but all attempts at dialogue failed.[21] With war looming in Europe, His Majesty's Government attempted to defuse the Palestine problem by unilaterally imposing a temporary settlement in the form of the MacDonald White Paper of May 1939. Both Jews and Arabs reacted with anger to the limits it placed on Jewish immigration and land ownership. For the Arabs, these limits did not go far enough, while for the Jews they went too far.[22]

Despite the optimism about ultimate Jewish-Arab reconciliation expressed for public relations or produced by wishful thinking, leading figures on both sides concluded, at an early stage, that Zionist and Palestinian goals in Palestine were simply incompatible. "We, as a nation, want this country to be *ours*," Ben-Gurion declared in 1919; "the Arabs, as a nation, want this country to be *theirs*." Even before his mid-1934 meeting with Ben-Gurion, Palestinian leader Awni Abd al-Hadi had similarly recognized the harsh reality that "the goal of the Jews was to take over the country and the goal of the Arabs was to fight against that takeover."[23]

Once the British decided in 1947 to turn the question of Palestine over to the United Nations, the struggle for Palestine shifted to two arenas: world capitals and the United Nations, where the Jewish Agency unleashed a vigorous lobbying campaign; and the battlefields inside and along the frontiers of Palestine, where both parties tried to create facts on the ground. The few high-level attempts at reconciliation at the eleventh hour proved too little, too late.[24]

ARAB-ISRAELI CONTACTS AND NEGOTIATIONS, 1948–1977

After several phases of fighting and ceasefires, the first Arab-Israeli war ended in early 1949 with separate armistices negotiated directly between Israel and each of four "confrontation states" with the help of United Nations mediator, Dr. Ralph Bunche. In January 1949, Egypt and Israel became the first of the antagonists to sit down to armistice negotiations on the Mediterranean Island of Rhodes. These talks became the model for similar agreements signed shortly thereafter by Jordan, Lebanon, and Syria, but also served as a prototype for a negotiating format recommended for years afterward by Israelis and would-be mediators.[25]

The United Nations Conciliation Commission for Palestine (or Palestine Conciliation Commission [PCC]) attempted to capitalize on the positive experience at Rhodes by putting the remaining unresolved issues of refugees and territorial claims on the agenda of successive peace conferences convened in Lausanne (1949), Geneva (1950), and Paris (1951). The Arab states' unwillingness to recognize and deal with the Jewish state and the Israelis' refusal to consider Arab demands for a return of Palestinian-Arab refugees led the PCC to abandon its quest for a comprehensive solution.[26]

Following the Egyptian revolution of July 1952, Prime Minister Gamal Abd al-Nasir and Israeli Foreign Minister Moshe Sharett explored the prospects of rapprochement through secret channels in Paris. In the deteriorating situation that preceded the 1956 Suez Crisis, British and US intermediaries engineered top-secret diplomatic maneuvers between Egypt and Israel, code-named "Operation Alpha." But many months of intensive Anglo-American mediation activity between Egypt and Israel ultimately failed to persuade Nasir to enter into direct negotiations with Israel.[27]

In late 1956, war erupted between Egypt and Israel. The "Sinai Campaign" (or "Suez War") ended with the withdrawal of invading Israeli, British, and French forces from Egyptian soil under combined US and UN pressure.[28] The UN created and sent a United Nations Emergency Force (UNEF) to take up positions along the Egyptian-Israeli border. Some of the Mixed Armistice Commissions (MACs), established under the 1949 armistice régimes to deal with routine issues of border control, continued to meet. Given the growing Arab rejection of direct dealings with Israel, these bodies were often the only points of contact between the unreconciled states, and the decade following the 1956 war saw few attempts at Arab-Israeli negotiation.

The June 1967 war between Israel and Egypt, Jordan, and Syria saw a decisive Israeli victory in six days, leaving Israel in control of the Sinai Peninsula, Gaza Strip, West Bank, and Golan Heights. This created a tangible quid-pro-quo situation, and would-be negotiators promoted the concept of a "land-for-peace" deal between Israel and the Arab states. No such exchange materialized, however. The Arab states persisted in their nonrecognition of the State of Israel, and Israel grew more attached to the territories that some diplomats hoped to use as bargaining chips.

On the diplomatic front, one could point only to the passage of UN Security Council (UNSC) Resolution 242 in November 1967, calling, among other things, for "the withdrawal of Israeli armed forces from

Courtesy of Dwane Powell, *News and Observer*

territories occupied in the recent conflict." (See Appendix, Document 1.) Resolution 242 became a benchmark for almost every attempt at Arab-Israeli peacemaking for the next quarter century. Crucial ambiguities in the text—notably, the omission of the definite article "the" from the phrase "withdrawal from territories occupied in the recent conflict"—led to legalistic wrangling over the obligations imposed on the parties, in particular whether the resolution obliged Israel to withdraw from *all* of the territories captured in the 1967 war.[29] The failure of the resolution to refer to the Palestinians or address any of their claims provided a source of future complications. Although many Israelis hoped that this resolution, asserting the right of "every state . . . to live in peace within secure and recognized boundaries" (and backed by their decisive victories on the ground), would convince Arab leaders that the Jewish state was here to stay and an inevitable partner for negotiations, Arab refusal to deal directly with Israel became even more entrenched in the aftermath of the 1967 war.

The war of October 1973 finally led to some moderately successful mediation activities and the hope of a breakthrough in the ever-worsening dispute. On the international-legal level, the UNSC passed Resolution 338, which extended the force of Resolution 242 (1967) by calling upon the parties to enter into negotiations.[30] In a flurry of postwar diplomatic maneuvering, US Secretary of State Henry Kissinger moved the ex-combatants from ceasefire accords toward disengagement agreements, while orchestrating a brief international conference in Geneva in December 1973. In the short term, it achieved little apart from the symbolic, momentary act of having an Israeli delegation in the same room as Egyptian and Jordanian delegations.[31] The true usefulness of Geneva, however, was its function as a legitimizing umbrella under which Kissinger embarked upon several rounds of personalized, jet-setting diplomacy, building upon progress made during direct Egyptian-Israeli military negotiations in the famous tent at kilometer-101 along the Cairo-Suez road, and producing parallel disengagement agreements between Israel and Syria and between Israel and Egypt.[32] The latter constituted the prelude to the dramatic breakthrough achieved by President Jimmy Carter, President Anwar Sadat and Prime Minister Menachem Begin during 1977–79.

NEGOTIATION PATTERNS 1918–1977

An overview of the cumulative negotiating experience of Zionists/Israelis and Arabs since 1918 reveals several repeating patterns that essentially constitute an operating manual for how to *fail* to achieve peace. By analyzing contemporary peacemaking efforts within the framework of this historical continuum, we can determine where they fall into the pattern of earlier failed diplomatic encounters, and where they deviate, encouragingly, from the historical model. We can best understand these patterns by first considering five familiar explanations for the lack of peace in Palestine prior to 1948, explanations that have their equivalents in the post-1948 period:

- Zionist/Israeli failure to appreciate the legitimacy of Palestinian-Arab national sentiment and aspirations;
- Arab failure to recognize the legitimacy of Jewish-Zionist national sentiment and aspirations;
- third-party pursuit of selfish interests and machinations that undermined chances for Zionist-Arab reconciliation;
- the lack of direct contact and resulting misunderstandings between Arabs and Zionists/Israelis; and
- the persistence of passionately held but genuinely irreconcilable national goals.

While there is some merit in all of these, the last explanation seems to us the most compelling on the basis of the historical record. Indeed, as the above-quoted remarks of David Ben-Gurion and Awni Abd al-Hadi illustrate, many leading Zionists and Palestinian Arabs themselves realized, quite clearly and long before 1948, the immensity of the gulf separating their minimum demands.

If the parties recognized that their goals are essentially incompatible, why, then, have there been so many negotiation attempts? The answer requires an appreciation of how early Arabs and Zionists re-interpreted the standard definition of "negotiation" to suit their purposes. Negotiation commonly refers to a process by which actors in conflict engage in a process of making concessions to each other in order to reach a mutually satisfactory agreement. In the Arab-Israeli case, however, "the object of negotiations has seldom been the conclusion of a definitive peace treaty to end the conflict. The tactical usage of the negotiating process for other ends is perfectly consistent with the mutual recognition . . . of the basic incompatibility of the parties' positions."[33] In other words, it is not surprising that the many negotiations failed because a mutually satisfying peace was rarely their purpose in the first place.

Futile Arab-Israeli diplomacy during the six decades prior to 1977 followed a pattern that lends itself to examination under the seven headings previously proposed: (1) previous negotiating experience, (2) purposes and motives, (3) questions of timing, (4) status of negotiating partners, (5) third-party considerations, (6) proposed terms of agreement, and (7) psychological factors. We shall briefly review the pattern that emerged under each of these headings.

Previous Negotiating Experience

The record of multiple failed negotiations suggests that neither a lack of direct communication nor unfamiliarity with the enemy has been responsible for the persistent failure to produce an Arab-Zionist or an Arab-Israeli accord. The record also shows that, contrary to popular belief, merely increasing the amount of contact between the two sides does not increase the likelihood of negotiators actually achieving a working agreement. Many times direct negotiations only clarified for the protagonists just how far apart, even irreconcilable, their positions really were.[34]

Purposes and Motives

Both sides in this conflict often entered the negotiating process for purposes other than actually making concessions to and peace with one another. The historical pattern finds that the parties usually came together when one or both wanted to forestall other, less appealing, initiatives. Most often they negotiated for appearances, trying to impress upon their constituents or upon a powerful third party the justness of their cause, the righteousness of their interpretation of events, and their flexibility and willingness to resolve matters, as opposed to the extremist, uncompromising posture of the other side. During the Mandate period, a mercenary instinct often brought Arabs to the table in search of Zionist resources, and Zionists often invited or entertained them out of a desire to weaken the Arab opposition by playing off rivals against one another. In the historic pattern, Arabs and Zionists sought to inverse von Clausewitz's dictum by employing "diplomacy and negotiation . . . as an extension of their basic 'war' by other (nonviolent) means."[35]

Timing

This factor, closely related to motives (above), refers to both those circumstances that propel an actor to the negotiating table, and those that advance or obstruct his flexibility once there. Historically, Arabs and Israelis have come to the table not so much when conditions seemed ripe for peace as much as when "the status quo seemed more painful or dangerous than a potential negotiated compromise."[36] Like protagonists everywhere, Arabs and Zionists/Israelis proved reluctant to negotiate from positions of perceived weakness. Unfortunately, they similarly lacked the incentive to make concessions from positions of perceived strength, illustrating the vicious circle captured in the Middle Eastern adage: "When I am weak, how can I compromise? When I am strong, why should I compromise?"[37]

Status of the Negotiators

Successful negotiation requires leaders to identify one another correctly as politically capable of persuading their followers to go along with whatever agreements they reach through the bargaining process.[38] Too often, Arab-Zionist and Arab-Israeli peace efforts have suffered from a "Groucho Marxist" dilemma: "Anyone willing to negotiate with me can't be worth negotiating with." Arabs and Jews often refused to meet with one another's hawks, while eschewing contact with the doves on the grounds that they were not truly representative or capable of "delivering the goods." Many times one or both of the people at the table simply did not have an adequate power base to carry out his side of a proposed deal.

A related problem has been asymmetry in the status of Arab and Jewish negotiators. Official spokespeople on both sides often found themselves engaging in "damage control" necessitated by unofficial representatives from their own camps making overtures to leading personalities on the other side. The desire of these "free-lancers" for personal gain or to "do good" many times led them to propose concessions that the recognized leadership then repudiated, understandably increasing the level of confusion and mutual suspicion between the two communities.

The intersection between Palestinian and inter-Arab politics created a special problem. Zionist diplomacy focused on non-Palestinian Arab leaders, hoping to find someone prepared to concede Palestine to the Jews in exchange for certain services to the Arab world as a whole, and able to influence Palestinian Arabs to go along with this arrangement. Such plans invariably fell flat when prominent Arab personalities outside of Palestine proved unable to deliver Palestinian acquiesence in this sort of exchange of services. Yet these encounters often appeared partially successful to Zionists and Israelis—not, of course, in the sense of producing a definitive or lasting peace agreement, but rather in terms of temporarily overcoming the specifically Palestinian resistance to Zionist aspirations to Jewish sovereignty and security.

Third-Party Considerations

There have always been powerful external forces intimately involved in the region, whether Turkish, British, French, Soviet, or American. It is a peculiar fact of Middle East politics that Arabs, Zionists, and later, Israelis, have usually sought to advance their interests by turning to these outside powers instead of to one another. Historically, the third party has been more of a hindrance than a help. It was, after all, the audience to which Arab, Zionist, and Israeli negotiators played for appearances, as noted above. Prior to 1948, both sides regularly petitioned the British to impose a solution wholly favorable to themselves. To the extent that His Majesty's Government allowed Arabs or Jews to believe it might impose their maximum demands upon the other, neither side felt compelled to make the hard choices and difficult concessions needed for a negotiated settlement. When British policy wavered, Arab and Zionist leaders displayed even greater hesitancy rather than risk getting out in front with a bold plan that did not enjoy the Mandatory's support.

Since 1948, the United States has replaced the British, while the US-USSR Cold War rivalry added a new third-party ingredient. Soviet and US diplomatic, financial, and military support for rival regional proxies encouraged at least some of those parties to persist in unrealistic expectations of a one-sided victory, and allowed them to cling to irreconcilable stances antithetical to the requirements of a negotiated compromise.[39]

Proposed Terms of Agreement

The historical record shows that, during the course of negotiations, would-be Arab, Zionist, and Israeli negotiators left themselves little room for any scaling back of their maximum demands. This refusal or inability to prioritize objectives and then compromise accordingly may reflect either the genuine incompatibility of the two sides' most basic goals, or the fact that the negotiators' aims were something other than a negotiated settlement. This zero-sum approach denied the opponent any benefit from an agreement, leading to recurrent instability marked by either constant deadlock or repeated requests for an imposed settlement.

The two most contentious and precious cards that the Zionists pressured the British to play, and that are the same ones Palestinian negotiators now demand of Israel, were control over immigration and the conditions for future independence. Prior to 1931, Arabs and Zionists clung stubbornly to their demands for a wholly Arab or Jewish Palestine, respectively. The 1930s witnessed deliberations as to possible compromises, although neither the main parties nor a flurry of well-meaning intermediaries produced a plan able to bridge the chasm between them. Clever strategists devised a variety of complicated principles for Arab-Jewish coexistence in Palestine, such as cantonization, non-domination, parity, binationalism, controlled Jewish immigration, and partition. "The range of logical possibilities seems to have been fully probed and exhausted in Arab-Zionist negotiations prior to 1948," and it is difficult to imagine a scenario for the post-1948 situation that had not been proposed, in some form, in the earlier period.[40] The problem has not been a lack of creative imagination in devising solutions, but rather the leaders' lack of flexibility in considering departures from entrenched positions.

Psychological Factors

For much of a century, the rigors of maintaining national cohesiveness and morale during their protracted conflict encouraged the rise of Arab, Zionist, and Israeli leaders well suited to wage war, but not necessarily peace. They have created instead a "dynamics of deadlock" under which leaders have rallied their communities, encouraged individual sacrifice for the national endeavor, and preserved for their respective peoples both physical survival and strong national identities.[41] Great leadership was measured by the ability to eliminate defeatism and foster optimism even when the realities of a situation dictated otherwise. By defining the conflict in existential terms, squelching dissent, and promising their people imminent victory, leaders failed to prepare their communities for the difficult choices and compromises required for negotiating with the enemy, as opposed to obliterating him.

The dynamics of deadlock is a vicious circle of hostility. The first step in breaking out of it is a psychological transformation on the part of the political élites. Once the leaders decide that peace will serve their personal and national interests, the second step requires their justifying the new diplomatic approach to followers who have been conditioned to distrust and revile the enemy. Whole generations of psychologically traumatized Israelis and Arabs have grown up in fear and distrust of one another, tutored as to the virtue of their own cause and the evil intentions of the other side. Underlining the centrality of these psychological factors, Mark Tessler has observed,

> The most important obstacles to the achievement of peace are attitudes, perceptions, fears, and symbols, rather than the incompatibility of existential interests. . . . The key to genuine peace is not to be found in the realm of novel diplomatic formulas or innovative insights about the structure of a solution. . . . [T]he most basic requirement for peace involves the intangibles of tolerance, empathy, trust or confidence.[42]

Any leader contemplating the peace option must consider the difficult tasks of building up a supportive political base and shaping a political environment that will support his diplomatic overtures. If negotiations succeed, a leader may find legitimizing the deal in the eyes of his people as difficult as negotiating it in the first place. The failure to persuade, overcome, or otherwise silence his opponents can cost a leader his political power, by ballots or bullets. Legitimization requires strategies that effectively wean public opinion away from anticipating the next war to accepting normal relations and peace with the erstwhile enemy.[43]

THE ARAB-ISRAELI PEACE PROCESS: CASE STUDIES, 1977–1996

If Arabs and Israelis are to negotiate lasting peace agreements, they must step out of their traditional diplomatic culture and onto new, untried terrain.

> What seems to be needed, in addition to the right political conditions among the main rivals for Palestine/Israel and interested third parties, is a new psychology and a new leadership factor which can alter the protagonists' way of thinking about this conflict.[44]

While it is difficult to determine what constitute the "right political conditions," Harold H. Saunders, a senior US State Department official intimately involved in American mediation efforts between Israelis and Arabs during the 1970s, has pointed to ways of moving well-entrenched adversaries from deadlock and to constructive bargaining. Saunders's recipe calls for:

- reshaping leaders' "pictures of the problem" to "include the other side's deepest fears and concerns";
- an acute awareness that the consequences of drift will be worse than the status quo;
- a sense that solutions are available;
- a demonstration that the adversaries are prepared to seek political solutions; and
- a sense that no party to the conflict will have unlimited support from any major power for anything other than a peaceful settlement.[45]

Despite the abundance of cooks in the kitchen over the years, Arab and Israeli leaders have not, until recently, met these conditions for fruitful negotiation.

Several systemic changes have occurred in recent decades to enhance the likelihood of successfully negotiated solutions to the Arab-Israel conflict. Of seminal importance are the dissolution of the Soviet Union, the emergence of the United States as the sole superpower, and all the political, military, and economic ramifications of this international metamorphosis. The Middle East in the last quarter century has also witnessed a number of violent disruptions: the 1973 Arab-Israeli war, the 1982 war in Lebanon, the 1987–91 Palestinian uprising (*Intifada*), the 1991 Gulf War, several political assassinations, and recurring terrorist attacks against innocent civilians. These events produced much anxiety and uncertainty, but also realignments, policy changes, and new opportunities for peacemaking. Important shifts in the regional balance of power, with Iraq, Egypt, and Syria vying for primacy in the Arab world, have had implications for Arab-Israeli relations. Shifts in the balance of power within each camp—between Likud and Labor in Israel, or between secular and religious forces in both Israel and the Arab countries—have also dramatically altered the diplomatic field.

To what extent have Arab and Israeli leaders taken advantage of these chances to strike out in new diplomatic directions? The following analysis examines six recent Arab-Israeli encounters, including both failures and successes, against the long legacy of failed peace attempts and counterproductive negotiating habits. Our case studies are:

1. the Camp David peace process, 1977–79,
2. the Israel-Lebanon treaty of 1983,
3. the Hussein-Peres London Document of 1987,
4. the 1991 Madrid conference and subsequent Washington talks,
5. the Israel-Jordan peace process, 1993–94, and
6. the Oslo peace process between Israel and the PLO, 1993–96.

NOTES

1. For an overview of the many-wars-little-peace phenomenon, see Itamar Rabinovich, "Seven Wars and One Peace Treaty," in Alvin Z. Rubinstein, ed., *The Arab Israeli Conflict: Perspectives*, 2nd ed. New York: Praeger, 1991, 34–58.

2. Neil Caplan, "Negotiation and the Arab-Israeli Conflict," *Jerusalem Quarterly* 6 (Winter 1978), 3–19.

3. Some of the classic works about Zionism are: Arthur Hertzberg, ed., *The Zionist Idea: A Historical Analysis and Reader*, New York: Meridian, 1960 (Atheneum reprint, 1982); Walter Laqueur, *A History of Zionism*, New York: Schocken, 1972; Howard M. Sachar, *A History of Israel from the Rise of Zionism to Our Time*, 2nd ed., New York: Knopf, 1996; and David Vital's trilogy, *The Origins of Zionism; Zionism: The Formative Years;* and *Zionism: The Crucial Phase*, Oxford: Oxford University Press, 1975, 1982, and 1987. For a Palestinian critique of Zionism, see Walid Khalidi, ed., *From Haven to Conquest: Readings in Zionism and the Palestine Problem until 1948*, Washington: Institute for Palestine Studies, 1971 (reprint 1987).

4. Some of the classic works about Arab Nationalism are: George Antonius, *The Arab Awakening*, 2nd ed., London: Hamish Hamilton, 1946; Sylvia G. Haim, ed.,

Arab Nationalism: An Anthology, Berkeley and Los Angeles: University of California Press, 1962; C. Ernest Dawn, *From Ottomanism to Arabism: Essays on the Origins of Arab Nationalism,* Urbana and Chicago: University of Illinois Press, 1973; Rashid Khalidi et al., eds., *The Origins of Arab Nationalism,* New York: Columbia University Press, 1993.

5. For works dealing specifically with the origins of Palestinian Arab nationalism and its confrontation with Zionism, see: Yehoshua Porath, *The Emergence of the Palestinian Arab National Movement, 1918–1929,* and *The Palestinian Arab National Movement, 1929–1939,* London: Frank Cass, 1974 and 1977; Ann Mosely Lesch, *Arab Politics in Palestine, 1917–1939: The Frustration of a National Movement,* Ithaca and London: Cornell University Press, 1979; Neville J. Mandel, *The Arabs and Zionism before World War I,* Berkeley: University of California Press, 1976; David Fromkin, *A Peace to End All Peace: The Fall of the Ottoman Empire and the Creation of the Modern Middle East,* New York: Avon, 1989; William B. Quandt, Fuad Jabber, and Ann Mosely Lesch, *The Politics of Palestinian Nationalism,* Berkeley: University of California Press, 1973.

6. See Kenneth W. Stein, *The Land Question in Palestine, 1917–1939,* Chapel Hill: University of North Carolina Press, 1984.

7. The landmark United Nations General Assembly (UNGA) Resolution 181, recommending a plan of "partition with economic union" for the future government of Palestine, dated 29 November 1947, was adopted with the required two-thirds majority: 33 in favor, 13 against, with 10 abstentions. The text is given in *The Israel-Arab Reader: A Documentary History of the Middle East Conflict,* 5th rev. and updated ed., eds. Walter Laqueur and Barry Rubin, New York: Penguin, 1995, 95–103.

8. For a selection of recent scholarship on the end of the Mandate period and the first Arab-Israeli war, see: William Roger Louis and Robert W. Stookey, eds., *The End of the Palestine Mandate,* Austin: University of Texas Press, 1986; Benny Morris, *The Birth of the Palestinian Refugee Problem, 1947–1949,* London: Cambridge University Press, 1987; Ilan Pappé, *The Making of the Arab-Israeli Conflict, 1947–1951,* London and New York: I. B. Tauris, 1992; Neil Caplan, *Futile Diplomacy, vol. III: The United Nations, the Great Powers, and Middle East Peacemaking 1948–1954* London: Frank Cass, 1997, chaps. 2–6; Barry Rubin, *The Arab States and the Palestine Conflict,* Syracuse: Syracuse University Press, 1981, chaps. 10–13.

9. The September 1967 Arab League Summit Conference, meeting in Khartoum, Sudan, resolved to abide by the principles of "no peace with Israel, no recognition of Israel, no negotiations with it, and insistence on the rights of the Palestinian people in their own country." For the text of the conference resolutions, see *The Israeli-Palestinian Conflict: A Documentary Record, 1967–1990,* ed. Yehuda Lukacs, Cambridge and New York: Cambridge University Press, 1992, 454–55.

On the 1967 Arab-Israeli war, see: Mark Tessler, *A History of the Israeli-Palestinian Conflict,* Bloomington: Indiana University Press, 1994, 378–464; Fred J. Khouri, *The Arab-Israeli Dilemma,* 3rd ed., Syracuse: Syracuse University Press, 1985, chap. 8; Richard B. Parker, *The Politics of Miscalculation in the Middle East,* Bloomington: Indiana University Press, 1993, chaps. 1–5, and Parker, ed., *The Six Day War: A Retrospective,* Gainesville: University Presses of Florida, 1996; Chaim Herzog, *The Arab-Israeli Wars,* New York: Random House, 1982, 145–91; Sachar, chaps. 21–22.

10. The complete text of the Balfour Declaration is as follows: "His Majesty's Government view with favour the establishment in Palestine of a national home for the Jewish people, and will use their best endeavours to achieve this object, it being clearly understood that nothing shall be done which may prejudice the civil and religious rights of the existing non-Jewish communities in Palestine, or the rights and political status enjoyed by Jews in any other country."

For a history of the Balfour Declaration and conflicting British promises to the Zionists and the Arabs in this era, see: Leonard Stein, *The Balfour Declaration*, London: Vallentine Mitchell, 1961; Elie Kedourie, *In the Anglo-Arab Labyrinth, The McMahon-Husayn Correspondence and Its Interpretations, 1914–1939*, Cambridge: Cambridge University Press, 1976; Ronald Sanders, *The High Walls of Jerusalem: A History of the Balfour Declaration and the Birth of the British Mandate for Palestine*, New York: Holt, Rinehart and Winston, 1983; Isaiah Friedman, *The Question of Palestine: British-Jewish-Arab Relations, 1914–1918*, 2nd expanded ed., New Brunswick, NJ: Transaction, 1992; Charles D. Smith, "The Invention of a Tradition: The Question of Arab Acceptance of the Zionist Right to Palestine during World War I," *Journal of Palestine Studies* (JPS) 22:2 (Winter 1993), 48–61.

11. For a selection of relevant documents and analysis, see Neil Caplan, "Faisal Ibn Husain and the Zionists: A Re-examination with Documents," *International History Review* 5:4 (November 1983), 561–614; Caplan, *Futile Diplomacy, vol. I—Early Arab-Zionist Negotiation Attempts, 1913–1931* London: Frank Cass, 1983, 51–61.

12. Caplan, *Futile Diplomacy* I:51–54, 221–24 and *Futile Diplomacy, vol. II—Arab-Zionist Negotiations and the End of the Mandate*, London: Frank Cass, 1986, 11–14, 40–42, 65–67, 92–95, 188–89, 203–206, 216–17, 238–39. Relations also had their economic dimension, when Zionists purchased an option to lease some of the amir's lands. See Anita Shapira, "The Option on Ghaur al-Kibd: Contacts between Emir Abdallah and the Zionist Executive, 1932–1935," *Studies in Zionism* 2 (Autumn 1980), 239–83.

13. Uri Bar-Joseph, *The Best of Enemies: Israel and Transjordan in the War of 1948*, London: Frank Cass, 1987. See also: Avi Shlaim, *Collusion across the Jordan: King Abdullah, the Zionist Movement, and the Partition of Palestine*, Oxford: Clarendon Press, 1988; Caplan, *Futile Diplomacy* II:145–48, 157–64, 268–71, 277–79; Avraham Sela, "Transjordan, Israel and the 1948 War: Myth, Historiography and Reality," *Middle Eastern Studies* 28:4 (October 1992), 623–88.

14. These leading figures included Nuri as-Sa'id and Tawfiq as-Suwaidi of Iraq; Mahmud Azmi, Abbas Hilmi, Ali Mahir, and Ismail Sidqi of Egypt; Syria's Shakib Arslan, Ihsan al-Jabiri, Amin Sa'id, Jamil Mardam, Shukri al-Quwatly, and Abd ar-Rahman Shahbandar; and Lebanon's Riad as-Sulh and Emile Eddé.

15. Laura Zittrain Eisenberg, *My Enemy's Enemy: Lebanon in the Early Zionist Imagination, 1900–1948*, Detroit: Wayne State University Press, 1994; Eisenberg, "Desperate Diplomacy: The Zionist-Maronite Treaty of 1946," *Studies in Zionism* 13:2 (Autumn 1992), 147–63; Ian Black, *Zionism and the Arabs, 1936–1939*, unpublished Ph.D. dissertation, University of London, 1978.

16. See, e.g., Caplan, *Futile Diplomacy* II:58–84, 130–64; Eisenberg, *My Enemy's Enemy*, 19–21.

17. Best known among the dissenters were Hayim Margaliuth Kalvaryski, Dr. Judah L. Magnes, and Aharon Cohen.

18. Caplan, *Futile Diplomacy* II:29–40, 73–77, 118–29.

19. See, e.g., Caplan, *Futile Diplomacy* I: 76–77, 101–106 and II: 5–11, 20–28, 70–84, 233–39.

20. See, e.g., Caplan, *Futile Diplomacy*, passim.

21. See, e.g., Caplan, *Futile Diplomacy* I:47–51, 168–87 and II:18–21, 85–118, 181–82, 240–62.

22. The main components of the MacDonald White Paper were: (1) Jewish immigration was to be restricted to 15,000 per annum for the coming five years, after which Arab consent would be required; (2) land sales were to be forbidden in certain zones, restricted in others, and unrestricted in a third area; and (3) self-government would be granted following a ten-year transition period during which relations between the Arab and Jewish communities would have to become

stabilized. The text of the White Paper (Cmd. 6019, 17 May 1939) is given in Laqueur and Rubin, 55–64. For discussions of its effect on the Arab and Jewish communities, see: Porath, *The Palestinian Arab National Movement*, 290–94; Philip Mattar, *The Mufti of Jerusalem: al-Hajj Amin al-Husayni and the Palestinian National Movement*, New York: Columbia University Press, 1988 (rev. ed. 1992), 84–85; Zvi Elpeleg, *The Grand Mufti: Haj Amin al-Hussaini, Founder of the Palestinian National Movement*, London: Frank Cass, 1993, 52–55; Yehuda Bauer, *From Diplomacy to Resistance: A History of Jewish Palestine, 1939–1945*, Philadelphia: Jewish Publication Society, 1970, chaps. 1–2; Caplan, *Futile Diplomacy* II:114–18.

23. David Ben-Gurion speech, 19 June 1919, cited in Caplan, "Negotiation," 4–5; Awni Abd al-Hadi, in conversation with Hayim Arlosoroff, quoted by Moshe Shertok (Sharett), 12 February 1932, reproduced in Caplan, *Futile Diplomacy* II:186. Cf. David Ben-Gurion, *My Talks with Arab Leaders*, Jerusalem: Keter, 1972; Caplan, *Futile Diplomacy* II:5–8, 189–96, 199–202.

24. For accounts of this important period, see: J. C. Hurewitz, *The Struggle for Palestine*, New York: W. W. Norton, 1950; Michael J. Cohen, *Palestine and the Great Powers, 1945–1948*, Princeton: Princeton University Press, 1982; Louis and Stookey, eds., *The End of the Palestine Mandate*; Pappé, *The Making of the Arab-Israeli Conflict*; Caplan, *Futile Diplomacy* II:139–64, 274–79.

25. See, e.g., Walter Eytan, *The First Ten Years: A Diplomatic History of Israel*, New York: Simon and Schuster, 1958; Saadia Touval, *The Peace Brokers: Mediators in the Arab-Israeli Conflict, 1948–1979*, Princeton: Princeton University Press, 1982, chap. 3; Neil Caplan, "A Tale of Two Cities: The Rhodes and Lausanne Conferences, 1949," *JPS* 21:3 (Spring 1992), 5–12. For examples of invocation of the Rhodes model three decades later, see Israeli Prime Minister Yitzhak Rabin's first meeting with Jimmy Carter, 7 March 1977, cited in William B. Quandt, *Camp David: Peacemaking and Politics*, Washington, DC: The Brookings Institution, 1986, 45; remarks of former Supreme Court justice and ambassador to the UN, Arthur J. Goldberg, in August 1977, cited in ibid., 104.

26. Neil Caplan, *The Lausanne Conference, 1949: A Case Study in Middle East Peacemaking*, Tel Aviv: Moshe Dayan Center for Middle Eastern and African Studies, Occasional Papers, No. 113, 1993; Caplan, *Futile Diplomacy, III*, chaps. 4–10.

27. For details of Egyptian-Israeli negotiation episodes between 1949 and 1956, see: Shimon Shamir, "The Collapse of Project Alpha," in *Suez 1956: The Crisis and Its Consequences*, eds. Wm. Roger Louis and Roger Owen, Oxford: Clarendon Press, 1989, 73–100; Michael Oren, "Secret Egypt-Israel Peace Initiatives Prior to the Suez Campaign," *Middle Eastern Studies* 26:3 (July 1990), 351–70; Michael B. Oren, *Origins of the Second Arab-Israel War: Egypt, Israel and the Great Powers, 1952–56*, London: Frank Cass, 1992, chap. 5; Mordechai Bar-On, *The Gates of Gaza: Israel's Road to Suez and Back, 1955–1957*, New York: St. Martin's, 1994, chaps. 7–8; Ben-Gurion, *My Talks*, chaps. 47–53; Neil Caplan, *Futile Diplomacy, vol. IV—Operation Alpha and the Failure of Anglo-American Coercive Diplomacy in the Arab-Israeli Conflict, 1954–1956*, London: Frank Cass, 1997.

28. Bar-On, *The Gates of Gaza: Israel's Road to Suez and Back, 1955–1957*; Mohamed Heikal, *Cutting the Lion's Tail: Suez through Egyptian Eyes*, London: Andre Deutsch, 1957; Keith Kyle, *Suez 1956*, New York: St. Martin's, 1991; Roger Louis, *Suez 1956: The Crisis and Its Consequences*; Earl Berger, *The Covenant and the Sword*, Toronto: University of Toronto Press, 1965; Khouri, chap. 7; Sachar, chap. 17

29. On the maneuvering and redrafting that led to the historic resolution, see Lord Caradon, Arthur J. Goldberg, Mohammed H. El-Zayyat, and Abba Eban, *UN Security Council Resolution 242: A Case Study in Diplomatic Ambiguity*, Washington, DC: Institute for the Study of Diplomacy, Edmund A. Walsh School of Foreign

Service, Georgetown University, 1981; Gideon Rafael, "UN Resolution 242: A Common Denominator," in Laqueur and Rubin, 197–212; Mahmoud Riad, *The Struggle for Peace in the Middle East,* London and New York: Quartet Books, 1981, 58–75; Henry Kissinger, *White House Years,* Boston: Little, Brown, 1979, chap. 10.

30. For the text of UNSC Resolution 338, see Lukacs, 13. For a firsthand account of some of the immediate postwar diplomatic activity, see Kissinger, *White House Years,* chap. 13. On the 1973 Arab-Israeli war, see: Tessler, 474–89; Walter Laqueur, *Confrontation: The Middle East and World Politics,* New York: Quadrangle Books, 1974; Mohamed Heikal, *The Road to Ramadan,* New York: Ballantine Books, 1975; Chaim Herzog, *The War of Atonement: October 1973,* Boston: Little, Brown, 1975; Naseer Aruri, ed., *Middle East Crucible: Studies on the Arab-Israeli War of October, 1973,* Wilmette, IL: Medina Press, 1975; Sachar, chaps. 24–25.

31. Texts of the addresses at the opening meeting (21 December 1973) are reproduced in *Israel's Foreign Relations: Selected Documents, 1947–1974,* vol. II, ed. Meron Medzini, Jerusalem: Ministry of Foreign Affairs, 1976, 1081–1109; Touval, 238–41. Cf. Kissinger, *White House Years,* chap. 17.

32. Kissinger, *White House Years,* chaps. 18, 21, 23. On the kilometer-101 talks, see Ensio Siilasvuo, *In the Service of Peace in the Middle East, 1967–1979,* London and New York: Hurst and St. Martin's, 1992, 196–217.

33. Caplan, "Negotiation," 5.

34. Kenneth W. Stein and Samuel W. Lewis (with Sheryl J. Brown), *Making Peace among Arabs and Israelis: Lessons from Fifty Years of Negotiating Experience,* Washington, DC: The United States Institute of Peace, 1991, v; Caplan, "Negotiation," 8, quoting Y. Harkabi, *Palestinians and Israel,* New York: John Wiley, 1974, 209.

35. Caplan, "Negotiation," 6. Cf. "[In the] Middle East diplomacy often times serves as a war of attrition by other means." Aharon Klieman, "Approaching the Finish Line: The United States in Post-Oslo Peace Making," Ramat Gan: The Begin-Sadat Center for Strategic Studies, Bar-Ilan University (Security and Policy Studies, No. 22), June 1995, 29.

36. Stein and Lewis, 14–15. Cf. Harold H. Saunders, *The Other Walls: The Arab-Israeli Peace Process in a Global Perspective,* rev. ed., Princeton: Princeton University Press, 1991, 24–25, 121.

37. Quoted in Thomas L. Friedman, *From Beirut to Jerusalem,* New York: Doubleday Anchor, 1990, 194. Cf. Saunders, 30–31, 49–51 ("Power for Negotiation or Power for Digging In?"), 124.

38. See, e.g., Saunders, 28–30, 123.

39. For a brief discussion of the role of third parties since 1967, see Saunders, 106–109, 125. A comprehensive examination of US involvement in Arab-Israeli diplomacy can be found in two seminal works by William B. Quandt: *Decade of Decisions: American Policy toward the Arab-Israeli Conflict, 1967–1976,* Berkeley: University of California Press, 1977, and *Peace Process: American Diplomacy and the Arab-Israeli Conflict since 1967,* Washington, DC: The Brookings Institution, 1993.

40. Caplan, "Negotiation," 18.

41. Caplan, *Futile Diplomacy* II:179.

42. Tessler, xv–xvi.

43. See Saunders, 116, 126–30. For an analytical study of the process of legitimizing the 1978–79 Egypt-Israel peace, see Yaacov Bar-Siman-Tov, *Israel and the Peace Process, 1977–1982: In Search of Legitimacy for Peace,* Albany: State University of New York Press, 1994.

44. Caplan, *Futile Diplomacy* II:180.

45. Saunders, 126–29, 142–47.

Chapter 1

HOT WARS AND A COLD PEACE

THE CAMP DAVID PEACE PROCESS, 1977–1979

Camp David is perhaps the best known and most written-about of all negotiation episodes between Arabs and Israelis. The unusual name refers to the US presidential retreat that was the site of intensive tripartite Israeli-Egyptian-American negotiations in September 1978. While the Camp David story may be familiar to students of the modern Middle East, it is nevertheless instructive to review this famous episode in terms of our historical model.[1]

The designation "Camp David" actually encompasses several stages of a complex peace process that succeeded in producing three agreements cosigned by Israel, Egypt, and the United States. Two were concluded in September 1978—A Framework for Peace in the Middle East and A Framework for the Conclusion of a Peace Treaty between Egypt and Israel (Appendix, Document 3)—and the third in March 1979—the Egyptian-Israeli Peace Treaty (Appendix, Document 4). All three agreements required a number of accompanying "side-letters" of understanding between Egypt and the United States, and between Israel and the United States. The net result was the first peace treaty ever between Israel and an Arab state.

PREVIOUS NEGOTIATING EXPERIENCE

In spite of the Arab world's almost total post-1948 ostracism of the Jewish state, Egyptians and Israelis were able in 1977 to look back over almost sixty years of intermittent contacts and negotiations. Egypt and Israel, it will be recalled, had been the first to sit down to direct bilateral negotiations with UN Acting Mediator Ralph Bunche and the first to conclude an armistice agreement to end the 1948–49 fighting. During 1949–51, Egyptian and Israeli delegations also shared many months of *negative* multilateral negotiating experiences while attending sterile peace conferences at Lausanne, Geneva, and Paris. At the same time, a fair amount of secret prenegotiation maneuvering involving US and British intermediaries took place between 1949 and 1956, especially surrounding the aborted "Operation Alpha," under which the US State Department and British Foreign Office conspired to arrange secret peace negotiations between Egyptian President Gamal Abd al-Nasir and Israeli Prime Minister David Ben-Gurion.

In the June 1967 war, Israel captured the Gaza Strip and the Sinai Peninsula from Egypt. Israeli Defense (and later Foreign) Minister Moshe Dayan expected negotiations to follow, based on a return of Egyptian territory in exchange for Egyptian recognition of, and peace with, the Jewish state. But Dayan waited in vain for his "phone call from Cairo." The Egyptians had no intention of suing for peace from their position of weakness after the 1967 defeat. Anwar Sadat assumed the presidency upon Nasir's death in 1970, and in 1972 made a play for US affections by ejecting thousands of Soviet advisors from Egypt and intimating that he was prepared to talk peace with Israel. Distracted by the growing Watergate scandal and the Viet Nam war, however, President Richard Nixon's administration did not pick up on the cue.[2]

Reverting to the military option, Egypt patched up its relations with the USSR, coordinated military plans with Syria, and surprised Israel in early October 1973 with a dramatic assault across Israeli lines on the east bank of the Suez Canal, in an effort to recapture Sinai. This war caught Israel unprepared and the first few days saw Israeli troops falling back along both the Egyptian and Syrian fronts. Although the Israeli counteroffensive ultimately succeeded, the Israeli people and the military and political establishments were deeply shaken by their close call. The Egyptians, on the other hand, felt that they had reclaimed their honor and could now face Israel in the diplomatic arena from a position of strength. The aftermath of the 1973 war thus left both sides more inclined to bargain.

After two decades of recurring Egyptian-Israeli battlefront contact, it was President Richard Nixon's National Security Adviser and Secretary of State, Henry Kissinger, whose visits as intermediary in the wake of the 1973 war helped the parties negotiate two disengagement agreements, Sinai I (1974) and Sinai II (1975). Most commentators designate Kissinger's 1973–75 "shuttle diplomacy" as the direct antecedent leading to the US-brokered peace between Egypt and Israel during the administration of President Jimmy Carter.[3] As Carter and his aides prepared their own Middle East peace probes in 1977, some observers wondered whether Egypt and Israel might be ready for a "Sinai III."

PURPOSES AND MOTIVES

Egyptian purposes for engaging in negotiations at this time were deliberately oriented to wider national goals. Since taking office, Anwar Sadat had been working to eliminate frustration with the legacy of Nasir's socialist experiment and the disappointing military alliance with the Soviet Union. Economic distress led to the cancellation of food subsidies, which precipitated widespread rioting in January 1977. With the rising prestige and economic power of the Gulf states during the 1970s—including their temporarily successful use of oil as a weapon against Israel's western allies—Egypt's aspirations to leadership of the Arab world were no longer as clear as they had once been.

The warm relations that developed between Anwar Sadat and Henry Kissinger during the latter's frequent visits following the October 1973 war offered a natural starting point for the Egyptian president's efforts at seeking closer political and economic relations with the US. Kissinger had reportedly advised the Egyptians that "the Soviet Union can give you arms, but [only] the United States can give you a just solution which will give you back your territories."[4] By 1977, the Egyptian leader was therefore primed to respond to Jimmy Carter's intentions to make that year the "year of Geneva."

Carter and Sadat held their first meeting in Washington in April 1977, opening an active channel of communication between them. Sadat intended to use these preliminary contacts with the Carter administration to realign Egypt with the US after breaking with the Soviets; regain the Sinai from Israeli control; settle his conflict with Israel in a way that would reassert Egypt's leadership in the Arab world; and relieve Egypt's financial plight.

The first two of these aims illustrate clearly the pre-1948 pattern in which would-be negotiators based their "peace" calculations on the desire to secure wider goals. The Egyptian delegation's strategy paper on the eve of the Camp David summit explicitly stresses Egypt's concern for impressing the Americans. Foreign Minister Muhammad Ibrahim Kamil recommended that Egypt's strategic aims for the summit be "to expose the Israeli intransigence before the US and before the world," and to show Egyptian flexibility "invariably in response to the American stand."[5]

Sadat also put a novel spin on the more common use by Arab régimes of militant posturing vis-à-vis Israel as a means of establishing their credentials for pan-Arab leadership. By using the diplomatic option and his "American card" to obtain the return of occupied Arab lands, Sadat hoped to demonstrate the futility of traditional Arab belligerence and reassert Egyptian regional leadership in the face of the rival aspirations of Syria's Hafiz al-Asad, who backed the PLO in its rejectionist stance.

In November 1977, Sadat stunned the world with the announcement that, in pursuit of peace, he would travel even to Jerusalem. Prime Minister Begin promptly extended an invitation. The most popular explanation for Sadat's surprise decision to journey to Jerusalem in November 1977 is that he wished to avoid the Geneva summit that the US and USSR were planning to convene. On 1 October 1977, a joint US-USSR communiqué calling for a new Geneva gathering did stimulate Sadat to chart a different course, but as much out of concern about losing his bid for Sinai to Syrian and Palestinian maneuvering at a multilateral conference as out of fear of giving his still-smarting former Soviet ally an influential role.[6]

In Israel, 1977 saw the election of a new right-wing government under Prime Minister Menachem Begin. Like the Labor Party that had governed the country since 1948, Begin's Likud Party was dedicated to maintaining Israel's regional military superiority and deterrence capability; optimizing Israel's "special relationship" with the United States; working toward nonbelligerency and peace with each of its Arab neighbors *separately*; and resolving the Palestinian issue short of recognizing the PLO and the Palestinians' right to statehood. Unlike their rivals in the Labor Party, however, Likud leaders maintained an ideological commitment to holding on to Judea and Samaria (their preferred Biblical terms for the West Bank), conquered in the 1967 war, as parts of Israel's historic patrimony.

In responding to 1977 US and Egyptian overtures, Menachem Begin saw an opportunity to end the state of war with Egypt, thereby detaching the most populous and powerful Arab state from the pan-Arab military coalition. Another attraction was the chance to earn credit for flexibility and cooperativeness in the eyes of the US administration, while at the same time sidestepping the Palestinian issue as much as possible. Begin calculated that making concessions to Egypt in Sinai would relieve international pressure for Israeli concessions on the West Bank.

In late December 1977, Begin armed himself with a twenty-six-point plan for limited Palestinian "self-rule" in "Judea, Samaria and the Gaza District,"[7] hoping that this, together with the moves for peace with Egypt, would nominally satisfy international pressure for a solution to the Palestinian situation, while allowing Israel to consolidate its hold over the West Bank through the continued development of Jewish settlements there. The Likud government's position on the territories conflicted sharply with that of Egypt and the United States. In the end, these differences were fudged rather than resolved at Camp David.

An important incentive for Begin in welcoming Sadat's personal mission to Jerusalem in November 1977 was his hope (soon fulfilled) that direct dealings would supersede US and Soviet plans to reconvene the Geneva Conference. Israel was suspicious of Soviet involvement, wary of being ganged up on by the Arabs, and worried about the American emphasis on a comprehensive solution. Thus, the powers' joint declaration, aborted in its intent, became the common catalyst that created one of the rare historic moments when two Middle Eastern leaders found the path of mutual recognition and direct negotiations preferable to all other available options.

TIMING

The Camp David peace process benefited from the convergence of conditions (above) that allowed Menachem Begin, Anwar Sadat, and Jimmy Carter to take risks toward a negotiated settlement. To differing degrees, all three had simultaneously come to believe that negotiations had a fair chance of succeeding, that the outcome would be an improvement over the status quo, and that the risks associated with potential failure would be manageable.[8] An important difference, however, turned out to Begin's advantage. While all three leaders found reasons why the timing was *attractive to enter* into talks, only Sadat and Carter actually found it *compelling to conclude* them with positive results.

Self-imposed deadlines created some of the timing constraints. Carter declared 1977 as the year for the resumption of the Geneva Conference, while Sadat pressed for some visible change in the Egyptian-Israeli status quo by early 1978, the nominal expiration date of the 1975 disengagement agreement. Other timing factors included political and economic cycles in the United States and in the Middle East. As a first-term president, Jimmy Carter had only a brief window of opportunity for foreign-policy risk taking before midterm congressional elections in November 1978 imposed limits on his freedom to maneuver.[9] Later, negotiations between the second and third of the Camp David Agreements coincided with a downturn in the president's domestic standing, and Carter desperately sought a major foreign-policy success to boost his chances for reelection.[10] For his part, Sadat needed to show quick and tangible progress on the Israel issue and in his rapprochement with the US in the hope of overcoming growing domestic discontent, a deteriorating economic situation, and mounting regional criticism of his diplomatic initiative. Menachem Begin was in an altogether different position, basking in the glow of negotiating one-on-one with Israel's mightiest enemy, thereby satisfying the Jewish state's long-standing yearning for acceptance and respect from the Arab world—regardless of the outcome of this round of negotiations.

STATUS OF THE NEGOTIATORS

Unlike many of the earlier unsuccessful negotiation attempts involving marginal political figures, this initiative was undertaken by heads of state whose leadership within their respective camps was virtually unchallenged. Anwar Sadat was, by 1977, in firm control in Egypt, able to outmaneuver, control, or replace (as needed) his prime minister, foreign minister, and top-ranking officials so as to keep a pro-peace team around him throughout the negotiations. Sadat felt strong enough to cope with domestic dissent and foreign criticism. Largely unmoved by accusations of treason, he pursued the peace process in defiance of a Syrian-led pan-Arab consensus against dealing with the enemy.[11]

At crucial moments during the slow negotiations at Camp David and afterward, Menachem Begin demonstrated his personal power by overruling compromises proposed by Foreign Minister Dayan and Defense Minister Ezer Weizman. While previous governments in Israel "had refrained from offering concessions for fear of criticism" from people like Begin, the Likud government elected in July 1977 "embodied the right wing and possessed impeccable ultranationalist credentials."[12] Yet, Begin's peace policy did encounter some opposition in the cabinet and Knesset and among some segments of the public. Although personally hurt by accusations of having "sold out" by some party loyalists, Begin deflected the criticism and persevered in his pursuit of a Sinai-for-peace settlement with Egypt.[13]

The distinction between Palestinian and non-Palestinian actors constituted the most problematic aspect of the status-of-negotiator factor. In this respect, the Sadat-Begin negotiations resembled the historical pattern by which Zionists and Israelis attempted to negotiate peace by circumventing the Palestinians through dealings with other leading Arabs. Despite the heightened sense of Palestinian consciousness that had developed since the Mandate period, and despite the creation of the Palestine Liberation Organization in 1964 as a vehicle for Palestinian power and demands, Anwar Sadat and Menachem Begin, each working to his own distinct agenda, skirted the Palestinian issue with relative ease. Unlike previous negotiation attempts that crumbled because of the absence of a credible Palestinian negotiating partner, the Camp David process held firm because—the Palestinian issue notwithstanding—it produced satisfactory results in terms of each side's immediate aims and those of their US patron.

Although Sadat and Carter had gone into negotiations with the intention of linking an Egyptian-Israeli treaty to a formula that would have obliged Israel to satisfy some Palestinian desiderata, Begin succeeded in watering down any linkage between Palestinian and Egyptian issues. In the face of Palestinian rejection and nonparticipation, Egyptian-Israeli talks about Palestinian autonomy, as called for in the Accords, quickly collapsed. The bilateral Egyptian-Israeli agreements, however, held. Given the relative weakness of the PLO and its allies, and the fact that the peace with Israel did satisfy Egypt's aspirations to closer ties with the United States, increased American aid, and the return of Sinai, Arab rejectionists proved unable to persuade Egypt to disavow Camp David and powerless to reverse the first negotiated peace treaty between Israel and an Arab state.

THIRD-PARTY CONSIDERATIONS

Secret prenegotiations in Morocco in September 1977 between Anwar Sadat's personal envoy, Hasan Tuhamy, and Israel's foreign minister, Moshe Dayan, preceded the Egyptian president's surprise announcement that he would travel to Jerusalem.[14] The Morocco meeting was kept from the Americans for fear of pressure to abandon bilateral Egyptian-Israeli approaches in favor of Carter's preferred Geneva Conference. Sadat and Begin's historic breakthrough succeeded in derailing the US plan, but when open Egyptian-Israeli negotiations faltered due to personality differences and conflicting expectations as to what should happen next, both sides turned to the Americans to salvage their initiative. At Carter's invitation, Egyptian, Israeli, and US teams, personally led by Sadat, Begin, and Carter, spent twelve days sequestered at Camp David before producing the first agreements. A strong component in their success was the willingness of both Israel and Egypt to please the United States in order to benefit from the familiar perks of a friendly alliance with a great power: loans and grants for economic development, arms purchases, and diplomatic support. As William Quandt has written:

> The US role became crucial because both Egypt and Israel wanted American involvement and hoped to win Washington to their point of view. Neither wanted the United States to be an entirely neutral intermediary. Neither expected the Americans to content themselves with the role of postman. Both hoped that the United States would advocate their views in their adversary's capital and would be generous in rewarding any of their concessions made in the course of negotiations.[15]

Each side's hope that a third power would impose a unilaterally pleasing solution constituted a clear repetition of the historical pattern. A variation was the occasional request by Arabs and Israelis that a third party "impose" terms which neither could appear, before domestic public opinion, to favor voluntarily. The parties were sometimes prepared to "reluctantly" accept a proposal coming from an outsider which would have been unacceptable had it emanated from their Middle Eastern opponent. Anwar Sadat enthusiastically adopted both maneuvers as part of his broader strategy of collusion with Carter against Begin.[16]

But Egyptians and Israelis differed on the exact nature of the US involvement they were seeking. The conflicting preferences of the two parties were, in fact, continuations of a pattern discernable between 1948 and 1956. Sadat and his advisers were keen on seeing the United States submit its own proposals and participate fully in the negotiations. One of the aims of the Egyptian delegation at Camp David was "to force the US to modify its role from that of mediator to that of full partner" on the grounds that "the formally declared American positions were closer to the Egyptian than the Israeli."[17] The Israelis, recognizing this closeness, worked against the imposition of any "externally devised formula." Both Menachem Begin and Ezer Weizman (but not Moshe Dayan) displayed extreme caution in avoiding moves that might expand the US role beyond that of helping to bring the parties to the table.[18]

While many of the attitudes displayed by the Middle Eastern protagonists toward great-power mediation represent a repetition of the pre-1977 patterns of futile diplomacy, the United States deviated from the historically unhelpful third-party role. Unlike in the 1950s and 1960s, during the 1970s the United States enjoyed the unique position of being both sought after "as the only party that could bring the Arabs and Israelis together,"[19] as well as trusted by both Israel and a number of Arab régimes. This element contributed to the success of Camp David, particularly since Sadat and Begin never overcame their mutual mistrust. Yet the parties' faith in the Americans was fragile and could not be taken for granted. Israelis worried about having their interests subverted by a United States vulnerable to disruptions in Arab oil supplies. Egyptians and Arabs harbored doubts about the ability of Carter himself and of the American foreign-policymaking machinery to withstand domestic pro-Israeli pressures and electoral politics. Despite these frailties, the Carter administration demonstrated unusual skill in sidestepping their respective fears without alienating Egyptian or Israeli leaders.

Even more important was the unprecedented level of personal activism displayed by Carter, who was supported by a skilled team that invested heavily in elaborate prenegotiation background preparations. Because the US president proved unusually prepared to risk failure and the resulting political backlash, he saved the frequently faltering negotiations from complete breakdown on more than one occasion.

The Carter administration was also unusual in its willingness to back up its diplomatic encouragement with security guarantees and financial incentives, taking the position that the United States was more than a simple intermediary, but rather a party with "a direct, substantial interest in a permanent peace in the Middle East."[20] American bilateral commitments to Egypt and to Israel were embodied in side-letters and memoranda of understanding, and played no small part in overcoming potential deadlock. In the end, Jimmy Carter found himself "buying" peace between Egypt and Israel.[21]

PROPOSED TERMS OF AGREEMENT

A comparison of the opening bargaining stances of the United States, Egypt, and Israel with the final terms of the Camp David Accords suggests that—unlike many instances of failed Arab-Israeli negotiation attempts—

the 1977–79 negotiators did display some tactical flexibility. The bottom line appears to have been Egypt's insistence on the return of all of Sinai to its full sovereign control and Israel's equally firm insistence on maintaining its full claim to Judea and Samaria. Nevertheless, protracted bargaining narrowed other gaps between the parties. Strategies were revised during the negotiating process, and all parties—some would argue Sadat and Carter more so than Begin—backed down from most of their opening bargaining positions.

The process of downscaling original demands for the sake of an accord is never mathematically even or symmetrical among the negotiating parties. This final agreement bore little resemblance to Sadat's and Carter's initial goals of linking developments on the Israeli-Egyptian front with progress on self-determination for the Palestinians. On this score, Menachem Begin achieved more of his original negotiating aims because he felt less pressure than his Egyptian and US counterparts to descend from the Camp David summit with an agreement in hand. Indeed, once Sadat had played his ace card by recognizing Israel de facto nine months earlier, the Egyptian president was under great pressure to justify his overture by bringing home a substantial quid pro quo. The Israeli prime minister was under no such constraint, and could have returned from Camp David without an agreement, justifying his position before his people as a defense of Israel's vital security interests in the face of unacceptably dangerous proposals cooked up between Sadat and Carter. The same imbalance characterized the pressures on the three parties as they struggled over the final terms of the peace treaty between October 1978 and March 1979.[22]

As the first official treaty of peace between Israel and an Arab state, the March 1979 Egyptian-Israeli Treaty is remarkable more for its very existence than for its content. While the Arab countries responded with dismay, euphoria gripped the West; the *New York Times* ran a bold, three-tiered headline quoting the agreement in Arabic, Hebrew, and English.[23] Applying UN Resolution 242's "land-for-peace" formula, Israel committed itself to a phased withdrawal from all of the Sinai Peninsula in return for a parallel phased normalization of relations leading to an exchange of ambassadors. Despite Begin's efforts to retain Israeli settlements around Yamit and two Sinai airbases, the final agreement included provisions for their evacuation, with a US commitment to finance the replacement of the latter on the Israeli side of the frontier. Israel held out for Egyptian and US pledges to guarantee it continued access to oil supplies to compensate for an anticipated double loss: the retreat from the Abu Rodeis oil fields in Sinai and the end of purchases from Iran in the wake of the shah's downfall.

There were several important issues that simply defied resolution. The Carter team gradually retreated from its ambitious hopes for a comprehensive solution and reverted, consciously or unconsciously, to Henry

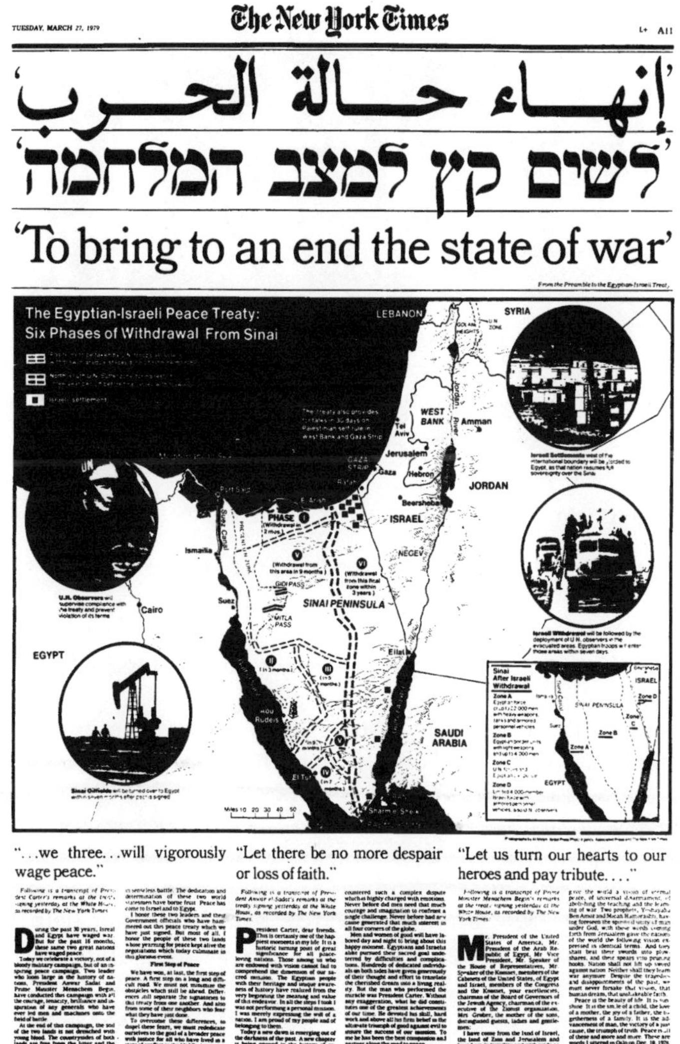

TUESDAY, MARCH 27, 1979 — The New York Times — A11

إنهاء حالة الحرب

לשים קץ למצב המלחמה

'To bring to an end the state of war'

"...we three...will vigorously wage peace."

"Let there be no more despair or loss of faith."

"Let us turn our hearts to our heroes and pay tribute...."

© 1979 by the New York Times Co. Reprinted by permission.

Kissinger's gradualist approach. This included the techniques of deferring difficult decisions to a later date (i.e., the status of Jerusalem), agreeing to disagree, and ambiguous verbal formulations designed to give each party the *impression* that its concerns were being met.[24] The Americans were especially concerned to provide Sadat with a "fig leaf"—ultimately inadequate—for what turned out to be an embarrassingly bilateral agreement and a separate peace difficult to justify before pan-Arab opinion.[25] Camp David's unresolved issues provided the irritants and flashpoints of future

"Enough is enough, Menachem. Get those settlements off Boardwalk."

© 1978 Dayton Daily News and United Features Syndicate,
Courtesy of Grimmy, Inc. / Mike Peters.

disagreement, conflict, violence and—finally, during the 1990s—resumed negotiation.

The joys of the Egypt-Israel success story were diminished by the shortcomings of Camp David on two other fronts: the failure to expand the framework to include other Arab states, and the continuing absence of any Palestinian participation.[26] Moderate, pro-US states like Jordan and Saudi Arabia were dissuaded from following in Sadat's footsteps by the outrage and ostracism Egypt suffered in the wake of what many Arabs perceived as an inadequate and humiliating agreement. It did not help that the confidence-building gesture of an Israeli freeze on the building of new settlements in the occupied territories turned out to be much shorter-lived than either Sadat or Carter had understood from Begin's commitment.[27] And since neither the Americans nor the Egyptians had succeeded in coaxing the Israelis to declare their readiness to withdraw on all fronts in exchange for peace, neither the Jordanians nor the Syrians saw any incentive to become involved in follow-up negotiations. In light of Jordan's steadfast rejection of the Camp David initiative, it initially seems peculiar that the architects of that initiative envisioned such an important role for Jordan, which is cited by name fifteen times in the Accords and which was the recipient of a special US questions-and-answers document about the meaning of the Camp David agreement.[28] This apparent divorce from reality can be explained by the fig-leaf-for-Sadat theory, and by Begin's preference for dealing with Jordan on Palestinian matters.

Palestinians rightly perceived the disinclination of the Camp David signatories to deal with the PLO or allow for the creation of an independent Palestinian state. Even advocates of "self-determination" for the Palestinians were disappointed with the much weaker permutations of the term employed in the Accords. Camp David supporters argued that by fully exploiting the agreement's autonomy provisions, the Palestinians would nevertheless vastly improve their situation on the ground, and perhaps build momentum for future claims. With their leadership clearly excluded from the process and no guarantee of post-autonomy independence, however, Palestinians remained overwhelmingly opposed to what they perceived as an Egyptian-Israeli deal that shortchanged their just requirements.

PSYCHOLOGICAL FACTORS

The breaking down of psychological barriers was a crucial element both in paving the way to Camp David and in producing an agreement. The respectable showing of the Egyptian military in October 1973 removed the stigma of the 1967 humiliation, allowing Anwar Sadat to pursue a negotiated solution without appearing to give in to dictated terms of surrender. Sadat had hinted at his readiness to consider the diplomatic route as early as February 1971;[29] in 1977 he made that crystal clear. Begin came around to the idea in response to the new opportunities presented by Sadat's unmistakable signals. Once convinced of the need to change the prevailing dynamics of deadlock, the leaders' task was to persuade their people to make the same psychological conversion.

As one scholar has pointed out, people respond better to "the gestures and speeches that make up the drama of the state" than to intellectual arguments, "factors," or "moral codes."[30] In this regard, Sadat's visit, and especially his 20 November 1977 speech to the Israeli Knesset—both heavily televised—played a crucial role in convincing Israelis of a new reality. The dramatic fact of the Egyptian president's presence in Jerusalem was an eloquent gesture that did much to break down what Harold Saunders, echoing Sadat, has called the "other walls." Along with a largely unwelcome rehash of Egypt's call for Israeli withdrawal from the occupied territories, Sadat's speech to the Knesset contained, more significantly, words that recognized the humanity of his Israeli adversaries. Israelis listened in amazement to the Egyptian president declaring, "You want to live with us in this part of the world. In all sincerity, I tell you, we welcome you among us, with full security and safety" (Appendix, Document 2). His language, coupled with several emotional exchanges with leading Israeli personalities, touched a chord within the Israeli people, allowing Begin to be more forthcoming in negotiations than he might otherwise have dared to be.[31]

Caught off guard by their president's sudden about-face, Egyptians struggled to assimilate the new interpretation of the old conflict. The public display of huge Cairo crowds proclaiming Sadat a "hero of peace" concealed deep divisions over the substance of his achievement.[32] Begin offered no dramatic equivalent to Sadat's Knesset speech. But tired of war and anxious to enjoy the economic benefits that Sadat promised would accrue from peace with Israel and its accompanying American largesse, many people were prepared to give Sadat's new gambit a chance. When tangible improvements did not immediately materialize, however, disappointment grew. While he was able to pilot his peace project over many hurdles by ignoring regional and suppressing internal criticism, on 6 October 1981 Sadat fell victim to assassins dedicated to an Islamic vision of Egypt militantly opposed to westernization, Americanization, and peace with Israel.[33] His successor, Hosni Mubarak, committed Egypt to its Camp David obligations, but at a more cautious pace.

The resounding speed and joy with which Israelis embraced their former enemy gave encouraging indications that even deeply held animosity is not impervious to change. Anwar Sadat's memoirs record the Egyptian leader's delighted appreciation of the broad public support his initiative received in Cairo and in Jerusalem, even if his estimation of the latter proved more accurate than of the former.[34] Yet, the move from war to peace and normalization is a slow and shaky process, involving the implementation of painful concessions, the healing of psychological wounds, and the reversing of negative stereotypes. Genuine reconciliation between the Egyptian and Israeli peoples has lagged behind the proper diplomatic formalities established between the Egyptian and Israeli governments; Camp David is a success in that Egypt and Israel remain at peace, but the Egyptian and Israeli people still hold one another at arm's length. It will take generations for average Egyptians and Israelis to overcome psychological barriers and what Raymond Cohen has termed their ingrained "cultural incompatibility" before an authentic and warm peace is within reach.[35] A cold peace is undoubtedly better than a hot war, but the chilly nature of Egyptian-Israeli relations two decades after Camp David demonstrates that negotiating and signing a peace treaty are seldom sufficient, in themselves, to bring about a definitive resolution to international conflict.

NOTES

1. Among the vast literature on Camp David, this section relies heavily on the perspectives offered in William B. Quandt, *Camp David: Peacemaking and Politics,* Washington, DC: The Brookings Institution, 1986, and Saadia Touval, *The Peace Brokers: Mediators in the Arab-Israeli Conflict, 1948–1979,* Princeton: Princeton University Press, 1982, chap. 10.

2. Henry Kissinger: *Years of Upheaval,* Boston: Little, Brown, 1982, chap. 6.

3. Roger Fisher, "Playing the Wrong Game," in *Dynamics of Third Party Intervention,* ed. Jeffrey Z. Rubin, New York: Praeger, 1981, 95–121; E. R. F. Sheehan, *The Arabs, Israelis and Kissinger: A Secret History of American Diplomacy in the Middle East,* New York: Reader's Digest Press, 1976.

4. M. Heikal, quoted in Touval, 277. Cf. Abraham Ben-Zvi, *Between Lausanne and Geneva: International Conferences and the Arab-Israeli Conflict*, Tel Aviv: Tel Aviv University, Jaffee Center for Strategic Studies (study no. 13) and Boulder, CO: Westview Press, 1989, 80.

5. Muhammad Ibrahim Kamil, Memorandum to the President of the Republic [of Egypt] on the Tripartite Camp David Meeting, 28 August 1978, reproduced in M. I. Kamil, *The Camp David Accords: A Testimony*, New York: KPI, 1986, 273, 276, 279.

6. This point is made clearly by Quandt, *Camp David*, 97, 109, 123–25, 146 (n. 12). Cf. William B. Quandt, "US Policy toward the Arab-Israeli Conflict," in *The Middle East: Ten Years after Camp David*, ed. William B. Quandt, Washington, DC: The Brookings Institution, 1988, 373; Ben-Zvi, 45–47, 51–53. For the text of the US-Soviet Joint Communiqué of 1 October 1977, see *The Israeli-Palestinian Conflict: A Documentary Record, 1967–1990*, ed. Yehuda Lukacs, Cambridge and New York: Cambridge University Press, 1992, 16.

7. Begin Autonomy Plan, 28 December 1977, text in Lukacs, 153–55.

8. Cf. Harold H. Saunders, *The Other Walls: The Arab-Israeli Peace Process in a Global Perspective*, rev. ed., Princeton: Princeton University Press, 1991, 36.

9. See, e.g., Quandt, *Camp David*, 8, 14–22, 198.

10. Ibid., 23–24.

11. See, e.g., Quandt's December 1977 assessment of Sadat's strategy, in Quandt, *Camp David*, 152. Cf. ibid., 211; Daniel Dishon, "Sadat's Arab Adversaries," *Jerusalem Quarterly* 8 (Summer 1978), 3–15.

12. Touval, 287–88.

13. Melvin A. Friedlander, *Sadat and Begin: The Domestic Politics of Peacemaking*, Boulder, CO: Westview Press, 1983, 240–43. The author credits both leaders for winning a national pro-peace consensus through their mastery of the techniques of domestic intra-élite bargaining.

14. Moshe Dayan, *Breakthrough: A Personal Account of the Egypt-Israel Peace Negotiations*, London: Weidenfeld and Nicolson, 1981, 38–54; Jay Rothman, "Negotiation as Consolidation: Prenegotiation in the Israeli-Palestinian Conflict," *Jerusalem Journal of International Relations* 13:1 (1991), 23. Cf. Touval, 288; Quandt, *Camp David*, 109–10; Mohamed Heikal, *Secret Channels: The Inside Story of Arab-Israeli Peace Negotiations*, London: HarperCollins, 1996, 255–57.

15. Quandt, *Camp David*, 4. Cf. ibid., 61, 213, 237.

16. See, e.g., ibid., 163, 174–77, 187, 195, 202–203, 215, 224.

17. Kamil, Memorandum to the President of the Republic, 28 August 1978, reproduced in Kamil, *Camp David Accords*, 273. See also Quandt, *Camp David*, 92, 95, 116, 174, 198, 207, 226; Touval, 296, 298–99.

18. See, e.g., Quandt, *Camp David*, 78, 180, 189, 224; Shibley Telhami, *Power and Leadership in International Bargaining: The Path to the Camp David Accords*, New York and Oxford: Columbia University Press, 1990, 121–22; Touval, 243, 298.

19. Quandt, *Camp David*, 33. Cf. Touval, 243–44.

20. Carter Press Conference, 16 September 1977, cited in Quandt, *Camp David*, 111. Cf. ibid., 315, 324–25, 333–35. This stance has been reiterated, with varying degrees of sincerity, by other presidents since Carter. Cf. Saunders, 112; Ambassador Martin Indyk (representing the Clinton administration's approach), The Jimmy Carter Lecture, Moshe Dayan Center for Middle Eastern and African Studies, Tel Aviv University, 16 May 1995.

21. As a result of Camp David, Israel and Egypt received a combined $5 billion per year during the 1980s. Quandt, *Camp David*, 241, 335; Touval, 317–18.

22. For different analyses of the gains and losses (and the relative backing down) of each of the parties involved at Camp David, see Quandt, *Camp David*, 324–27; Telhami, *Power and Leadership*, chap. 7 and pp. 206–209; Yaacov Bar-Siman-Tov, *Israel and the Peace Process, 1977–1982: In Search of Legitimacy for Peace*, Albany:

State University of New York Press, 1994, chaps. 7, 9. An interesting collection of interviews with leading Egyptian and American participants is in Zahid Mahmood, "Sadat and Camp David Reappraised," *JPS* 15:1 (Autumn 1985), 62–87.

23. *New York Times,* 27 March 1979, p. A11.

24. Janice Gross Stein, "Structure, Tactics and Strategies of Mediation: Kissinger and Carter in the Middle East," *Negotiation Journal* 1:4 (October 1985), 340; Ben-Zvi, 21–22.

25. Quandt, *Camp David,* 118, 169–70, 188, 226, 251, 262, 283, 329–32; Touval, 291, 296, 301–302; Saunders, 95.

26. For a US assessment of Camp David's failure to win any Palestinian backing, see Saunders, 60–62.

27. Jimmy Carter, *Keeping Faith: Memoirs of a President,* New York: Bantam, 1982, 409; Jimmy Carter, *The Blood of Abraham: Insights into the Middle East,* Lafayetteville: University of Arkansas Press, 1993, 50.

28. American Answers to Jordanian Questions, October 1978, in Quandt, *Camp David,* 388–96 (app. H). Cf. Friedlander, 243–48.

29. See, e.g., Anwar el-Sadat, *In Search of Identity: An Autobiography,* New York: Harper and Row, 1978, 279–81; Heikal, *Secret Channels,* 164–65; Telhami, *Power and Leadership,* 7. One active diplomat who did *not* view Sadat's signals as being clear enough was Henry Kissinger. See his *Years of Upheaval,* chap. 6.

30. Murray Edelman, quoted in Bar-Siman-Tov, 12.

31. For discussions of the effect of Sadat's Knesset speech of 20 November 1977 (Appendix, Document 2), see Quandt, *Camp David,* 147–48; Touval, 289; Saunders, xii–xiii; Bar-Siman-Tov, 58–59.

32. Friedlander, 238–40.

33. For an analysis of Egyptian impulses and constraints in making peace with Israel, see Fouad Ajami, *The Arab Predicament: Arab Political Thought and Practice Since 1967,* rev. ed., Cambridge: Cambridge University Press, 1992, sections 2 and 3.

34. Sadat, *In Search of Identity,* 310–11.

35. Raymond Cohen, *Culture and Conflict in Egyptian-Israeli Relations: A Dialogue of the Deaf,* Bloomington: Indiana University Press, 1990, 6–8. On the Israeli process of legitimizing peace with Egypt between 1979 and 1982, see Bar-Siman-Tov, 188–242. For continuing evidence of the incompleteness of the process on both sides, see Alan Cowell, "To Egypt, Peace Pact Is a Stigma on Its Arab Soul," *New York Times (NYT),* 19 March 1989, p. 6; Adam Garfinkle, *Israel and Jordan in the Shadow of War: Functional Ties and Futile Diplomacy in a Small Place,* New York: St. Martin's, 1992, 3–4; interview with Elyakim Haetzni of the ultra-nationalist Tehiya Party, 16 July 1991, in Shibley Telhami, "Israeli Foreign Policy after the Gulf War," in *The Arab-Israeli Search for Peace,* ed. Steven L. Spiegel, Boulder, CO and London: Lynne Rienner, 1992, 49; *al-Ahram Weekly* poll conducted in December 1994, discussed in Fawaz A. Gerges, "Egyptian-Israeli Relations Turn Sour," *Foreign Affairs* 74:3 (May-June 1995), 74–75; Amos Elon, "The Thinking Men's War," *New York Times Magazine,* 11 May 1997, 40–43.

Chapter 2

MISSION IMPOSSIBLE

THE 1983 ISRAEL-LEBANON AGREEMENT

The Israel-Lebanon Agreement of 17 May 1983 (see Appendix, Document 6) is what we might call a perfect failure. The negotiations leading to this agreement involved virtually all characteristics of the early pattern of unsuccessful Arab-Zionist encounters. The presence of so many elements that permitted negotiations to persist for the "wrong" reasons, i.e., those other than actually making peace, allowed these talks to progress all the way through ratification of a formal agreement, which then failed entirely.

The May 17 agreement came in the wake of the 1982 Israeli invasion of Lebanon. Operation "Peace for the Galilee" aimed to destroy the Palestine Liberation Organization, thereby securing Israel's northern border from attacks by PLO guerillas. Secondary goals were to drive the Syrians out of Lebanon (thereby reducing Syrian regional influence) and to win Israel a peace treaty with a newly liberated Lebanon, its second with an Arab country. The campaign's supporters also believed that the elimination of the PLO, whose leadership operated freely in Beirut and whose fighters used southern Lebanon as a training and staging ground,[1] would deal a mortal blow to Palestinian morale and thus Palestinian resistance to continued Israeli control of the West Bank.[2] Israel's strongest opponent in Lebanon, and ultimately the party with the staying power to prevail after the Israelis and Americans had cut and run, was Syria. Syria objected to Israeli and US privileges and proxies in Lebanon, which it considered part of the historic Syrian patrimony, and refused to countenance a central Lebanese government independent of Syrian influence and inclined toward Washington and Jerusalem. At the time of the Israeli invasion, some 30,000 Syrian troops were ensconced in eastern Lebanon, having been dispatched by Syrian President Asad in 1976 to protect Syrian interests during the Lebanese civil war.[3]

Israel undertook the 1982 operation in collaboration with Bashir Gemayel, the charismatic young scion of one of the leading Maronite Catholic families in Lebanon. Bashir headed the Phalange, an ultranationalist Maronite militia founded by his father in the 1930s,[4] which during the 1970s and 1980s emerged as the leading opponent of the PLO in Lebanon. Israel entered into an alliance with the Phalange under the (mistaken) impression that, once installed as president of a PLO- and Syria-free Lebanon, Gemayel would commit his country to an open peace with the Jewish state. But doubts about Bashir's ability to fulfil that promise arose during the war when, on several occasions, he refused to commit his troops to operations agreed upon with the Israel Defense Forces.[5] His assassination on 14 September 1982 further jeopardized the Israeli-desired outcome when his brother Amin, more cautious and even less enthusiastic about a Lebanese-Israeli relationship, assumed the presidency. Nevertheless, after repeated delays and false starts, Israel and Lebanon entered into negotiations on 28 December 1982, ostensibly seeking border security, peace, and the withdrawal of all foreign forces from Lebanese territory.

PREVIOUS NEGOTIATING EXPERIENCE

Israelis and Lebanese came together in the early 1980s with a considerable wealth of experience negotiating together. The decades before Israel's birth in 1948 witnessed close Lebanese-Zionist relations, particularly between the Maronites and the Jewish Agency for Palestine (JA). Representatives of both sides made periodic attempts to achieve a political alliance based upon the similar minority positions of Palestinian Jews and Lebanese Christians and their shared fears of a perceived common Muslim enemy.[6] Lebanon, then as now, was divided among a variety of religious and ethnic sects locked in constant rivalry for political power. Increasingly desperate Maronite bids to ward off challenges to the political predominance they enjoyed under the French Mandate led to closer relations with the Zionists in Palestine. A 1946 treaty between the politically active Lebanese Maronite Church and the JA foreshadowed the fate of the May 17 Agreement thirty-seven years later: both documents were meticulously negotiated, signed, and accepted by the respective leaderships—and soon after disavowed from the Lebanese side, leaving them entirely inoperative.[7]

In the 1930s and 1940s, Jewish settlements in northern Palestine enjoyed good neighborly relations with Christian and Muslim villages across the border in Lebanon. Zionist emissaries met frequently with representatives of groups besides the Maronites and found several parties interested in talking, with whom they occasionally negotiated draft agreements. None was as far-reaching as the 1946 accord with the Maronite church, but all were equally ineffective—an outcome that the Zionists chalked up to Palestinian and Syrian pressure on their would-be Lebanese friends.[8]

Lebanon entered the first Arab-Israeli war of 1948–49, but its nominal participation and the generally smooth negotiation of the Israeli-Lebanese armistice afterward reinforced pre-state Zionist assumptions that grounds for a mutually acceptable bargain with Lebanon existed. In fact, the negotiation of the armistice between the two countries had been fairly painless, and in alternating negotiating sessions between Ras al-Nakoura and Rosh Hanikra, on the Lebanese and Israeli sides of the border, respectively, these 1949 talks established the precedent for the 1983 meetings, which similarly alternated between Khalde, Lebanon, and Kiryat Shemona and Netanya in Israel. In sitting down face-to-face in 1983, Lebanese and Israelis further replicated the 1949 formula, in which they had negotiated directly with one another, often bypassing the UN mediator by addressing one another in Arabic.[9] The Israel-Lebanon Mixed Armistice Commission (ILMAC), set up in 1949 to monitor and remedy border violations, functioned effectively and afforded Lebanese and Israeli officials a regular point of contact until 1967.

Contacts between Israel and different Lebanese groups lingered after 1948. In 1950 the Phalange engaged the new Israeli government in a brief flurry of exploratory negotiations, looking for assistance in the upcoming Lebanese elections, but with no significant results.[10] A huge influx of PLO fighters into southern Lebanon and Beirut in 1970 tipped the fragile balance among Lebanon's rival sects; by 1976 civil war had erupted and sent the Christian militias in search of external allies. A mutinous army major, Sa'ad Haddad, declared south Lebanon "Free Lebanon," and with aid and encouragement from Israel led a band of local Maronites and Shi'a dedicated to keeping the PLO out of the immediate border region.

In response to a spectacular terrorist attack originating from Lebanon, Israel invaded that country in March 1978 to push PLO forces north of the Litani River, creating a ten-kilometer-wide *cordon sanitaire* along the Israeli border. Haddad's troops were only marginally helpful during "Operation Litani," but Israel continued to back them as the preferred alternative to the United Nations Interim Force in Lebanon (UNIFIL), which took up positions after the Israeli withdrawal in June.[11] The militarily more powerful Phalange approached Israel again as well. With an interest in seeing the Maronites take on the PLO in Lebanon, Israel responded this time by establishing close clandestine contacts with Gemayel and with the other leading Christian families. By 1982, the Maronite-Israeli relationship was quite the open secret, with Maronite militiamen training in Israel and high-level Israeli and Maronite leaders making regular reciprocal visits to one another's homes and headquarters.[12] Lack of familiarity was thus *not* a factor accounting for the ultimate failure of the 1983 negotiations to produce a lasting agreement.

PURPOSES AND MOTIVES

Israeli purposes and motives for entering into post-invasion negotiations with the Lebanese changed over time. Initially, Defense Minister Ariel Sharon and Prime Minister Menachem Begin set out to win far-reaching political, military, and economic concessions first from Bashir and then from Amin Gemayel.[13] Their primary goal was an open and full-fledged treaty of peace between Israel and a newly reconstituted (with the help of the IDF) pro-Israeli Lebanese government. This treaty would assuage Israeli security concerns regarding the PLO and the northern border with Lebanon by allowing for Israeli access, patrols, overflights, early warning stations, and other surveillance facilities in southern Lebanon. Israel's freedom of action in southern Lebanon, coupled with a Lebanese commitment to thwart anti-Israeli activity in its territory, would serve Israeli military interests by blocking Syrian, as well as PLO, movement in Lebanon. Sharon and Begin aimed for an eventual Syrian withdrawal from Lebanon, concomitant with a similar Israeli pull-out.

Another of Israel's objectives was to see its long-time friend, the renegade Major Sa'ad Haddad, rewarded with a high position in Gemayel's new government, possibly that of defense minister, and his south Lebanon militiamen incorporated into the Lebanese army. That Begin believed he could manipulate the composition of Gemayel's cabinet, and impose upon the weak new president a controversial major-gone-AWOL as minister of defense, speaks to the breadth, depth, and arrogance of Israeli plans for Lebanon. The purpose in entering into negotiations may have been peace, but this was to have been a peace dictated to the Lebanese rather than one negotiated with them. The Begin-Sharon team also expected its preferred arrangement with Lebanon to create economic benefits for Israel, by opening new markets for Israeli products and produce. This, in fact, happened in the first heady weeks after the invasion, while a good many Lebanese were still prepared to view the IDF as their liberator from PLO (and Syrian) domination.[14]

As both the fighting and the negotiating dragged on, however, it became clear that the chances for an active and open peace with Lebanon were slim to none. Nevertheless, there were other strong Israeli motives for continuing the negotiations. Among these were hopes of delaying attempts to implement the Reagan Plan of 1 September 1982 (discussed on page 48, under Timing) and, paradoxically, the desire to appear flexible and forthcoming in American eyes, thus repairing US-Israeli relations which were then suffering from American unhappiness with having been dragged into Lebanon by Israel in the first place.[15]

Lebanese purposes and motives evolved similarly. Bashir Gemayel believed he had the "unique ability to reconcile a pro-Israel orientation with authoritative national leadership."[16] He had planned to use Israeli resources and assistance in consolidating his control over civil-war-torn Lebanon and driving the Syrians and the PLO from the country. Amin Gemayel, although lacking the personal and political strength of his late brother, devised a similarly ambitious agenda, which included:

- securing multisectarian support for his presidency;
- ending the violence wracking the country;
- assimilating the fractious confessional groups into a united Lebanon;
- negotiating the withdrawal of all foreign forces from Lebanese territory; and
- presiding over the physical and political reconstruction of the nation.

Another aim was to diffuse the Israeli-Palestinian spillover into Lebanon, which had contributed so much to Lebanon's own inter-confessional tensions and tragedies. For Amin, even more than for Bashir, a peace treaty with Israel was a bitter pill to force down the throat of a skeptical nation, but one that he thought the people could swallow if a treaty meant a speedy Israeli withdrawal from Lebanon, and possibly a Syrian pull-back as well.

Gemayel's people exhibited an initial temptation to indulge in a classic "exchange of services" with the Israelis, i.e., trading peace for services such as Israeli influence with the Americans and the sharing of intelligence. This faded in the face of stiff Arab opposition to the entire endeavor. Yet, even as the negotiations foundered and the chances for a complete Israeli withdrawal dimmed, other Lebanese concerns—primarily the need to win legitimacy and American backing for the shaky Gemayel administration, and particularly American economic aid with which the government hoped to rebuild the shattered nation—dictated a continuation of the negotiations.

Thus, neither side approached these negotiations with a compelling desire to settle the differences between them and replace hostility with diplomacy. Instead, a multitude of shifting goals held by both Israel and Lebanon reflected the historical pattern whereby Arabs and Israelis negotiated at length for many reasons—none of which was the quest for an honorable and mutually satisfying peace.

TIMING

The timing of the negotiations, particularly the great delay in getting them underway, contributed to the course they took and the failure of the agreement eventually reached. After the resounding defeat of Syrian forces in the first days of the June 1982 campaign and the expulsion of thousands of PLO fighters from Beirut that September, Israel felt strong enough to press Lebanon for maximum concessions while giving up few of its own. Once US mediators got involved in the negotiating process, they too bought into Israel's perception of a permanently weakened PLO and, more importantly, of an indefinitely disabled Syria. Many scholars and diplomats believe that, had Lebanon and Israel moved quickly to hammer out an accord (i.e., within the first three months after the departure of the PLO from Beirut), they might indeed have been able to achieve the withdrawal of Syrian and Israeli troops, some quiet cross-border traffic between Israel and Lebanon, and a stable border region. The key to that three-month window of opportunity, analysts agree, was the weakness and disorganization of Syria and its Lebanese allies.[17] Those three months, and the five months it took to conclude the agreement, however, were time enough for Syria to rearm and reestablish its position. By May 1983, Syria had sufficiently recovered so that it could thwart the implementation of the accord.

Another event whose timing affected this agreement in a variety of ways was President Ronald Reagan's speech of 1 September 1982 (Appendix, Document 5). The announcement of the president's plan came on the heels of the evacuation of PLO cadres from besieged Beirut,[18] which the Reagan administration saw as "an opportunity for a more far-reaching peace effort in the region." Expressing the assumption that the Lebanon problem was all but taken care of, Reagan focused on a resumption of the stalled Palestinian autonomy talks (mandated by Camp David but boycotted by the PLO and Jordan)[19] "to pave the way for permitting the Palestinian people to exercise their legitimate rights." Reagan called upon the Israeli government to freeze further settlement activity in the occupied territories, and for the question of the future self-government of the Palestinians there to be decided "in association with Jordan."

One of the purposes of Israel's invasion of Lebanon and the destruction of the PLO infrastructure had been the consolidation of Israeli control over the West Bank. The Reagan Plan's focus on autonomy for the Palestinians in the occupied territories and its proposal that those lands be federated with Jordan thus came as a rude shock to the Begin government.[20] By making peace in Lebanon a stepping-stone to a resolution of the Palestinian problem, the Reagan Plan hampered Israeli-Lebanese negotiations by encouraging the Israelis to stall in Lebanon so as to postpone action on the West Bank. The Arab response to the plan was less categorical. King Hussein expressed noncommittal interest; eight days later, the Arab states responded with their own plan issued from their summit meeting in Fez, Morocco; and opponents of the President Reagan's initiative sat back quietly and let the Begin Government bury it for them.[21]

Poor American timing, in the most literal sense, also had a negative impact upon the Israeli-Lebanese negotiations: coincidentally, US Ambassador Samuel Lewis officially apprised Begin of Reagan's agenda only hours before the Israeli prime minister was to meet Bashir Gemayel to congratulate him personally upon his election to the Lebanese presidency.

Equally infuriated by the substance of the Reagan Plan as by its preparation behind his back, Begin arrived for what was to have been a victory celebration with Bashir in a black and bitter mood. Several accounts describe the disastrous meeting in which the ill-tempered Begin brusquely lectured the young president-elect on Israeli demands and the need for the immediate signing of a formal peace treaty.[22] This unpleasant encounter further spoiled Gemayel's already tenuous readiness to cooperate with his Israeli allies.

A relentless succession of bloody setbacks in Lebanon constituted a timing factor in that each new catastrophe pushed the negotiators to try to wring from this mess something tangible that might stop the violence and justify the war. Bashir's assassination by Syrian agents and the Phalange's massacre of Palestinian civilians in the Sabra and Shatilla refugee camps (September 1982), the bombing of the US embassy in Beirut (April 1983), and the steadily rising casualty rate among American servicepeople, IDF soldiers, Lebanese civilians, and dueling Lebanese militias weighed on American, Israeli, and Lebanese shoulders as the diplomats hunched over tables and maps, trying to forge an accord. The worsening of the situation in Lebanon and its increasingly high cost in blood, money, and reputation were apparently not enough to bring the parties to an agreement during those first three months after the PLO evacuation, but were pressure enough to keep negotiators at the table long after it was clear that a workable settlement was not possible at that time.

STATUS OF THE NEGOTIATORS

Traditional problems with the status of the negotiators greatly contributed to the accord's failure. Many Arab régimes, and indeed many Lebanese, considered the Gemayel government illegitimate and representative of one narrow Maronite faction at best, Israeli-installed puppets at worst. Aware of this, and hoping to broaden the base of support for his policy, Gemayel attempted to draw representatives from all of Lebanon's major sects into the negotiating process. The result, complained David Kimche, then director-general of the Israeli foreign ministry, an architect of the Israeli-Maronite alliance and leader of the Israeli negotiating team, was that

> the composition of the Lebanese delegation [including Chaldeans, Shi'a, Sunnis, Maronites and Greek Orthodox Catholics] destroyed any thought of rapid progress. . . . Each member had to report to his respective community leaders and to ask for their approval before he could agree to anything.[23]

The president similarly ran every proposal by his Sunni prime minister, Shafiq al-Wazzan. Although Bashir had been inclined to challenge Syrian sway in his country, Amin walked in the shadow Syria had cast over the

Lebanese presidency for decades, and Hafiz al-Asad was pressing hard for the cancellation of the Lebanese-Israeli negotiations. The Lebanese delegates to the talks (including, finally, the president himself) proved unable to make good on their end of the May 17 obligations.

Israel correctly perceived the weakness and malleability of the Lebanese government, but incorrectly calculated that Israel could use this frailty to its advantage. The asymmetry in status between Lebanon's representatives and the high-ranking Israeli delegates, occasionally including Menachem Begin and Ariel Sharon themselves, further encouraged the Israelis in the belief that they could dictate terms rather than negotiate them. This showed a lack of appreciation for the fact that Lebanon's very weakness, which made it vulnerable to Israeli pressure, also mitigated against its ability to fulfil its treaty obligations. In lording their perceived superiority over first Bashir and then Amin Gemayel, Begin and Sharon repeatedly angered, embarrassed, and humiliated their Lebanese partners, who chafed at being treated like "spineless vassals."[24]

The counterproductive US pressure to produce an agreement increased commensurately with the status of each new mediator to come on the scene, from diplomat Morris Draper, to Ambassador Philip Habib, and finally to Secretary of State George Shultz himself. No matter how high Israel and the United States raised the ante, however, war-ravaged Lebanon simply could not produce one individual capable of striking a deal, selling it to the severely factionalized Lebanese people, and delivering upon his end of the bargain.

THIRD-PARTY CONSIDERATIONS

As already indicated, extensive mediation activity by the United States meant that third-party considerations played a decisive part in these negotiations. US goals also evolved over time and in response to developments on the ground. On the Lebanese front, American aspirations included Israeli, Syrian, and PLO withdrawals, a quiet Israeli-Lebanese border, the restoration of a central Lebanese government, and the rebuilding of the Lebanese army so that it could extend the new central government's role beyond the confines of the presidential palace. Reagan's personal envoy, Philip Habib, had made a start by negotiating the evacuation of the PLO from the city in late September 1982.[25] The PLO fighters exited Beirut under the watchful eyes of the US-led Multinational Force, which itself departed from Beirut several days later, its mission apparently a success.

The Reagan Plan, however, added even more far-reaching goals for a resolution of the broader Israeli-Palestinian conflict. President Reagan acknowledged that, in explicitly enunciating detailed proposals for an Arab-Israeli settlement, he was pushing the United States beyond its normally cautious mediatory position. Indeed, the Plan spelled out concrete suggestions for implementing the unfinished Palestinian agenda contained in the Camp David framework and committed the United States to an active leadership role. Rashid Khalidi has argued that a history of multiple failed attempts over the years by external powers to manipulate events in Lebanon to their advantage boded ill for the ambitious US agenda from the outset.[26] From a different angle, William Quandt has detailed the many mistakes that sabotaged Reagan's policy in Lebanon, among them errors of analysis, judgment, and execution, a mistaken assumption that limited force could achieve political objectives, and a lack of presidential leadership. Quandt suggests, however, that a more limited and realistic US policy, carefully pursued, was not beyond reach.[27]

Unfortunately, the role that US diplomacy played followed the historically unhelpful model. Appreciating the importance of American support for their respective interests, both sides followed the pre-1948 pattern of directing more effort toward persuading US intermediaries to accept and impose their versions of a settlement than toward compromising with one another. Amin Gemayel angled for concrete American support for his régime; Israel tried to salvage at least some of its original goals in launching the invasion in the first place, while simultaneously shoring up its frayed relationship with the United States. Perhaps the strongest card the United States had to play was the threat to favor one side over the other.[28] Once Secretary of State George Shultz took personal control of the negotiations, committing the prestige of his office to their success, both Israel and Lebanon felt the pressure to hand the American secretary of state a win—or at least not appear responsible for his failure. For some Lebanese and Israelis, the "success" of the document finally signed on 17 May 1983 lay more in terms of enhancing (Lebanon) or repairing (Israel) relations with the United States than in dealing with one another. Ironically, Shultz's vigorous efforts were at odds with the lackluster interest displayed by the administration. Despite his steely declaration of the Reagan Plan, President Reagan never committed the resources to a serious follow-through. US ambivalence about the course of events in Lebanon fit the Great Power pattern for irresoluteness.[29]

Recognizing at the outset of the negotiations that stated American policy had come to correspond more closely with Lebanese priorities (Israeli withdrawal) than with Israeli goals (a peace treaty), Ariel Sharon initially tried to limit US involvement by secretly negotiating an accord with Amin Gemayel's personal emissary, and then presenting US envoy Philip Habib with a fait accompli.[30] But Sharon's suspicions that US support would embolden the Lebanese to resist Israeli pressure for concessions proved accurate. Once Gemayel had similarly discerned that US policy inclined toward his position, he dismissed the secret protocol as merely preliminary planning and went on to solicit full American partici-

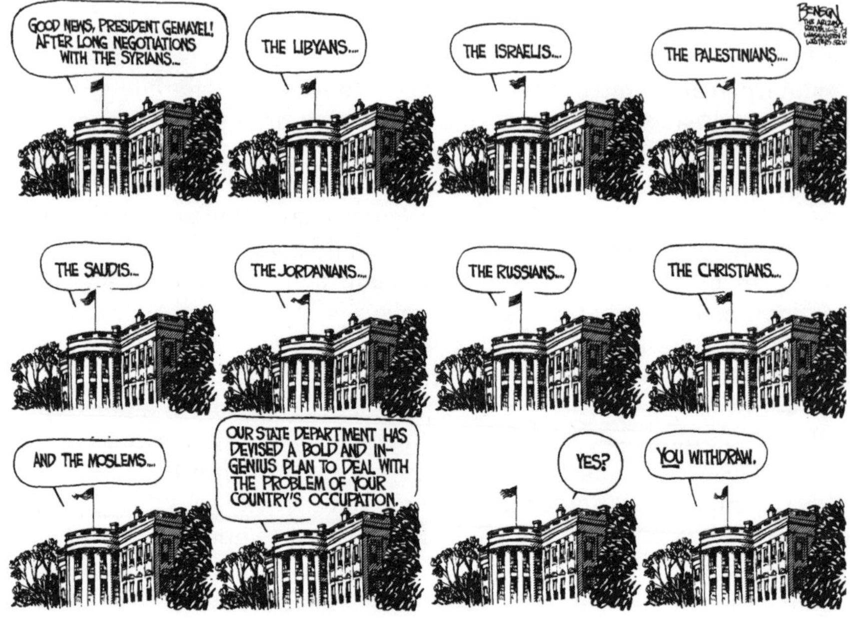

Courtesy of Steve Benson, *Arizona Republic*

pation in tripartite negotiations. During this early phase of the talks, Lebanon tried to use its perceived common cause with the United States for leverage against the Israelis, and held to hard-line positions that had worked for Sadat.[31] Like the Egyptian leader before him, Gemayel at first refused to consider Israeli demands to maintain troops, proxies, or surveillance stations on sovereign Lebanese soil and rejected language that would have favored Lebanon's treaty obligations with Israel over its relations with the Arab states or the Arab League.[32]

As US involvement in Lebanon increased, so did US pressure on Israel and Lebanon to deliver something to vindicate its increasingly costly and unpopular role as peacekeeper in a land not at peace. The return of the Multinational Force after Bashir's assassination handed the United States the lead role in trying to untangle the Lebanese skein. But a devastating suicide bomb attack against the US Marines' barracks in October of 1983, and firefights with the Druze and Syrian forces in September and December of that year sapped the US resolve to see the Lebanese imbroglio through to a peaceful resolution. At the same time, in taking the side of Gemayel's government and firing upon its Druze and Syrian opponents, the United States lost whatever trust it once enjoyed as mediator and became, in the eyes of Gemayel's many enemies, irrevocably associated with his government and its allies, the Israeli invaders.[33]

American interests in producing an agreement extended the Lebanese-Israeli negotiations long after the irreconcilable nature of the parties' minimum objectives and the resurgence of Syrian influence had precluded any hope of a successful accord. In the end, however, the United States could not maintain the political or physical presence required to fortify Amin in the face of overwhelming Syrian opposition, and proved unable to shepherd the agreement signed on 17 May 1983 through to implementation.

PROPOSED TERMS OF AGREEMENT

Israel and Lebanon also stumbled badly over differing expectations regarding the terms of the agreement. Reminiscent of the establishment of the old ILMAC, Lebanese officials initially tried to deny any political color to the 1983 talks, assigning a *military* man to head their delegation and arguing for an agenda restricted to military matters.[34] Israeli interests necessitated a *political* arrangement, however, and Israel's agenda prevailed. Between December 1982 and May 1983, 138 hours of Israeli-Lebanese talks under US auspices ultimately produced the ill-fated May 17 agreement.

Neither Israel nor Lebanon was happy with the document. In terms of security, Israel gave up on retaining a direct presence in south Lebanon and early warning stations, in return for joint Lebanese-Israeli patrols. Ze'ev Schiff and Ehud Ya'ari point out that, on the political side as well, the agreement fell far short of Israeli hopes:

> The principle of a "package deal" had been whittled down to . . . unofficial relations . . . underwritten by American guarantees. Amin Gemayel was not required to commit himself publicly to an open border with Israel; a joint supervisory committee took the place of diplomatic missions; and the framework that was supposed to formulate a peace treaty vanished altogether.[35]

Despite Israeli misgivings, the outcome of the Israeli-Lebanese negotiations resembled the Camp David process in that Israel moved the least in scaling back its original demands, while Lebanon (and the United States) retreated on many key points in order to secure a signed agreement. Criticizing the accord for satisfying too many of Israel's demands and leaving the Lebanese open to scathing condemnation by Amin's many foes, Michael Hudson writes,

> Under the terms of that agreement, the southern third of the country [Lebanon] would be a "security zone" in which Lebanese troop deployments or overflights would require Israeli approval. The Israel-supported South Lebanon Army would be incorporated into the Lebanese Army. Lebanon's treaties with Arab countries not in conformity with the May 17 Agreement would be nullified; military transfers from other Arab countries would be curbed, as would anti-Israel political activity or publishing. The new Lebanese govern-

ment, having come to power under the shadow of Israeli tanks, [apparently] considered this to be the best deal obtainable.[36]

The May 17 document was a peace treaty in all but name. But it was simultaneously a disappointment to the Israelis, who had hoped to claim their second official peace accord with an Arab neighbor; an embarrassment to most Lebanese, who rejected its tight Israeli embrace; and an offense to those in the Arab world who objected to a Lebanese-Israeli peace while Syrian, Jordanian, and Palestinian claims against Israel were left unresolved. Sensitivity toward public opinion led negotiators to reveal publicly only the least forthcoming of the Lebanese concessions. "As finally constituted, the May 17 agreement was merely the wrapping around a series of secret understandings."[37]

Uneasy over the terms of an agreement they could only guess at, Saudi Arabia and Jordan, whose support the United States had expected, declined to endorse the accord. The Americans, Israelis, and Lebanese had anticipated Syria's rejection of the agreement, but especially in the case of the first two, seriously underestimated Syria's recuperative powers and ability to derail it. An unwritten Israeli caveat hinging the IDF's withdrawal from Lebanon upon a Syrian pull-out was yet another nail in the coffin, handing the Syrians an unexpected veto over implementation of the accord.

PSYCHOLOGICAL FACTORS

Israeli and American leaders tried to exploit the psychological aspect of the negotiations by depicting the direct Lebanese-Israeli talks and the agreement as a breakthrough in Arab-Israeli relations: a second "Camp David." In reality, however, Lebanese willingness to deal with Israel reflected not reconciliation but the country's relative weakness, its president's decision to seek US backing, and a lack of alternatives for securing an Israeli withdrawal. The Lebanese leadership downplayed the negotiations accordingly, presenting them, when at all, as a joint American-Lebanese venture.

In thinking that Gemayel could or would sell his people on full peaceful relations with Israel, the architects of the May 17 agreement displayed a gross misreading of anti-Israel sentiment in Lebanon. Observing that sometimes "nothing fails like success," Robert Gromoll contends that Begin erred in trying to impose his version of a prefabricated Camp-David-like formula on a uniquely Lebanese situation.[38] In pressuring Bashir Gemayel to follow Sadat's footsteps to Jerusalem and in demanding of him, and later of Amin, the conclusion of a separate and open peace treaty with Israel, Begin ignored the reality that weak, factionalized Lebanon was not Egypt, leader of the Arab world, and that neither of the

Gemayel brothers ever commanded the kind of control over his country and countrymen that Sadat did.

In addition to the traditional opponents of Israel in the Lebanese body politic, there was now a new foe in the south with which to contend: the fundamentalist Shi'a Muslim group Hizballah. The Shi'a had initially welcomed the IDF with rice and flowers for freeing them from PLO domination. But as the war and negotiations dragged on, they changed their perception of the heavy-handed Israeli troops hunkered down among them from liberators to occupiers.[39] Hizballah suicide bombers and guerillas in Israel's south Lebanese "security zone" made more persistent and deadly enemies for the IDF than the PLO there had ever been. Israel's indefinite control over the security zone and the collateral damage to south Lebanese villages from Israel-Hizballah firefights and Israeli retaliatory operations further embittered Lebanese public opinion against Israel.

The May 1983 accord failed to overcome a growing Israeli antipathy for the Lebanese, as well. Prior to the war, many Israelis had harbored a romantic impression (dating back to the 1930s) of a beleaguered Christian Lebanese enclave anxious to make peace with Jewish Israel, but constrained by their common Muslim enemy. The Begin government designed, described, and defended "Peace for the Galilee" as a strategic attack against the PLO, but was not beyond trying to rally support for the operation by capitalizing on popular positive perceptions of the Lebanese Maronites. Several times the prime minister expressed satisfaction at the IDF's role in rescuing the Christians from alleged Muslim oppression, comparing their situation to the plight of European Jewry in World War II.[40] But when Gemayel's forces balked at openly siding with the IDF, and when the expulsion of the PLO failed to elicit an outpouring of Christian gratitude, the Israeli public began to rethink its previously rosy image of its neighbor to the north. After the Christian militias massacred Palestinians at the Sabra and Shatilla camps under Israeli control, Israelis staged massive demonstrations against their own government's involvement in a Lebanon where each community was now seen as unsavory as the next. On 25 September 1982, 10 percent of the entire population of Israel—some 400,000 people—turned out in Tel Aviv for a massive rally against the war.[41] Bloodshed continued in tandem with the negotiations, and public opinion revolted against the mounting IDF casualties. By 17 May 1983 the collective psychological trauma of the Lebanese fiasco had inured most Israelis to their government's attempts to celebrate the accord with Lebanon as a worthwhile outcome of the war.

Efraim Inbar has suggested that the Israeli-Lebanese accord is a case where the operation succeeded but the patient died.[42] Repeating historically unsuccessful patterns of Arab-Israeli negotiating behavior, Israeli and Lebanese representatives painfully negotiated a sterile and inoperative accord. The Lebanese and Israeli cabinets ratified the agreement; Syria condemned it. Bowed and bloodied, the American troops in Lebanon "redeployed" to their ships between February and March of 1984 and quietly set sail for home. In the face of the abrupt US departure from Lebanon, and unable to withstand alone the unrelenting Syrian pressure, Gemayel's government officially abrogated the May 1983 agreement on 5 March 1984 and shut down the Israeli mission in Lebanon established to administer the treaty. In 1985 the IDF undertook a unilateral, three-stage withdrawal, leaving in its wake the self-declared security zone patrolled by small IDF units supporting the Israeli-sponsored South Lebanese Army.

Facts on the ground defeated fantasies. A potent combination of all-too-familiar dubious purposes, ulterior motives, external pressures, ineffective leadership, and poor timing perpetuated negotiations and propelled the parties all the way to signatures on a dotted line. They could not, however, paper over the gaps in power and priorities that defied diplomatic solutions.

NOTES

1. See Raphael Israeli, ed., *PLO in Lebanon: Selected Documents,* London: Weidenfeld and Nicolson, 1983; Rex Brynen, *Sanctuary and Survival: The PLO in Lebanon,* Boulder, CO: Westview Press, 1990.

2. Richard B. Parker, *The Politics of Miscalculation in the Middle East,* Bloomington: Indiana University Press, 1993, 171, 176; Ze'ev Schiff and Ehud Ya'ari, *Israel's Lebanon War,* New York: Simon and Schuster, 1984, 42–43, 71, 304–305; Itamar Rabinovich, *The War for Lebanon, 1970–1983,* Ithaca: Cornell University Press, 1984, 133; David Kimche, *The Last Option: After Nasser, Arafat, and Saddam Hussein, The Quest for Peace in the Middle East,* New York: Scribner's, 1991, 144–45, 153–58; Barry Rubin and Laura Blum, *The May 1983 Agreement over Lebanon,* Baltimore: Foreign Policy Institute, Johns Hopkins University, Pew Charitable Trusts, 1988, 6–7.

See also M. Thomas Davis, *40 KM into Lebanon,* Washington, DC: National Defense University Press, 1987; Richard A. Gabriel, *Operation Peace for Galilee,* New York: Hill and Wang, 1984; Jonathan C. Randal, *Going All the Way: Christian Warlords, Israeli Adventurers and the War in Lebanon,* New York: Vintage Books, 1983; Ze'ev Schiff, "Lebanon: Motivations and Interests in Israel's Policy," *Middle East Journal* 38 (Spring 1984), 220–27.

3. On Syrian involvement in Lebanon in the 1970s, see Walid Khalidi, *Conflict and Violence in Lebanon: Confrontation in the Middle East,* Cambridge: Center for International Studies, Harvard University, 1979, chaps. 2–3, and pp. 82–84; Patrick Seale, *Asad: The Struggle for the Middle East,* Berkeley: University of California Press, 1989, chap. 17. On Syrian opposition to the May 17 Agreement, see ibid., chaps. 22, 23; Avner Yaniv, *Dilemmas of Security: Politics, Strategy, and the Israeli Experience in Lebanon,* Oxford: Oxford University Press, 1987, 153. See also As'as Abukhalil, "Determinants and Characteristics of Syrian Policy in Lebanon," in *Peace for Lebanon? From War to Reconstruction,* ed. Deirdre Collings, Boulder, CO: Lynne Rienner, 1994, 123–36.

Additional analysis of the Lebanese civil war and beyond can be found in Halim Barakat, ed., *Toward a Viable Lebanon,* Washington, DC: Georgetown University, Center for Contemporary Arab Studies, 1988; Robert Fisk, *Pity the Nation: Lebanon at War,* London: Deutsch, 1990; David Gilmour, *Lebanon: The Fractured*

Country, New York: St. Martin's, 1984; David C. Gordon, *The Republic of Lebanon: Nation in Jeopardy,* Boulder, CO: Westview Press, 1983; Edward P. Haley and Lewis W. Snider, eds., *Lebanon in Crisis,* New York: Syracuse University Press, 1979; William Harris, *Faces of Lebanon: Sects, Wars and Global Extensions,* Princeton: Marcus Wiener, 1997; Rosemary Hollis and Nadim Shehadi, eds., *Lebanon on Hold: Implications for Middle East Peace,* London: Royal Institute of International Affairs, 1996; Augustus Richard Norton, "Lebanon after Ta'if: Is the Civil War Over?" *Middle East Journal* 45 (Summer 1991), 457–73; Kamal Salibi, *A House of Many Mansions: The History of Lebanon Reconsidered,* Berkeley: University of California Press, 1988.

4. Contacts between the Jewish Agency for Palestine and the Phalange under Pierre Gemayel occurred during the pre-1948 period, but, as a rule, Gemayel's battle against Muslim rule in Lebanon did not translate into a pro-Zionist orientation on the Palestine question. See Laura Zittrain Eisenberg, *My Enemy's Enemy: Lebanon in the Early Zionist Imagination, 1900–1948,* Detroit: Wayne State University Press, 1994, 83–84, 126, 135, 137; L. Z. Eisenberg, "Desperate Diplomacy: The Zionist-Maronite Treaty of 1946," *Studies in Zionism* 13:2 (Autumn 1992), 152, 154 (n. 22).

5. Schiff and Ya'ari, 15, 22–25, 46–51, 56–57; Kimche, 154–56; Yaniv, 152–53. Already in the first week of the war, Bashir gave an interview to American television in which he denied the existence of an alliance with Israel. Extracts of the interview, broadcast on ABC news, 27 June 1982, and ABC's *20/20* program, 9 July 1982, are in Israeli, 256–59.

6. Eisenberg, *My Enemy's Enemy,* esp. 28–36; Eisenberg, "Desperate Diplomacy," 147–51.

7. Eisenberg, *My Enemy's Enemy,* 136–41, 163–69; Eisenberg, "Desperate Diplomacy," 147–63.

8. Eisenberg, *My Enemy's Enemy,* 32–33, 65–66, 110–11; Neil Caplan and Ian Black, "Israel and Lebanon: Origins of a Relationship," *Jerusalem Quarterly* 27 (Spring 1983), 48–58; Yoav Gelber, "Antecedents of the Jewish-Druze Alliance in Palestine," *Middle Eastern Studies* 28:2 (April 1992), 352–73.

9. Shabtai Rosenne to Eliahu Sasson, 13 March 1949 (Report on Talks at Ras al-Nakoura), Israel State Archives, *Documents on the Foreign Policy of Israel, vol. III—Armistice Negotiations with the Arab States, December 1948–July 1949,* ed. Yemima Rosenthal, Jerusalem: 1983, 309–11. A selection of documents pertaining to the negotiation of the Israeli-Lebanese armistice agreement appears in ibid., 279–326.

10. Benny Morris, "Israel and the Lebanese Phalange: The Birth of a Relationship, 1948–1951," *Studies in Zionism* 5:1 (Spring 1984), 125–44; B. Morris, "The Phalange Connection," *Jerusalem Post Magazine,* 1 July 1983, pp. 7–8; Eisenberg, *My Enemy's Enemy,* 159; David Ben-Gurion, *Min ha-Yoman* [From Ben-Gurion's Diary, The War of Independence], eds. G. Rivlin and E. Orren, Tel Aviv: Misrad ha-Bitachon, 1986, 444.

11. W. Khalidi, chap. 6; Ezer Weizman, *The Battle for Peace,* New York: Bantam, 1981, chap. 21; Brynen, 115–19.

12. Schiff and Ya'ari, chap. 1; Rabinovich; Kimche, 125–26, 130, 132–33, 153–55, 157, 164–68; Parker, 171; Yaniv; Yair Evron, *War and Intervention in Lebanon: The Israeli-Syrian Deterrence Dialogue,* Baltimore: Johns Hopkins University Press, 1987.

13. Schiff and Ya'ari, 41–43; Rubin and Blum, 6–7; Robert H. Gromoll, *The May 17 Accord: Studies of Diplomacy and Negotiations on Troop Withdrawals from Lebanon,* Pittsburgh: Graduate School of Public and International Affairs, Pew Charitable Trusts, 1987, 6.

14. According to one Israeli account, for a short while Lebanese tourists crossed into Israel, and Lebanese merchants imported Israeli goods not only for the

Lebanese markets, but also to re-export to Arab countries after suitable repacking and relabeling. Trade between the two countries soared, exceeding that between Israel and many of her traditional European trading partners. Kimche, 167; "First Boomlet in Tourism from Lebanon," *Jerusalem Post,* 30 November 1982, p. 3.

15. See, e.g., Ze'ev Schiff, "The Green Light," *Foreign Policy* 50 (Spring 1983), 73–85; Raymond Tanter, *Who's at the Helm? Lessons of Lebanon,* Boulder, CO: Westview Press, 1990, 31–35, 110–13.

16. Rubin and Blum, 3.

17. Kimche, 164; Rubin and Blum, 28; Parker, 180, 198–99 (quoting US Ambassador to Israel, Samuel Lewis, and US Ambassador to Lebanon, Robert Dillon).

18. See Rashid Khalidi, *Under Siege: PLO Decisionmaking during the 1982 War,* New York: Columbia University Press, 1986.

19. For documentation on the conflicting Israeli and Egyptian interpretations of the nature of future Palestinian "autonomy," see Yehuda Lukacs, ed., *The Israeli-Palestinian Conflict: A Documentary Record, 1967–1990,* Cambridge and New York: Cambridge University Press, 1992, 160–70. Cf. Begin's December 1977 autonomy proposals in ibid., 153–55 (discussed above, Chapter 1).

20. See, e.g., Israel Cabinet communiqué, 2 September 1982, in Lukacs, 200–203.

21. See William B. Quandt, *Peace Process: American Diplomacy and the Arab-Israeli Conflict since 1967,* Washington, DC: Brookings Institution, 1993, 344–45; Mark Tessler, *A History of the Israeli-Palestinian Conflict,* Bloomington: Indiana University Press, 1994, 600–609; Lukacs, 478–79.

22. Gromoll, 21–23; Kimche, 157–58; Parker, 183; Schiff and Ya'ari, 233–36; Yaniv, 152.

23. Kimche, 166–67.

24. Schiff and Ya'ari, 235.

25. R. Khalidi, *Under Siege*; Tanter; Philip Habib, *Diplomacy and the Search for Peace in the Middle East,* Georgetown: Institute for the Study of Diplomacy, 1985.

26. Rashid Khalidi, "Problems of Foreign Intervention in Lebanon," *American Arab Affairs* 7 (Winter 1983–84), 24–29.

27. William B. Quandt, "Reagan's Lebanon Policy: Trial and Error," *Middle East Journal* 38 (Spring 1984), 237–54.

28. Rubin and Blum, 26.

29. In addition to the sources cited above, see the following for their interpretations and critiques of US policy: Ronald J. Young, *Missed Opportunities for Peace: US Middle East Policy: 1981–1986,* Philadelphia: American Friends Service Committee, 1987; Michael C. Hudson, "The United States' Involvement in Lebanon," in *Toward a Viable Lebanon,* ed. Halim Barakat, Washington, DC: Georgetown University Center for Contemporary Arab Studies, 1988, 210–31.

30. Seale, 404–405; Parker, 184; Schiff and Ya'ari, 290–91; Kimche, 164–65; Gromoll, 32–33; Rubin and Blum, 14–15.

31. In many respects the dynamics among the three parties resembled those of Sadat, Begin, and Carter five years earlier. The United States quickly assumed the role of mediator, and eventually only US pressure, namely the personal commitment of the highest officials (Carter and then Shultz) kept the negotiations going until the end. Again the US position was closer to that of the Arab partner, leading Israel to work as hard to limit US involvement as Egypt and then Lebanon worked to expand it. Reflecting both the implications of having the United States as mediator as well as dubious Lebanese purposes in negotiating with Israel (see above, "Purposes and Motives"), Amin Gemayel had, in the words of Schiff and Ya'ari, "an eye more to Washington than Jerusalem and, like Sadat before him, regarded as his primary goal not an accommodation with Israel but the attainment of American support for his regime." Schiff and Ya'ari, 293.

32. Schiff and Ya'ari, 292. David Kimche, who had developed a close relationship with both Bashir and Amin Gemayel, claims that US envoy Philip Habib actually urged Gemayel *not* to sign a separate peace with Israel so as not to estrange Lebanon from the Arab world, adding that the United States had given Sadat the same advice in 1978, much as the British had advised King Abdallah of Transjordan three decades earlier. Kimche, 172, 182.

33. Anthony McDermott and Kjell Skjelsbaek, eds., *The Multinational Force in Beirut, 1982–1984,* Miami: Florida International University Press, 1991.

34. Another parallel may be drawn with the 1949 Egyptian foreign minister's appointment of three military men and one civilian to his country's Rhodes delegation (while the Israelis did the reverse: four foreign ministry officials and one senior military officer). See Neil Caplan, "A Tale of Two Cities: The Rhodes and Lausanne Conferences, 1949," *JPS* 21:3 (Spring 1992), 7–8.

35. Schiff and Ya'ari, 296.

36. Michael C. Hudson, "Lebanon's US Connection in the New World Order," in Collings, 143.

37. Schiff and Ya'ari, 296–97.

38. Gromoll, 17–19.

39. Augustus Richard Norton, *Amal and the Shi'a: Struggle for the Soul of Lebanon,* Austin: University of Texas, 1987, 84–85, and esp. chap. 7. See also Frederic C. Hof, *Galilee Divided: The Israel-Lebanon Frontier, 1916–1984,* Boulder, CO: Westview Press, 1985; Fida Nasrallah, *Prospects for Lebanon: The Questions of South Lebanon,* London: Centre for Lebanese Studies, 1992 (includes documents); Laura Zittrain Eisenberg, "Israel's South Lebanon Imbroglio," *Middle East Quarterly,* 4:2 (June 1997), 60–69.

40. Scholars are divided over the extent to which the Phalange-Israeli relationship in the 1980s constituted a modern-day incarnation of the old idea for an alliance among non-Muslim religious minorities. Our research persuades us to the contrary: that the contemporary arrangement was based overwhelmingly on *strategic* calculations and the anti-PLO and anti-Syrian stances of the two sides. See Laura Zittrain Eisenberg, "History Revisited or Revamped? The Roots of Contemporary Israeli Interests in Lebanon," lecture delivered at the Moshe Dayan Center for Middle Eastern and African Studies, Tel Aviv University, 20 October 1993.

41. For an evocative description of the protest, see "Eyewitness," in Shulamith Hareven, *The Vocabulary of Peace: Life, Culture and Politics in the Middle East,* San Francisco: Mercury House, 1995, 157–63. For the findings of an official Israeli Commission of Inquiry investigation into Israeli culpability for the Sabra and Shatilla massacres, see *The Beirut Massacre: The Complete Kahan Commission Report,* New York: Karz-Cohl, 1983. No one in Lebanon has ever been arrested, charged, or tried for the murders.

42. Inbar, 81.

Chapter 3

PREMATURE PEACEMAKING

THE 1987 HUSSEIN-PERES AGREEMENT (THE LONDON DOCUMENT)

In 1987, Jordan's King Hussein and Israeli Foreign Minister Shimon Peres personally drafted an accord in a secret London meeting, the culmination of many months of intense communication between the two men and their trusted aides. "The London Document" of 11 April 1987 (Appendix, Document 7) broke new ground in a number of ways, but ultimately fell victim to several traditionally flawed conditions of Arab-Israeli negotiation.

PREVIOUS NEGOTIATING EXPERIENCE

The scope and depth of Zionist-Transjordanian and Israeli-Jordanian contact since the 1920s have been remarkable. Israel and Jordan are, after all, the Solomonic baby who survived. In 1921 the British divided the territory of the Palestine Mandate in two: the territory west of the Jordan remained "Palestine," but that part east of the Jordan River became the Hashemite Amirate of Transjordan, with Abdallah ibn Hussein as ruler (see Map 2). In bequeathing a kingdom and a throne to Abdallah, the British were repaying a debt owed to Abdallah's father, Sharif Hussein of the Hashemite family that ruled the Hejaz area of the Arabian Peninsula. The sharif had rallied an Arab revolt on behalf of the British and against the Turks during World War I.[1]

But Abdallah was not content to govern only his assigned desert principality. Hegemonic ambitions to rule over "Greater Syria" made the ultimate disposition of western Palestine a matter of continuing interest to him. In the 1930s he solidified a budding political relationship with the Jewish Agency Executive through a land-sales option.[2] For the amir, an alliance with the Jews offered a common front against the Palestinian Arabs, who were demanding Palestinian-Arab sovereignty over the land Abdallah coveted and who absolutely rejected any formula for sharing Palestine with the Zionists. In his desire to outflank the Palestinians and extend his kingdom to the Mediterranean coast, he was prepared to accept a Jewish autonomous unit within western Palestine under his sovereignty—a scenario that had little appeal to Zionists.

But the Zionists and the amir had reason to find one another appealing partners nevertheless. There is evidence that Abdallah held traditionally exaggerated beliefs about the wealth and influence the Jews could put at his disposal, perhaps reinforced by the gifts he was offered and accepted. For the Zionists, Abdallah was the pan-Arab, non-Palestinian leader who might eventually accommodate a Jewish National Home in Palestine in the classic "exchange of services" mode.[3] Abdallah and members of his inner circle met often with Jewish Agency for Palestine officials, exchanging ideas and proposals for resolving the conflict over Palestine to the satisfaction of both Zionist and Hashemite aspirations.[4]

As the first Arab-Israeli war approached, a plan took shape whereby Transjordan would not fight against Israel and in return would take that territory designated as Arab Palestine by the UN Partition Plan of 29 November 1947 (see Map 3). Historian Avi Shlaim has claimed that military activity during the ensuing war was governed by "an explicit agreement . . . between the Hashemites and the Zionists on the carving up of Palestine following the termination of the British mandate, and that this agreement laid the foundation for mutual restraint during 1948 and for continuing collaboration in the aftermath of war."[5] Yet despite extensive discussions—including the last-minute May 1948 visit to Abdallah in Amman by future Israeli prime minister Golda Meir, disguised as an Arab peasant woman—Abdallah sent the Arab Legion into battle against Israeli positions when the war broke out.[6]

The war on Israel's eastern front ended with a Jordanian-Israeli armistice, officially signed at Rhodes under Dr. Bunche's mediation on 3 April 1949. The negotiations at Rhodes had been phantom talks, however: in reality, Lieutenant Colonel Moshe Dayan and Colonel Abdallah al-Tal negotiated the armistice agreement directly, with personal input from the king during occasional visits to his winter palace at Shuneh.[7] The Rhodes agreement established the Jordanian-Israeli Mixed Armistice Commission and a "Special Committee," both of which met near the Mandelbaum Gate of the Old City of Jerusalem and provided official points of contact between Israeli and Jordanian officials for several years.[8] After concluding the armistice, Abdallah and his old friends in the new Israeli government entered into extensive talks, resulting ultimately in a draft treaty of peace between the two nations.[9] The negotiations had already run into familiar problems—i.e., the questionable ability of the king to deliver his end of the bargain; negative pressures from third parties, both Arab and Western; and the psychological gap between élite proposals and Jordanian public opinion—when Abdallah's assassination by a Palestinian nationalist in July 1951 ended this chapter in Jordanian-Israeli relations.[10]

Two years later, Abdallah's grandson Hussein assumed the throne and quietly resumed the historical pattern of clandestine, frequent meetings with Israeli officials. When it launched the June 1967 war on its Syrian and Egyptian fronts, the Israeli government communicated to Hussein that if he kept out of the war, Israel would not move against his troops. The pressures for pan-Arab unity were too great, however, and the king committed his army to battle on Israel's eastern front. In the course of the fighting, Jordan lost the precious Old City of Jerusalem and the West Bank to Israel. In the aftermath of the war, the Israeli and Jordanian leaderships resumed their quiet contacts, working together to administer the West Bank, which Israel now controlled, but in which Jordan retained much interest and influence.

By all accounts Hussein has met with every Israeli prime minister over the years, creating ongoing relationships that have weathered wars and regional crises. Informal Jordanian-Israeli cooperation in fields such as border security and the environment created a functional relationship of such depth and breadth that, writing in 1978, Ian Lustick doubted whether any open, negotiated settlement between the two countries could provide as satisfactory an arrangement.[11]

Nevertheless, there have been efforts to negotiate a formal Jordanian-Israeli peace. Although evidence suggests that familiarity alone does not presage a successful negotiating experience, in this unusual case the two parties had been not just periodically talking to but actually cooperating with one another for many years. Israel and Jordan thus shared what Aharon Klieman has described as a durable "adversarial partnership" built on "a policy of de facto disengagement and conflict avoidance." This policy reflected "a basic affinity of core political interests and concerns," namely:

- the long border between them;
- mutual interests in the West Bank;
- a common aversion to the internationalization of Jerusalem;
- the preponderant Palestinian impact upon their politics and societies;
- a common American patron;
- similar fears regarding Syrian intentions; and
- (more recently) challenges from Islamic fundamentalism.[12]

By the 1980s, fifty years of high-level Jordanian-Israeli contacts were an open secret. But although leaders had come to know and understand one another well, the relationship resisted official rapprochement; technically the two states remained at war.[13]

PURPOSES AND MOTIVES

The London Document represents one of the more concerted efforts to advance Jordan and Israel from war to peace. A novel feature in this round of Arab-Israeli talks was the primary motivation of the parties themselves. Departing from the historical pattern in which Arabs and Israelis negotiated with one another for the purpose of endearing themselves to an interested third party or out of common antipathy to an imminent external proposal, Jordanian and Israeli leaders now came to the table with similar primary goals of reaching a Jordanian-Israeli peace and finding a diplomatic mechanism that would allow for a comprehensive settlement of the larger conflict. This new motivational element gave the Hussein-Peres initiative an auspicious start. Familiar constraints, however, soon ensured its impotency.

Strangely enough, the story of the London Document begins with an effort by Hussein to build a partnership with the PLO, with himself as the senior partner, aimed at resolving the Arab-Israeli conflict and regaining the West Bank from Israeli control. Jordan's self-exclusion from Camp David required that the king find a new avenue into the peace process. The PLO's near-demise in the ashes of Israel's invasion of Lebanon and the intensification of Israeli settlement activities in the West Bank led Hussein to think that PLO Chairman Yasir Arafat might be weak and desperate enough to accompany him to the negotiating table as his junior partner and political cover. The king's diplomatic initiatives bore fruit in the form of a February 11, 1985, accord with Arafat.[14] The fifth of the agreement's five points repeated King Hussein's public calls for an international conference, at which the PLO would be represented under the umbrella of a joint Jordanian-Palestinian delegation. Hussein hoped that an international conference would be acceptable to the Syrians, as well, thereby securing a second political fig leaf for Jordanian-Israeli negotiations under a multilateral screen.[15] Not wishing to limit his options, Hussein's flirtations with Arafat went parallel with continuing secret contacts with Israeli emissaries.

Deadlocked Israeli elections in 1984 necessitated the creation of a National Unity Government under whose terms Labor leader Shimon Peres and rival Likud leader Yitzhak Shamir became prime minister and foreign minister, respectively. After a two-year period, they were to exchange positions for another two years. Labor's Yitzhak Rabin retained the defense portfolio for the entire period. Peres began his tenure with a series of gestures designed to tempt King Hussein into negotiating an Israeli-Jordanian peace, among them, voicing possible Israeli support for an international conference, such as the king had in mind. Another consideration in Peres's overtures was to exploit his Jordanian connection to build an acceptable Palestinian component into future negotiations, thus leapfrogging over the hurdle left behind by the unconsummated post–Camp

David autonomy talks.[16] To the extent that Peres hoped to circumvent the PLO by dealing with a joint Palestinian-Jordanian delegation, he risked repeating the traditional pattern of failed negotiations. Yet, in taking the gamble that a joint delegation would prove a politically safe vehicle for conducting PLO-Israeli negotiations, he departed from the historical path in a significant way.

But as long as the king's primary peace efforts focused on coordinating Jordanian-PLO activities, Peres's overtures remained unanswered.[17] Within a year of the signing of the Jordanian-PLO agreement, however, the king grew disappointed with what he perceived as a lack of cooperation and vision on Arafat's part, and announced the abrogation of their entente. Thereafter Hussein concentrated his attentions on the back-channel with Israel.[18] Hussein found a ready partner in Prime Minister Peres, who had been wooing the king for over a year and whose "own schooling in the arts of back-channelling date[d] back to the early 1950s."[19]

Drawing upon decades of tacit cooperation and on the preparatory groundwork laid by Jordanian, Israeli, and American officials since early 1984, Hussein met with Yitzhak Rabin during the first week of April 1986 to consider a concerted Jordanian-Israeli approach to peace. By the spring of 1987, Hussein and Peres had finalized their London Document, which expanded upon the parties' previous negotiating experiences and represented a test of whether the time was ripe for removing the unrealistic and inconvenient formality of the state of war between them.

PROPOSED TERMS OF AGREEMENT

The terms of the London agreement, subtitled "A Three-Part Understanding between Jordan and Israel," reflect considerable flexibility, indicative of the unusually straightforward goals (primarily a formal, bilateral peace, and secondarily a new burst of high diplomacy vis-à-vis the Arab-Israel conflict) held by both sides. Breaking the historical pattern wherein parties presented and adhered to maximal, irreconcilable demands, this case found Shimon Peres departing from a number of entrenched Israeli positions by agreeing to sign a document calling for the "legitimate rights of the Palestinian people" (a formula consistent with the Camp David Accords but since avoided by the Likud), a comprehensive solution to the "Palestinian problem," the formation of a joint Jordanian-Palestinian delegation, and the holding of an international conference.

The latter, which was to have been held under the auspices of the UN Security Council, represented a far-reaching concession for Israel, whose leaders, especially those in the Likud Party, had consistently rejected such a format for peace talks on the grounds that:

- the participation of the Soviet Union would likely embolden the Arab delegations and stiffen their bargaining positions;

- the UN seemed heavily tilted in favor of promoting Palestinian rights to self-determination; and
- the multilateral format would crystallize a pan-Arab anti-Israel stance based on a consensus reflecting the most hard-line position.[20]

Shimon Peres hoped to persuade his ministerial colleagues and his public that Israel had nothing to fear, since the conference envisaged would be explicitly barred from imposing a settlement or vetoing any bilateral agreements reached.[21]

Given expressions of pan-Arab support for an international conference at this time,[22] King Hussein could point to substantial achievements in his draft agreement with Shimon Peres: namely, recognition of the centrality of the Palestinian issue and Israel's acquiesence to an international conference. A significant innovation was the king's acceptance of the first proviso of Part C of the agreement, which opened the way to negotiating a Jordanian-Israeli peace *independent of* success or failure on other Arab-Israeli fronts. This creative formula utilized the international conference as a legitimizing umbrella for de-linking a Jordanian-Israeli accord from other Arab issues. Despite public statements to the contrary,[23] this represented an important departure from the historical pattern by reverting to Jordan's 1948–51 inclinations for a separate deal. In so doing, Hussein offered Israel the welcome opportunity of negotiating with each of its neighbors individually, as had happened at Rhodes and, more recently, at Camp David.[24]

THIRD-PARTY CONSIDERATIONS

The United States at first welcomed the protagonists' early steps toward the goal of an Israeli-Jordanian peace treaty, playing (as in the Camp David peace process) the role of trusted facilitator. Professional US diplomats quietly shuttled between the king's circle and the Israeli foreign ministry for months, trying to craft a common basis for a Jordanian-Israeli understanding. US Ambassador to Israel Thomas Pickering, Secretary of State George Shultz, and even Vice-President George Bush were called upon at times to lend the weight of their offices to the operation.[25] Good relations had long existed between Jordan and the United States, and the United States was happy to shepherd the Jordanians further into the American fold. Peres informed the Reagan administration of his plans every step of the way and coordinated "his moves with Washington . . . via highly restricted diplomatic channels." Under his stewardship, the already unique relationship between Israel and the United States reached new "heights of intimacy."[26] The form of the accord itself—Parts A and B treated as US proposals accepted by Israel and Jordan and Part C presented as a proposal to the United States—testifies to mutual Jordanian and Israeli reliance on, and expectations of, active and high-level US support. Peres, in particular, needed the appearance of a "made-in-the-USA" label in hopes of overcoming Shamir's determined opposition to his bilateral dealings with Jordan.[27] In fact, Israeli analyst Abraham Ben-Zvi has treated the document as a "trilateral," rather than a bilateral, agreement.[28]

But, despite this new and promising cooperation among the two parties and their chosen intermediary, the United States was, in the end, reluctant to endorse the Hussein-Peres accord over which American diplomats had long labored in the shadows. Privately, the Reagan White House simply could not bring itself to support a process that invited the Soviets back into the Middle East. Publicly, the reasons given for the lukewarm US reaction cited official misgivings about the proposed international conference. The White House was unwilling to stake its prestige on what it feared might become yet another failed Middle East peace plan, and hesitated to interfere in the domestic tug-of-war between Peres and Shamir. This unexpected American ambivalence contributed to the "rapid erosion of the entire diplomatic momentum" of the Hussein-Peres accord.[29]

By withholding its blessing, the United States unwittingly recreated one of the unhelpful traditional patterns of Arab-Israeli negotiations: namely, hesitancy on the part of the third party, which invariably caused Arabs and Israelis to pull back and resume status-quo attitudes, for fear of getting out ahead on a plan to which the Great Power was not firmly committed. Washington's lack of open, enthusiastic support for the London Document made King Hussein uneasy and, more importantly, denied Peres the political ammunition he needed to sway Israeli public opinion in favor of his initiative and to impose his plan over the objections of his rival, Yitzhak Shamir. Ironically, when the Reagan administration decided to re-engage in Middle East peace efforts in early 1988, the Shultz Initiative[30] borrowed liberally from the London Document, and ultimately failed for many of the same reasons.

TIMING

The unusual rotation requirements of Israel's National Unity Government created special obstacles in terms of the timing and status-of-negotiator factors. The timing of the accord could not have been less propitious. Israeli-Jordanian relations reached the takeoff point just as Peres's term as prime minister was ending. Duly switching posts with Shamir, Peres pressed on with his agenda and "operated abroad almost as if no rotation had occurred."[31] This created a chaotic bargaining situation, with Yitzhak Shamir completely opposed to the framework Peres and Hussein had been devising. Shamir particularly objected to the Palestinian focus, the international conference framework, the inclusion of the Soviets, and the fact

Jeff MacNelly © Tribune Media Services. All Rights Reserved. Reprinted with permission.

that the accord had been negotiated behind his back. The dueling prime minister and foreign minister each appealed to the US administration to impose his preferred solution upon the other.[32] Shamir and Peres sent separate envoys to Washington to argue their positions, and each privately assured the Reagan administration that his position enjoyed public support and would prevail. This schizophrenic Israeli diplomacy unnerved the Americans and contributed to their reluctance to issue a definitive endorsement of the London Document, anticipating the inevitable problems such backing would create with half the Israeli government.[33]

The Shamir inner cabinet's rejection of the London Document on 13 May 1987 and Washington's aloofness came against a background of violent acts that unsettled all would-be peacemakers: the murder of three Israelis at Larnaca by PLO operatives, the Israeli bombing of PLO headquarters in Tunis, the Palestinian hijacking of the Italian cruise liner *Achille Lauro* and the subsequent murder of an elderly Jewish passenger, and Palestinian terrorist attacks at the Rome and Frankfurt airports. Before the year's end, the outbreak of a Palestinian uprising in the occupied territories (the *Intifada*) reshaped political options in the region, effectively overtaking the Hussein-Peres initiative. Confirming a shift away from any "Jordanian options," King Hussein publicly renounced most of Jordan's legal and administrative responsibilities for the West Bank in July 1988.[34] The unsuccessful initiative of US Secretary of State George Shultz earlier that year[35] and—more importantly—the Palestinian Declaration of Independence and the acceptance by the Palestine National Council (PNC) of a two-state solution in November 1988 further helped to bury the ill-fated London Document. "King Hussein's initiative rapidly receded into an increasingly turbulent regional background, while the Israeli Labor Party lost much of its influence in the shaping of foreign policy in the wake of the 1 November 1988 Israeli elections."[36] For Hussein and Peres, the window of opportunity had opened and shut.

STATUS OF THE NEGOTIATORS

Ultimately, the old status-of-the-negotiators conundrum drove the last nail into the coffin of the London Document. While King Hussein authoritatively represented Jordan, he had no mandate to commit the Palestinians or other Arab states to the procedures called for in the agreement. Both the king and his Israeli interlocutors preferred to see the problem of the occupied territories solved in a way that would enhance Jordanian influence there at the expense of the PLO. Hussein labored mightily to draw the PLO into an unequal partnership that would give him the legitimacy he required and the control he desired in negotiating an Israeli withdrawal from the West Bank. He had long counseled a parade of Israeli prime ministers, "For 100% you can talk to me. For anything less, you have to talk to Arafat." Despite his efforts to supplant PLO loyalty in the West Bank, Hussein could neither replace Arafat, nor win his blessing for Jordanian-Israeli talks.[37]

The king's failure to secure Syrian backing for his plan, and his hesitancy to proceed without it or without PLO support, highlight the many differences between Egypt and Jordan, and between Anwar Sadat and Hussein. Economically, Jordan could not withstand the isolation that Sadat-style negotiations and a Jordanian-Israeli "Camp David" would provoke. Gulf Arab outrage would threaten the millions of dollars in subsidies upon which Jordan was dependent; unhappy Palestinians within Jordan could foment anti-royalist sentiment; and an angry Syria and Iraq could easily menace their weaker neighbor economically, politically, and militarily. Writing in 1978, while the Camp David troika was still working hard to pull Jordan into the club, Ian Lustick calculated that for Jordan, "if the costs of negotiating à la Sadat are high, the risks of accepting a territorial compromise . . . are almost certainly intolerable."[38] Ultimately, Sadat's bold journey to Jerusalem demanded political daring simply uncharacteristic of Hussein, or of Peres either, for that matter.

Peres's status proved even more problematic than Hussein's. Simply put, although Peres began his Jordanian diplomacy as prime minister, he signed the agreement in the diminished capacity of a foreign minister operating in defiance of his prime minister's will. But even had Peres retained his role as prime minister, the fact he was presiding over a National Unity Government, and not a Labor government, might have been enough to nix the plan. The Likud side of the cabinet, rejecting an international conference, Soviet participation, and the very essence of the land-for-peace option, would have vehemently opposed the London

Document. In either case, without the approval of the Israeli government, the agreement remained an inoperative piece of paper. Once again, Arab-Israeli negotiations faltered due to the inability of one signatory or the other (or both) to deliver his end of the bargain.

Not surprisingly, Shimon Peres saw the status issue—the fact that Prime Minister Shamir refused to endorse his accord with Hussein—as the single most important reason for the London Document's demise. Looking back with some bitterness in 1993, Peres wrote, "We could have saved ourselves and the Palestinians six years of *intifada,* and the loss of so much human life, had the former head of the Likud-run government not undermined the agreement I had worked out with King Hussein of Jordan."[39]

PSYCHOLOGICAL FACTORS

Activating the London Document required of Hussein and Peres immense leadership skills in creating both élite and popular constituencies to support the plan. For Peres, the former presented the greater obstacle, for this meant persuading the Likud half of the government not to torpedo his efforts. For the king, the greater challenge was the latter, which meant winning over the Palestinians on the West Bank and at least part of the PLO. But Jordanians, Israelis, and Palestinians were never required to respond to this proposal, since it was effectively killed by Israel's inner cabinet in mid-May 1987. One can only hypothesize as to how public opinion in each country might have reacted had leaders in Jordan and Israel unveiled their secret accord.

Were Israelis and Jordanians ready to scale the psychological wall separating them, or would they have retreated into their familiar fortresses of mutual mistrust and official animosity? In 1992 Adam Garfinkle observed that,

> while the Hashemite hierarchy operates in a normal, civilized and pragmatic manner toward its neighbors, including Israel, the attitudes of the population of Jordan do not exactly follow suit. Rather, there is a kind of inverse proportionality at work.

He went on to attribute this phenomenon to the facts that: (1) East Bankers resented that Israel foisted a huge West Bank Palestinian population upon them; (2) Palestinians, who constituted more than 50 percent of the Jordanian population, retained a high level of anger at Israel for their families' displacement, and for the treatment of their brothers and sisters under Israeli occupation; and (3) the Jordanian government tolerated extensive Israel bashing in the media, perhaps as a counterbalance to general public knowledge of its extensive contacts with Israel.[40] Ironically, Israeli public opinion has always thought highly of King Hussein and looked to Jordan as the preferred negotiating partner in any deal over the West Bank. Jordan holds a special place in the collective Israeli imagination, as well, with many Israeli youths over the years attempting, occasionally with tragic results, to reach the famous red rocks of Petra. Likudniks may have objected to the international conference and land-for-peace components of the London Document, but a straightforward peace with Jordan was not in itself controversial.

Since the agreement remained a private and unconsummated understanding among leaders, efforts to prepare the populations for peace were indirect, at best. In terminating his agreement with the PLO, the king tried to ready his subjects for direct Jordanian-Israeli talks and perhaps even a separate peace. In a three-hour radio and television address to the nation on 19 February 1986, Hussein sharply criticized the PLO, blamed it for the failure to move ahead with the peace process, and stressed Jordan's commitment to finding a path to peace with or without Arafat's cooperation.[41] Although the fact of Jordanian-Israeli ties was widely known, prior to 1986 most cooperative ventures were based on oral agreements; after the dissolution of the PLO pact, political insiders were tipped off as to the changing policy toward Israel by the king's new willingness to put their mutual understandings on paper. Garfinkle calls this "an important psychological development" and cites paperwork regarding Amman's debt to the Jerusalem Electric Company as precedent-setting. An Israeli-Jordanian agreement about opening branches of the Cairo-Amman Bank in the West Bank "was actually committed to paper and signed—the first such document ever in the history of Israeli-Jordanian relations."[42]

Shimon Peres had preached peace with the Arabs for so long and had claimed so often to be on the verge of a breakthrough that he ran the risk of becoming the "little boy who cried wolf" of Arab-Israel relations. In 1985 he presented his own peace plan, foreshadowing the terms of the London Agreement, and spoke repeatedly of imminent opportunities for Arab-Israeli rapprochement. He endeavored to prepare the Israeli people for the reality of peace by example as well as with words. Visiting Morocco and Egypt in July and September 1986, Peres declared that normal relations with the Arab world were indeed feasible and might soon become commonplace. Reporting to the Knesset following an enchanted encounter with King Hassan in the cedar-forested town of Ifrane, Peres emphasized the Moroccan king's resounding message to the Arab world that it was time for the boycott on dialogue with Israel to end.[43] But such messages were not enough to win the hearts of skeptical parliamentarians, the Israeli public at large, or—most significantly—Peres's Likud coalition partners. For King Hussein, waiting for Peres before pressing ahead with their agreed plan was not unlike waiting for Godot. In the end, this negotiation attempt revealed a dire weakness in the Israeli political structure of that time, in which the second highest-ranking Israeli leader could not even sell his initiative to the first, and the first used all the resources at his command to make sure the démarche went no further.

Notwithstanding the pattern-breaking intersection of a number of positive factors—good intentions on the part of the negotiators, a not insignificant degree of assistance from a mutually acceptable third party, and a shared vision of the terms of an agreement—none of the parties involved was able to generate the energy and momentum necessary for changing the dynamics of deadlock and establishing the new psychological environment necessary for seeing the accord through to completion. The dejected authors of the London Document did not know then that circumstances five years later would offer Israelis and Jordanians a second chance to follow through and make good on the Peres-Hussein initiative.

NOTES

1. Avi Shlaim, *Collusion across the Jordan: King Abdullah, the Zionist Movement, and the Partition of Palestine,* Oxford: Clarendon Press, 1988, 24–32; Adam Garfinkle, *Israel and Jordan in the Shadow of War: Functional Ties and Futile Diplomacy in a Small Place,* New York: St. Martin's, 1992, 16–19; Christopher Sykes, *Crossroads to Israel, 1917–1948,* Bloomington: Indiana University Press, 1965, 44–49. Regarding the British pledge of Arab independence in return for Hashemite support against the Turks (the Hussein-McMahon Correspondence of 1915) see Sykes, 27–39, 63–66; George Antonius, *The Arab Awakening,* 2nd ed., London: Hamish Hamilton, 1946, chap. 9, App. A; and Isaiah Friedman, *The Question of Palestine, 1914–1918: British-Jewish-Arab Relations,* New York: Schocken, 1973.

2. Anita Shapira, "The Option on Ghaur al-Kibd: Contacts between Emir Abdallah and the Zionist Executive, 1932–1935," *Studies in Zionism* 2 (Autumn 1980), 239–83; cf. Neil Caplan, *Futile Diplomacy, vol. II—Arab-Zionist Negotiations and the End of the Mandate,* London: Frank Cass, 1986, 11–14, 40–42. On Abdallah's contacts with Zionists during the 1920s, see Caplan, *Palestine Jewry and the Arab Question, 1917–1925,* London: Frank Cass, 1978, 171–82; Caplan, *Futile Diplomacy, vol. I—Early Arab-Zionist Negotiation Attempts, 1913–1931,* London: Frank Cass, 1983, 51–54, 106.

3. Caplan, *Futile Diplomacy* I:51–54; Garfinkle, 20–24.

4. Representing Abdallah at different times were Muhammad al-Unsi, Hasan Khaled, and Dr. Shawkat Sati, while Moshe Shertok (Sharett), Reuven Shiloah, Eliahu Sasson, Ezra Danin, A. H. Cohen, and Golda Myerson (Meir) participated on behalf of the JA.

For discussion of early Zionist-Transjordanian relations, see Shlaim; Garfinkle; Yoav Gelber, *Jewish-Transjordanian Relations, 1921–1948,* London: Frank Cass, 1997; Martin Sicker, *Between Hashemites and Zionists: The Struggle for Palestine, 1908–1988,* New York: Holmes and Meier, 1989; and Joseph Nevo, *King Abdallah and Palestine: A Territorial Ambition,* New York: St. Martin's, 1997.

5. Shlaim, 1.

6. This point is well presented by Avraham Sela, "Transjordan, Israel and the 1948 War: Myth, Historiography and Reality," *Middle Eastern Studies* 28:4 (October 1992), 623–88. For background on Zionist-Israeli contacts with Abdallah at this time, see Zeev Sharef, "Negotiations with King Abdullah and the Formation of a Governmental Structure," in *Israel in the Middle East: Documents and Readings on Society, Politics and Foreign Relations, 1948–Present,* eds. Itamar Rabinovich and Jehuda Reinharz, New York and Oxford: Oxford University Press, 1984, 32–36; Sykes, 327–30, 342–43, 361–62; Caplan, *Futile Diplomacy* II:157–64, 277–79; Garfinkle, 24–26; Uri Bar-Joseph, *The Best of Enemies: Israel and Transjordan in the War of*

1948, London: Frank Cass, 1987; Itamar Rabinovich, *The Road Not Taken: Early Arab-Israeli Negotiations*, New York and Oxford: Oxford University Press, 1991, 15–16, 113.

7. Bar-Joseph, chap. 6; Shlaim, 400–28; Garfinkle, 26–27; Neil Caplan, *The Lausanne Conference, 1949: A Case Study in Middle East Peacemaking*, Tel Aviv: Moshe Dayan Center for Middle Eastern and African Studies (Occasional Papers, No. 113), 1993, 38–41; Abdallah al-Tal, "The Jordanian-Israeli Negotiations," in Rabinovich and Reinharz, 71–73.

8. Garfinkle, 29–32; Shlaim, 442–47.

9. The two basic primary documents are: (1) Initialled Non-Aggression Pact between Israel and Hashemite Jordan, 24 January 1950, reproduced in Garfinkle, Appendix C, 197–98, and (2) Draft of a Peace Treaty between Israel and Hashemite Jordan, 28 February 1950, doc. 105 in *Documents on the Foreign Policy of Israel*, vol. 5 (1950), ed. Yehoshua Freundlich, Jerusalem: 1988, 140; translation in Garfinkle, Appendix D, 199–204.

10. Shlaim, 513–612; Rabinovich, chap. 4; Garfinkle, 26–27; Robert B. Satloff, *From Abdullah to Hussein: Jordan in Transition*, New York and Oxford: Oxford University Press, 1994, 8–29.

11. Ian Lustick, *Israel and Jordan: The Implications of an Adversarial Partnership*, Berkeley: Institute of International Studies, University of California, 1978, 1, 14–16, 22–29. In 1992, Garfinkle (p. 2) listed the following issues on which Jordan and Israel enjoyed functional contact: agricultural development, pest control, water conservation and allocation, pollution control, intelligence, navigation, air-traffic control, mining, utilities management, banking and commerce policy, and scientific and technical exchange.

12. Aharon Klieman, *Statecraft in the Dark: Israel's Practice of Quiet Diplomacy*, Jerusalem: Jerusalem Post, and Boulder, CO: Westview Press, for Jaffee Center for Strategic Studies, Tel Aviv University, 1988, 103–108; Lustick, chap. 3.

13. See, e.g., Klieman, chap. 7; Garfinkle, loc. cit.; Moshe Zak, "A Survey of Israel's Contacts with Jordan," in Rabinovich and Reinharz, 337–42; Moshe Zak, "Talking to Hussein," *Jerusalem Post International Edition (JPI)*, w/e 4 May 1985, pp. 10–12 (reprinted from the *Washington Quarterly* [Winter 1985]); Moshe Zak, "Secret courtship," *JPI*, w/e 18 December 1993, p. 12A.

14. For a brief discussion of the initiative, see Garfinkle, 106–10; Emile Sahliyeh, "Jordan and the Palestinians," in *The Middle East: Ten Years after Camp David*, ed. William B. Quandt, Washington, DC: The Brookings Institution, 1988, 279–318; Mark Tessler, *A History of the Palestinian-Israeli Conflict*, Bloomington: Indiana University Press, 1994, 648–62; Ann M. Lesch, "The Reagan Administration's Policy toward the Palestinians," in *US Policy on Palestine from Wilson to Clinton*, ed. Michael W. Suleiman, Normal, IL: AAUG Press, 1995, 182–83. The text of the Jordanian-Palestinian Accord, 11 February 1985, is given in *The Israeli-Palestinian Conflict: A Documentary Record, 1967–1990*, ed. Yehuda Lukacs, Cambridge and New York: Cambridge University Press, 1992, 488–89.

15. Sahliyeh, 303; William B. Quandt, *Peace Process: American Diplomacy and the Arab-Israeli Conflict since 1967*, Washington, DC: The Brookings Institution, 1993, 360–61.

16. Shimon Peres, "A Strategy for Peace in the Middle East," *Foreign Affairs* 58 (Summer 1980), 896; Helen Davis, "Israelis Get the Feeling Peace Has a Chance," *Gazette* (Montreal), 5 October 1985, p. B4; Lars-Erik Nelson, "Israel Puts Its Enemies on the Spot," *Gazette* (Montreal), 25 October 1985 (reprinted from the *New York Daily News*); Quandt, 360.

17. Samuel W. Lewis, "Israel: The Peres Era and Its Legacy," *Foreign Affairs* 65:3 (1987), 597–600, and S. W. Lewis, "The United States and Israel: Constancy and

Change," in *The Middle East: Ten Years after Camp David,* ed. William B. Quandt, 247–48; Garfinkle, 111–13.

18. Tessler, 662–66; Quandt, *Peace Process,* 360–62; Garfinkle, 125–26.

19. Klieman, 52.

20. In "An International Conference on the Middle East," *Jerusalem Quarterly* 37 (1986), 14–28, Moshe Zak makes an especially strong case for the first of these objections. See also Abraham Ben-Zvi, *Between Lausanne and Geneva: International Conferences and the Arab-Israeli Conflict,* Tel Aviv: Tel Aviv University, Jaffee Center for Strategic Studies (Study No. 13), and Boulder, CO: Westview Press, 1989, 59–60, 66–67.

21. Sahliyeh, 303; Shimon Shamir, "Israeli Views of Egypt and the Peace Process: The Duality of Vision," in Quandt, *The Middle East,* 211–13; Ben-Zvi, 8–9, 65–66, 68–70. The London Document called, in Ben-Zvi's terminology, for a "minimalist" rather than a "maximalist" type of international conference.

22. See, e.g., Valerie Yorke, "Domestic Politics and the Prospects for an Arab-Israeli Peace," *JPS* 17:4 (Summer 1988), 17–19.

23. In arguing for an Arab-Israeli settlement via an international peace conference, Hussein's brother Crown Prince Hassan argued that the resolution of the Palestinian-Israeli tier of the conflict ought not to be pursued in isolation from the Arab-Israeli tier: "Decoupling those two tiers is not only inadvisable, it may be detrimental to the process as a whole." Speech at the Washington Institute for Public Policy, 12 September 1989, quoted in Asher Susser, "Jordan, the PLO and the Palestine Question," in *Jordan in the Middle East: The Making of a Pivotal State,* eds. Joseph Nevo and Ilan Pappé, London: Frank Cass, 1994, 225.

24. Ben-Zvi, 26–35, makes this point, while underlining Hussein's shifting position on the conference format.

25. Lewis, "The United States and Israel," 247–48; William B. Quandt, "US Policy toward the Arab-Israeli Conflict," in Quandt, *The Middle East,* 373. Americans most heavily involved behind the scenes were Assistant Secretary of State Richard Murphy, Murphy's special assistant Wat Cluverius, and legal advisor Abraham Sofaer.

26. Lewis, "Israel," 598, 603.

27. Heikal suggests that Shamir hoped, in vain, to present his own plan, on different terms, to King Hussein after the failure of Peres's London Document. Mohamed Heikal, *Secret Channels: The Inside Story of Arab-Israeli Peace Negotiations,* London: HarperCollins, 1996, 379–82.

28. Ben-Zvi, 8–9, 69.

29. Ben-Zvi, 88–89; Laurie Mylroie, "Israel in the Middle East," in *Israel after Begin,* ed. Gregory S. Mahler, Albany: State University of New York Press, 1990, 146; Shamir, 212–13; Quandt, *Peace Process,* 362–63; Quandt, "US Policy," 374–75; Lewis, "Israel," 600.

30. Quandt, *Peace Process,* 364–67, 486–87; Tessler, 713, 716; Lukacs, 104–15.

31. Lewis, "The United States and Israel," 252; S. Shamir, 210.

32. It is ironic that Peres and Shamir—in appealing to a powerful third party to impose their preferred policy on one another, instead of directly negotiating a compromise between the two of them—followed the traditionally flawed pattern of Arab-Israel negotiations. See Quandt, *Peace Process,* 362. Regarding Shamir's efforts to undermine Peres's achievement, see Glenn Frankel, *Beyond the Promised Land: Jews and Arabs on the Hard Road to a New Israel,* New York: Simon and Schuster/Touchstone, 1996, 37–38.

33. Lewis, "The United States and Israel," 249, 252; Mylroie, 146.

34. Text of Hussein's speech, 31 July 1988, reproduced in Harold H. Saunders, *The Other Walls: The Arab-Israeli Peace Process in a Global Perspective,* rev. ed.,

Princeton: Princeton University Press, 1991, 197–203 and in Quandt, *The Middle East,* 494–98. Cf. Susser, 218–21; Garfinkle, 137–38 and chap. 4.

35. Text of Schultz initiative, 4 March 1988, in Ben-Zvi, 155–56, and in Quandt, *The Middle East,* 488–89. For a discussion, see Quandt, "US Policy," 376–79, 383–84; Lesch, 184–89.

36. Ben-Zvi, 104.

37. Garfinkle, 114–15, 132–33, 137.

38. Lustick, 13–16.

39. Shimon Peres, *The New Middle East,* New York: Henry Holt, 1993, 16.

40. Garfinkle, 83–89.

41. Text of Hussein's speech, 19 February 1986, given in Ben-Zvi, 118–52. Cf. ibid., 34–35; Tessler, 665.

42. Garfinkle, 129, 131–32.

43. On the Peres-Hassan meetings, see Joint Communiqué on 22–23 July Summit at Ifrane, Morocco: Rabat and Jerusalem, 23 July 1986 and Peres, Knesset Statement, 28 July 1986, Israeli Ministry of Foreign Affairs (MFA), http://www.israel-mfa.gov.il or http://www.israel.org/peace or by e-mail from ask@israel-info.gov.il.

Chapter 4

SETTING THE PEACE TABLE

THE MADRID CONFERENCE AND WASHINGTON TALKS, 1991–1993

On 30 October 1991, official Arab and Israeli delegates gathered together around a common negotiating table in Madrid, Spain. The Madrid Conference represented a victory for those who championed a multilateral format and a comprehensive solution to the Arab-Israeli conflict. It also reflected the recent victory of the US-led multinational coalition in liberating Kuwait from Iraq's President Saddam Hussein, whose troops had invaded and occupied the tiny Persian Gulf sheikdom in August of 1990. Because of the unique alliance between the United States and a majority of the Arab states forged in the Gulf War, President George Bush and Secretary of State James Baker III believed that heightened American influence in the immediate postwar environment boded well for a new attempt at bringing the Arabs and Israelis together to resolve their differences. On 18 October 1991, in nominal partnership with the Soviet Union, Bush and Baker issued invitations to Madrid, which neither the Arabs nor Israel could refuse (Appendix, Document 8).

The Madrid peace process launched a complex series of negotiations aimed at bringing together all the interested parties and tackling all the unresolved issues that kept the Arab-Israeli pot bubbling on the front burner of international concern. Although its formal sessions were concluded in a matter of three days, many months of serious (although not totally successful) negotiations in Washington, DC followed. The name "Madrid" quickly found its place alongside other noteworthy venues and benchmarks for Arab-Israeli peacemaking: Rhodes, Geneva, Lausanne. While there is no "Madrid Agreement" to point to as the crowning success of the negotiations, the Madrid format facilitated a breakthrough that led, in a few short years, to the signing of peace agreements between Israel and

Jordan and—something of an anathema to at least some of the Madrid participants—between Israel and the Palestine Liberation Organization.

PREVIOUS NEGOTIATING EXPERIENCE

Given the historical record of failed international conferences aimed at overambitious targets, the organizers of the Madrid Conference, Secretary of State Baker and his Soviet counterpart, Boris Dmitriyevich Pankin, had little reason to expect this format to produce successful Arab-Israeli negotiations. The record of failure dates back to Britain's doomed St. James' Palace Conference of 1939 and was reinforced in September 1949 when the Lausanne Conference left all parties frustrated. Even less potent than the British before them, the United Nations Conciliation Commissioners failed even to seat the parties around the same table, let alone resolve any of the basic problems (boundaries, refugees, Jerusalem) resulting from the birth of Israel and the first Arab-Israeli war. Two further conferences under PCC auspices at Geneva (1950) and Paris (1951) led nowhere, illustrating the counterproductive dynamics whereby "the least compromising party set the pace of negotiations" during such multilateral gatherings.[1] These experiences also confirmed the Israeli conviction that only separate negotiations with each Arab state could produce results and, conversely, crystalized the Arab refusal to meet directly with Israel at all.

The 1973 Geneva Conference offered a slightly more promising model for the 1991 Madrid talks. By cleverly recasting an essentially American mediation process in an international format, Henry Kissinger, Secretary of State and National Security Advisor to President Nixon, created in Geneva a blueprint that became one of the preferred options promoted by other would-be peacemakers during the coming decade. Although the conference broke up after the second day, the very fact that Arabs and Israelis had openly gathered together in the same room for the first time in twenty-five years constituted a notable psychological accomplishment, for which the United States eagerly took credit. The Ford and Carter administrations inherited Kissinger's model of a "minimalist" conference, one that would be largely "symbolic, a cover for serious negotiations which would take place elsewhere"; yet, during his first eleven months in office, Jimmy Carter set out along the road to a more ambitious, "maximalist" type of conference.[2] By the end of 1977, however, Carter's gallop to Geneva was effectively sidetracked by Sadat's journey to Jerusalem. For both Anwar Sadat and Menachem Begin, "Geneva" symbolized everything undesirable in peacemaking, namely, predicating movement on any one Arab-Israeli front on success on all the others, thereby putting the entire process at the mercy of the most intransigent Arab state, or the most intractable Arab-Israeli problem.

In the aftermath of the Camp David Accords, which failed to engage other Arab actors besides Egypt, US policymakers in the 1980s returned to the vision of the ("minimalist") Geneva Conference as the best way to engage all the relevant parties. The Madrid format followed the minimalist format.[3] For the United States, a drawback to the multilateral conference idea had always been the risk of enhancing Soviet influence in the Middle East; but from its post–Gulf War apogee of international power, the Bush administration calculated that it could safely convene such a conference under its own aegis and terms. In the end, it was the American fine-tuning of the original Geneva idea in light of the experiences of the late 1970s and 1980s that laid the groundwork for Madrid.

MOTIVES AND TIMING

Why did the Madrid planners achieve 100 percent attendance at their assembly, when similar calls in the past had proven non-starters? The key to Madrid's initial success lay largely in the motives of the invited participants and in a unique configuration in the international balance of power. At first glance, success did not appear likely. Almost all of the would-be negotiating parties perceived themselves to be in unfavorably weak positions after the war with Iraq, and were "reluctant and ambivalent about the necessity of talking."[4] Yet all parties apparently calculated that the alternative of refusing to participate in the proposed US-inspired talks carried with it far greater potential costs or feared losses than did participation in what would probably be another round of sterile Arab-Israeli negotiations. Hence, all the required actors were brought to the table in short order.

On the world stage, the era of superpower confrontation and Cold War had come to a close. The dissolution of the Soviet Union "eliminated the ability of Middle Eastern countries to manoeuver between the superpowers"[5] and left each of the Arab invitees with an especially strong interest in upgrading its relations with the United States. With the US-led coalition's defeat of Sadam Hussein in the Gulf War of early 1991, the United States became the sole and victorious superpower influencing regional developments. American diplomats saw this as a golden opportunity to use their best endeavors to bring so many almost-willing parties together and start them talking as part of the construction of the much-heralded "New World Order."[6]

The PLO was particularly needy of American favors, "desperate for political rehabilitation—and Arafat for a personal comeback."[7] Almost mortally weakened by having bet on the wrong horse in the Gulf War, the organization was suffering stiff rebuffs from its former benefactors among the Arab Gulf states. By 1991, the *Intifada* showed signs of exhausting itself and no longer attracted the same positive international media attention it had generated for the Palestinian cause during 1988 and 1989. Israeli

Courtesy of Rob Rogers, *Pittsburgh Post Gazette*

settlement activity in the occupied territories had meanwhile intensified, raising the prospect that the longer Arafat waited, the less there would be to negotiate about. The Palestinians could ill afford to absent themselves from this forum, notwithstanding their dissatisfaction with the perceived pro-Israel tilt of its American sponsors and certain restrictions that the conference format placed upon their participation. Among these were the requirement for a joint Jordanian-Palestinian delegation[8] (instead of a separate Palestinian delegation) and the proviso that only Palestinians from the occupied territories (as opposed to those from East Jerusalem or the Palestinian diaspora) were eligible to be delegates to this opening phase of the Madrid process. In the words of Camille Mansour, a leading Palestinian academic attached to the delegation, preparations for the Madrid Conference came at

> an extremely difficult period for the Palestinian people, adding the worst conjunctural conditions to an already profound crisis. . . . [F]or the Palestinian leadership, while the prospect of accepting the US terms was bleak, refusing the initiative would [have] be[en] even bleaker.[9]

The Arab countries received the Madrid invitation with varying degrees of interest. Egypt responded enthusiastically, seeing in it the long-overdue vindication of Sadat's decisions to choose the Americans over the Soviets and to make peace with Israel. Still smarting from Arab rejection and isolation after Camp David, and eager to play the important intermediary role that Sadat had envisioned, Egypt came willingly to the conference table. Jordan also replied in the affirmative, seeing an opportunity to pursue a peace option as part of a pan-Arab consensus rather than in defiance of same as Sadat had done a dozen years earlier.[10] Sandwiched between an angry Saddam Hussein and his own large Palestinian population, King Hussein had broken with his traditional US ally and supported Iraq during the Gulf War of 1991. The United States and the Gulf states had responded by slashing or halting their financial support to Jordan. Reeling from this blow, coupled with the influx of several hundred thousand Palestinian refugees evicted from Kuwait and Saudi Arabia, the Jordanian economy suffered tremendously during 1991. King Hussein had always been interested in exploring different potential avenues to peace; now his desire to regain US diplomatic and economic favor sent Jordan to Madrid at an especially quick pace.

Syria's agreement to attend the peace parley came reluctantly. President Asad's decision to join the American-led coalition against Iraq had put Syria in the unusual and awkward position of allying with Israel's chief benefactor and against the Palestinians, whose cause Syria claimed to champion. Nevertheless, with the Soviet Union fading fast and no hope whatsoever of achieving military parity with Israel, Asad had no choice but to continue to try and improve Syria's standing with the only remaining superpower. If the Golan Heights could not be won back from Israel militarily, Syria would have to try to regain them diplomatically. Independent in name only, Lebanon followed Syria's lead. Although not among the "confrontation states," Saudi Arabia and the other Gulf Arab countries, grateful for American support and Israeli restraint during the war with Iraq, accepted invitations to come to Madrid as observers and to participate in the multilateral working groups that were to be created.

Crises in Israel's "strategic confidence" and in its relations with the United States immediately after the Gulf War led to the Shamir government's grudging agreement to attend Madrid.[11] American reluctance to include Israel in the alliance against Iraq raised the question of Israel's continued relevance as a US ally, potentially undermined Israel's primacy in US strategic planning, and made the refurbishing of the American-Israeli relationship of paramount importance for Israel.[12] Also disquieting for Israeli policymakers was the revelation that Israel depended so greatly upon US economic assistance for its domestic development and weapons programs that the desire for good relations with Washington, as opposed to independent strategic or military planning, had dictated Israeli policy during the war.

The Bush administration was not beyond using the fact of Israeli dependence to prod Israel down certain policy paths. In September 1991, the White House refused to approve $10 billion in loan guarantees for Israel, linking the loan request, and continued high levels of US financial support in general, to a freeze on Jewish settlement activity in the occupied territories. Overt linkage between the US-Israeli relationship and progress in the peace process constituted a new (and for the Israelis, disturbing) feature in US policy.[13]

Courtesy Rob Rogers, *Pittsburgh Post Gazette*

Baker's invitation to Madrid had to be weighed against the new readiness of the Bush administration to use sticks as well as carrots in persuading Israel to advance the peace process. It also had to be factored into the strategic interests of the right-wing Shamir government, which included protecting its claims to the West Bank, absorbing the flood of Russian immigrants, repairing relations with the United States, and reducing the Palestinian problem to an issue of limited autonomy only.[14] Israel's strong historic and strategic reservations about sending its representatives to face a roomful of hostile delegations, combined with the Likud government's opposition to any land-for-peace policy, forced Washington to engage in extensive prenegotiations before obtaining Israeli agreement to attend the Madrid Conference.[15] In the end, however, Israel could not afford the costs associated with a refusal to join its neighbors at the bargaining table. The best the Shamir government could do was to try and protect its interests by insisting on several conditions regarding the composition of delegations and Palestinian representation (discussed above).

Yitzhak Shamir's attitude toward the conference eloquently illustrated the historic pattern whereby reluctant protagonists have felt forced to give the *appearance* of being flexible and wanting to negotiate—regardless of the intractability of their positions and/or their distaste for their negotiating partners. After his electoral defeat in June 1992, Shamir admitted that he had agreed to attend Madrid and go through the motions without ever intending to give up Israel's plans to consolidate and expand in the occupied territories through immigration and settlement. In an unusually frank confession, he stated:

> In my political activity I know how to display the tactics of moderation, but without conceding anything on the goal—the integrity of the Land of Israel. . . . I would have carried on autonomy talks for ten years and meanwhile we would have reached half a million [Jewish] people in Judea and Samaria.[16]

But opinion polls and election results soon showed that Yitzhak Shamir's ideological attachment to the territories was no longer in tune with a public more interested in exchanging its vulnerability (due at least partly to Israel's rule over the West Bank and Gaza and the Likud's settlements policy) for peace and security.[17] Shamir's replacement in June 1992 by a Labor government under Yitzhak Rabin heralded an important turning point in the motivation of the Israeli delegates to the various follow-up talks in Washington and elsewhere. Rabin distanced himself from his predecessor by explaining to the Knesset on 13 July: "We inherited the framework of the Madrid Conference from the previous government. But there is one significant change: the previous government created the tools, but they never intended to use them in order to achieve peace" (Appendix, Document 11).[18] By September 1992, the atmosphere of the Washington talks had noticeably improved.

STATUS OF THE NEGOTIATORS

The invitations sent out by the United States and the USSR called for a conference at the foreign-minister level. The high status of the summit's participants could only benefit the chances of success, insofar as these were the men who could deliver on their end of a bargain, should they choose to make one. The trickiest issue was how the Palestinians would be represented. The vehicle for Palestinian participation constituted a highly charged issue for everyone involved. The Palestinians, of course, demanded full recognition of their national right to self-determination and the right to choose their own representatives; Shamir's government had a stake in obstructing Palestinian nationalist claims and in denying the PLO any role whatsoever. The Arab states, which have historically conditioned their commitment to the Palestinian cause on its enhancement of their various national interests, did not form a common front demanding full status for PLO participants. The form and degree of Palestinian participation in the Madrid Conference were ultimately determined by a combination of factors, including:

- the mixed bag of PLO relations with each of the Arab states,
- the US-Israel understanding, dating back to the 1975 Sinai Disengagement Agreement, banning official US dealings with the PLO,[19] and
- the sometimes differing priorities of "outside" (PLO, Tunis) and "inside" (the occupied territories) Palestinians.

The winning formula that satisfied all the various conditions set down by the conference invitees (albeit without fully satisfying all the parties) was a joint Jordanian-Palestinian delegation, whose Palestinian component consisted of West Bank or Gaza residents having no formal affiliation with the PLO. In fact, all delegates soon realized that there was some "constructive ambiguity" at play here: the Palestinian negotiators had indeed been designated by the PLO, but they discreetly avoided declaring so publicly. Four Palestinian residents of East Jerusalem and three prominent Palestinians from the diaspora (with whom the Israelis refused to deal) constituted an unofficial Palestinian "steering committee," whose media spokesperson, Hanan Ashrawi, soon overshadowed most of the official delegates. With the help of several subtle procedural maneuvers, the Jordanian-Palestinian delegation began functioning on two tracks as separate Jordanian and Palestinian negotiating teams once the talks moved to Washington. In May 1992, the charade of the non-involvement of the PLO broke down when members of the Palestinian delegation attended the PLO Central Council meeting in Tunis; the council passed a resolution expressing its appreciation of the performance of its negotiating team "which is the delegation of the PLO and of the people."[20] Months of Palestinian-Israeli negotiations would ultimately lead the Rabin government to the conclusion that only a PLO team, directly authorized by Yasir Arafat, could make the hard concessions and choices that the negotiations required. But Madrid's creative inclusion of a PLO-sanctioned Palestinian team was an important step leading to eventual PLO-Israeli talks, and probably the most the Shamir government could stomach.

The Madrid process thus set in place a new mechanism for direct dealings between official Israeli and Palestinian representatives regarding exclusively Palestinian matters. Even though Israel continued to insist on solving relevant aspects of its wider dispute with the Arabs through bilateral negotiations with each Arab state, its negotiators in Washington were forced reluctantly to break one of the well-worn negotiation patterns. For the first time in the contemporary period, Israelis dropped their reliance on outsiders like Anwar Sadat or King Hussein and went face to face with authorized Palestinian representatives to negotiate the issues of Palestinian self-rule and the fate of the occupied territories.

THIRD-PARTY CONSIDERATIONS

Extensive US activity in planning the conference and in seeing it through to completion continued the pattern of escalating American involvement in the search for a Middle East settlement since the days of Jimmy Carter and Camp David. Careful US preparations took into account the constraints under which the would-be Arab and Israeli participants were operating. In order to overcome reservations expressed by the invitees and ensure their attendance, the official invitation stressed the flexibility and non-coercive nature of the conference's format and aims. American officials also conducted extended prenegotiations which produced a series of secret letters offering various "assurances" about the proposed conference to the Palestinians, Israelis, Lebanese and Syrians—each letter delicately phrased differently to correspond to the particular sensitivities of the recipients (Appendix, Documents 9, 10).[21] The heavy hand of a third party fits the traditional pattern of Arab-Israeli negotiations; however, the US decision to declare a clear policy preference and then commit precious resources to making it work is a new feature evidenced only rarely since Camp David.

Another constructive aspect of US involvement was the confluence between the conference at Madrid and the fact that the Bush administration was pursuing American global interests in cooperation, not confrontation, with its European, Soviet, and Japanese allies. Unlike previous situations in which co-sponsorship with the Soviets gave Arab leaders opportunities to play one superpower off the other, Madrid saw the evolution of "dual sponsorship . . . from an impediment to peace into a catalyst for successful negotiations."[22] Another fortuitous circumstance was the absence of any competing European initiatives or declarations. This may have been because the phased format of the Madrid process satisfied other third-party wanna-bes that America's allies would be able to make their own contributions through their participation in the later, multilateral, stages of the peacemaking effort.

But the most valuable form of American involvement came after the formal sessions had ended, when US officials were called upon to supply ample quantities of patience, continuity, and ingenuity to help overcome the recurring deadlocks and slowdowns in the bilateral negotiations that the Madrid Conference had set into motion in Washington. As Israeli scholar and analyst Galia Golan correctly predicted in early 1992, "it will probably be . . . the United States that will have to continue to provide the procedural solutions to the problems of keeping the various sides at the negotiating table when crises arise in the talks."[23] Commenting on the potential "traps" inherent in the US mediation role at Madrid, I. William Zartman pointed to behavior consistent with the historical patterns already highlighted:

> Both sides expect to have the luxury of talking themselves into a deadlock and then being saved by . . . the United States, upon whom the blame for an imposed solution can then be heaped. The mediator's role is critical but misperceived by the parties, necessary but habit-forming and dangerous.[24]

But in retrospect, we can see that the United States performed effectively as a procedural facilitator, without succumbing to the temptation of becoming an arbitrator on matters of substance. American officials took full advantage of Israeli and Arab desires for good relations with and dependence upon the United States, shepherding sometimes reluctant delegations to the bargaining table with a combination of carrots and sticks. In clearly enunciating a specific format, issues, and schedule for negotiations, and acting resolutely to achieve them, the United States departed from the historic model in a positive way.

PROPOSED TERMS OF AGREEMENT

The success of the Madrid Conference cannot be gauged by the standard measure of analyzing agreements reached or treaties signed. When negotiators in Washington finally settled down to dealing with the hard issues separating them, the historic incompatibility of basic aims became evident and quickly produced deadlock in three of the four sets of talks. In the cases of the Syrians and (by extension) Lebanese, negotiations foundered over Israeli withdrawal from the Golan Heights and arrangements for returning the Israeli-imposed security zone in South Lebanon to effective Lebanese sovereignty, in exchange for a normalization of relations between Israel and Syria and Israel and Lebanon, respectively. Israeli and Syrian negotiators dug themselves into a Catch-22 rut, going around in circles shadowboxing over how much of a withdrawal for how much peace, and how soon. But, while progress in narrowing differences has been slight and slow, the delegations have remained in contact and "on stand-by," waiting for green lights from their leaders in the Middle East to signal changes in acceptable compromise formulae.

The Israeli-Palestinian talks finally began dealing with matters of substance in mid-January 1992. The subsequent exchanges of position papers revealed the irreconcilability of the delegations' positions over the nature, scope, and purpose of an "interim self-government" for the Palestinians, as called for in the letter of invitation to the conference. The Israelis sought at first to keep all discussions limited to the Begin-ite concept of "personal autonomy," while the Palestinians aimed all their arguments at achieving territorial sovereignty. The only small break from the historic pattern of the negotiating partners remaining locked into rigid opening positions came in April 1993, with the agreement to form three separate Israeli-Palestinian working groups on self-government, land and water, and human rights. Late in coming, this procedural step undoubtedly helped the parties focus on narrower practical issues more amenable to resolution, but the gap between them was a long way from being bridged. Only the Jordanian-Israeli talks seemed to break with the historic Arab-Israeli negative negotiating pattern; in that case, delegates kept some "give-and-take" in reserve behind their opening stances, thereby allowing the parties room for some real bargaining and the narrowing of differences.

The real success of the Madrid Conference was the breakthrough achieved on a number of procedural issues that had for years blocked the way to the very pursuit of negotiations. The participation of an official Palestinian delegation was one such triumph. The formal sessions that assembled the delegations together represented another important advance by sweeping aside long-standing taboos of mutual non-recognition. Even so, old habits die hard, and the precedent being set by the Madrid Conference seems to have been lost on several delegates, particularly the Israeli prime minister and Syrian foreign minister, who paid lip service to the "historic" nature of the occasion but went on to devote the bulk of their remarks to "histrionics," rehashing old grievances, accusations, and counterclaims.[25] A particularly dramatic moment came when Syrian Foreign Minister Farouq al-Sharaa suddenly produced what he said was a 1947 British "wanted" announcement featuring a young Yitzhak Shamir, accused by the British of underground terrorist activities against their troops in Palestine.[26] While indicating the presence of an astute archivist at the Syrian foreign ministry, the main effect of the presentation was to underscore the lack of trust and goodwill between the two parties, despite their presence at the same peace table. Nevertheless, once the rhetorical salvos had all been fired during the formal sessions, another important landmark passed quietly on 3 November 1991, when Israeli delegations sat down to parallel sets of direct bilateral talks in Madrid with representatives of Syria, Lebanon, Jordan and the Palestinians.

The architects of the Madrid Conference could point with pride to three primary accomplishments. First, they managed to assemble the reluctant delegations and, even more significantly, to retain their participation until the conference's scheduled conclusion, despite the strain of unabated mutual antagonism. Second, the conference set in motion the mechanism and rules for continuing Arab-Israeli peace negotiations into the 1990s. Third, the conference planted important seeds for the Jordanian-Israeli and Israeli-PLO peace processes.

The procedures adopted at Madrid represented the fine-tuning of aspects of both the "maximalist" and "minimalist" types of international conferences promoted actively by various parties between 1985 and 1988.[27] The major innovation was a structural formula that assigned delegations to separate but parallel bilateral and multilateral tracks.[28] The bilateral talks, which began in Madrid on 3 November, soon moved to Washington, where another ten rounds of talks took place between December 1991 and July 1993.

The multilateral track, which was inaugurated in Moscow in January 1992, introduced a useful novelty into the peacemaking process. In addition to involving the expected regional states (with the defiant exception of Syria and Lebanon), these multilateral negotiations broadened the base of participation by including eleven Arab states and twenty-seven other states and international agencies. The work was divided into five separate forums—water, refugees, environment, regional economic development, and arms control and regional security. The eighth round (the environmental working group) of the Madrid multinationals convened in Amman in June 1995.[29] The twin goals of the negotiations in these working groups were to find solutions for regional problems and to serve as "confidence-building measures" for the normalization of Arab-Israeli relations. In addition, a major multilateral economic summit took place in Casablanca in October 1994 and was followed by a second in Amman a year later.

PSYCHOLOGICAL FACTORS

In breaking sacred taboos and dealing directly with one another, leaders and negotiators created a huge gap between élite behavior and public attitudes. This presented a novel challenge requiring special efforts by would-be peacemakers. "The genius of the [Madrid] process," wrote one observer, "is that it is evolutionary." Rather than decrying the frustrating lack of visible progress in late 1992, Graeme Bannerman went on to suggest that this slow pace was an asset that "allow[ed] national leaders to prepare public opinion for change."[30] Indeed, the diplomatic activity set off by the Madrid process in foreign capitals was mirrored by an uphill public-relations campaign—including an unfreezing of high-level Israeli-Egyptian diplomatic visits—aimed at convincing disbelievers throughout the region that benefits of peace were attainable and did warrant an end to the state of belligerency and some territorial sacrifices. In January 1993, the Israeli Knesset removed a significant legal obstacle to normalization by voting to revoke a 1986 law banning contacts between Israelis and PLO representatives.

Given the drastic nature of the changes that the prospect of peace introduced into both the foreign and domestic policy of Israel, decision makers and opinion makers in the 1990s had only one precedent from which to try to draw useful lessons: the Begin government's 1979–82 campaign to legitimize its pioneering peace with Egypt. In his examination of how Begin sold Camp David to the nationalist skeptics, Yaacov Bar-Siman-Tov pointed to, among other things, "the perceived rationality of the proposed peace policy . . . [and] the conscious manipulation of national symbols, language, rituals, and ideology."[31]

The Rabin government that inherited the Shamir Madrid legacy faced formidable obstacles in pursuit of the "fundamental, stable, and comprehensive national consensus" to which Bar-Siman-Tov also referred. The wisdom of the post–Camp David experience was not so easily applied to legitimizing the Madrid peace process in the 1990s. The split within the Israeli population between those favoring and opposing continued negotiations in the Madrid-Washington framework, in the opinion of Tel Aviv University anthropologist Shlomo Deshen, reflected a schism far more profound than the classic difference of opinion on political options between "doves" and "hawks." The chasm between the two camps was, in his view, based largely on a clash between two *worldviews*—one secular-socialist, the other religious—which carried the risk of a violent showdown between religious opponents to the land-for-peace formula and the secular government.[32] The Rabin government's attempts to manipulate "national symbols, language, rituals, and ideology" in the process of legitimizing the Madrid peace process failed, however, to win over its ultranationalist and religious opponents.

The leaders of the Arab states and the Palestinians participating at Madrid and in the follow-up negotiations had similarly challenging tasks before them in persuading their constituents that the time was right to engage the Israelis in the conference room instead of on the battlefield. "Although Israel [was] still viewed with considerable suspicion in Damascus," some observers saw evidence that the Asad regime was beginning to prepare the Syrian people "to accept the new official goal of getting the Golan Heights back by negotiation, not war."[33] Like its Israeli counterpart, Palestinian public opinion was also fractured. In the Palestinian case, the tension was between diaspora refugees demanding a return to territory within Israel proper and those on the land in Gaza and the West Bank. The former demanded an all-Palestine solution, setting their sights on locations within Israel's borders. The latter, especially the secular pragmatists among them, were more prepared to accept a narrow West Bank/Gaza compromise that improved their quality of life and satisfied basic requirements of dignity and self-determination. Another division was between these secular pragmatists and the religious or ideological fundamentalists, who clung to maximalist visions of the destruction of Israel and the establishment of an independent Palestinian state in its place. The Palestinian delegates in Madrid and in Washington had presented the Palestinian case vigorously and eloquently. But if Palestinians in the occupied territories and in the diaspora were to make the huge psychological transformations demanded by the give-and-take of negotiations, they required strong leadership of no less than the PLO and Yasir Arafat himself.

Could Arafat extend the hand of peace to Israel? And could Rabin reciprocate? The Madrid Conference and follow-up talks in Washington succeeded in establishing direct lines of communication between Arab and Israeli élites, and creating an ongoing mechanism by which Arab and Israel negotiators could continue to wear away at the issues and chasms separating them. This was indeed progress, and an essential step. But much work still lay ahead in terms of breaking the dynamics of deadlock.

NOTES

1. M. Graeme Bannerman, "Arabs and Israelis: Slow Walk toward Peace," *Foreign Affairs* 72:1 (1992–93), 143. Cf. Abraham Ben-Zvi, *Between Lausanne and*

Geneva: International Conferences and the Arab-Israeli Conflict, Tel Aviv: Tel Aviv University, Jaffee Center for Strategic Studies (Study No. 13) and Boulder, CO: Westview Press, 1989, 15–17.

2. William B. Quandt, *Camp David: Peacemaking and Politics,* Washington, DC: The Brookings Institution, 1986, 36, 108, 113, 115, 198; Ben-Zvi, 17–22.

3. For details of the changing positions of the US, USSR, and Middle Eastern parties regarding an international conference prior to 1988, see Ben-Zvi, 26–104; Valerie Yorke, "Domestic Politics and the Prospects for an Arab-Israeli Peace," *JPS* 17:4 (Summer 1988), 17–20.

4. Galia Golan, "Arab-Israeli Peace Negotiations: An Israeli View," in *The Arab-Israeli Search for Peace,* ed. Steven L. Spiegel, Boulder and London: Lynne Rienner, 1992, 38.

5. Bannerman, 144. Cf. Golan, 46.

6. See, e.g., Steven L. Spiegel and David J. Pervin, "Introduction: The Search for Arab-Israeli Peace after the Cold War," in Spiegel, 1–4; Shlomo Gazit, "After the Gulf War: The Arab World and the Peace Process," in ibid., 18–20.

7. Efraim Karsh, "Peace Not Love: Toward a Comprehensive Arab-Israeli Settlement," *Washington Quarterly* 17:2 (Spring 1994), 151.

8. Cf. Asher Susser, "Jordan, the PLO and the Palestine Question," in *Jordan in the Middle East: The Making of a Pivotal State,* eds. Joseph Nevo and Ilan Pappé, London: Frank Cass, 1994, 226.

9. Camille Mansour, "The Palestinian-Israeli Peace Negotiations: An Overview and Assessment," *JPS* 22:3 (Spring 1993), 5–7. Cf. ibid., 30–31; Ziad Abu-Amr, "Palestinian-Israeli Negotiations: A Palestinian Perspective," in Spiegel, 27.

10. Marwan Muasher, "Jordanian Attitudes to the Peace Process," lecture by the Ambassador of Jordan to Israel, Tel Aviv University: Moshe Dayan Center for Middle Eastern and African Studies, 12 June 1995.

11. Shibley Telhami, "Israeli Foreign Policy after the Gulf War," in Spiegel, 49.

12. Laura Zittrain Eisenberg, "Passive Belligerency: Israel and the 1991 Gulf War," *Journal of Strategic Studies* 15:3 (September 1992), 315–16, 318–19.

13. Ibid., 317; Glenn Frankel, *Beyond the Promised Land: Jews and Arabs on the Hard Road to a New Israel,* New York: Simon and Schuster / Touchstone, 1996, 307.

14. Telhami, 51–53, 59–60; cf. Eisenberg, 305–306.

15. Frankel, chap. 12.

16. Interview with Yosef Harif, *Maariv,* 26 June 1992, quoted in Avi Shlaim, "Prelude to the Accord: Likud, Labour, and the Palestinians," *JPS* 23:2 (Winter 1994), 10–11; Bannerman, 150; Frankel, 309.

17. See, e.g., Golan, 42–44; Frankel, 221.

18. Cf. Shlaim, 11.

19. These restrictions still carried some weight, in spite of the attempts by the Palestine National Council and Arafat to satisfy American criteria for recognition and the start of a fledgling US-PLO dialogue in late 1988. See Mohamed Rabie, *US-PLO Dialogue: Secret Diplomacy and Conflict Resolution,* Gainsville, FL: University Press of Florida, 1995; Mahmoud Abbas [Abu Mazen], *Through Secret Channels: The Road to Oslo: Senior PLO Leader Abu Mazen's Revealing Story of the Negotiations with Israel,* Concord, MA: Paul (Reading: Garnet), 1995, 24–35; Mark Tessler, *A History of the Israeli-Palestinian Conflict,* Bloomington: Indiana University Press, 1994, 717–25; Ze'ev Schiff and Ehud Ya'ari, *Intifada: The Palestinian Uprising—Israel's Third Front,* New York: Simon and Schuster, 1990, 300–306.

20. Mansour, 18. Chairman Arafat met the entire delegation publicly in Cairo in April, and in Amman in June 1992. Cf. ibid., 18, 28–29; Abbas, chap. 6.

21. For a comprehensive selection of Madrid-related letters, speeches, statements, and draft proposals, see *The Palestinian-Israeli Peace Agreement: A Documen-*

tary Record, 2nd ed., Washington: Institute for Palestine Studies, 1995, section A; see also "The Madrid Peace Conference: Special Document File," *JPS* 21:2 (Winter 1992), 117–49. Cf. Mansour, 30.

22. Bannerman, 145. Cf. Golan, 46.

23. Golan, 46.

24. I. William Zartman, "The Negotiation Process in the Middle East," in Spiegel, 65.

25. Thomas L. Friedman, "Amid Histrionics, Arabs and Israelis Team Up to Lose an Opportunity," *NYT*, 3 November 1991, p. A1; texts of Arab and Israeli delegates' speeches are reproduced in "The Madrid Peace Conference: Special Document File," *JPS* 21:2 (Winter 1992), 128–49.

26. Alan Cowell, "Syria Offers Old Photo to Fill an Empty Chair," *NYT*, 2 November 1991, p. 4. Photo, p. 1.

27. The minimalist-maximalist dichotomy is taken from Ben-Zvi, passim.

28. This "two-tier" approach became part of American proposals in March 1989. See Cheryl A. Rubenberg, "The Bush Administration and the Palestinians: A Reassessment," in *US Policy on Palestine from Wilson to Clinton*, ed. Michael W. Suleiman, Normal, IL: AAUG Press, 1995, 199.

29. For a detailed chart of the participants in the five working groups, their key projects, and the venues of some three dozen meetings between January 1992 and June 1995, see *The Middle East Peace Process: An Overview*, Jerusalem: Israel Ministry of Foreign Affairs, December 1995, 42–43. See also Joel Peters, *Pathways to Peace: The Multilateral Arab-Israeli Peace Talks*, Washington, DC: The Brookings Institution, 1996.

30. Bannerman, 152. Cf. Golan, 39–40; Zartman, 69; Harold H. Saunders, *The Other Walls: The Arab-Israeli Peace Process in a Global Perspective*, rev. ed., Princeton: Princeton University Press, 1991, 36–37. Klieman argues, however, that optimism about the gradual, "evolutionary" nature of such agreements is based on the dubious assumptions that time can "stand still," that "it is on the side of peace," and that "regulating it is the prerogative of superpowers." Aharon Klieman, "Approaching the Finish Line: The United States in Post-Oslo Peace Making," Ramat Gan: Begin-Sadat Center for Strategic Studies, Bar-Ilan University (Security and Policy Studies, No. 22), June 1995, 26–28.

31. Yaacov Bar-Siman-Tov, *Israel and the Peace Process, 1977–1982: In Search of Legitimacy for Peace*, Albany: State University of New York Press, 1994, 243–44.

32. Shlomo Deshen, "Applied Anthropology in International Conflict Resolution: The Case of the Israeli Debate on Middle Eastern Peace Settlement Proposals," *Human Organization* 51:2 (Summer 1992), 180–84. Deshen's analysis of the depth of this rift, seen with hindsight after the events surrounding the November 1995 assassination of Yitzhak Rabin, is eerily prophetic. See also Ilana Kass and Bard O'Neill, *The Deadly Embrace: The Impact of Israeli and Palestinian Rejectionism on the Peace Process*, Lanham, MD: University Press of America, 1997, 101–106, and 175, where the authors quote Yitzhak Rabin's July 1995 comment on his government's troubles dealing with settler rabbis: "We must realize that we are headed toward a confrontation between two world views."

33. Sam Cahnman, "Inching toward Peace," *Jerusalem Report* (JR), 28 January 1993, pp. 30–31.

Chapter 5

OUT OF THE SHADOWS AND INTO THE LIGHT

THE JORDANIAN-ISRAELI PEACE PROCESS, 1993–1994

The Peace Treaty of 26 October 1994 (Appendix, Document 14) between the State of Israel and the Hashemite Kingdom of Jordan is one of the most promising negotiated settlements to emerge in the post-Madrid period. The treaty is actually the fourth in a series of Jordanian-Israeli agreements that grew out of the bilateral talks set in motion at Madrid.[1] The surprise PLO-Israeli agreement of September 1993 (see chapter 6) served as a catalyst for the Jordanian-Israeli deal. In gauging the stability of this diplomatic package, one can optimistically note that it breaks with tradition in almost every category of the historically failed pattern of Arab-Israeli negotiations.

PREVIOUS NEGOTIATING EXPERIENCE

The quartet of documents concluding with the peace treaty was, in effect, public affirmation of a private relationship long recognized as "the worst kept secret dialogue in the Middle East"[2]—remarkable for both "the longevity of the connection, and the many functional accomplishments" that it produced.[3] The 1993–94 Jordanian-Israeli peace process evolved against the background of extensive Transjordanian-Zionist and Jordanian-Israeli relations discussed at length in Chapter 3 (the London Document), and including that experience. In fact, the successful agreements of the early 1990s represent the continuation and belated fruition of the stillborn Peres-Hussein accord of 1987. Although that attempt at formal peacemaking failed, it did not deplete the reservoir of goodwill, at least

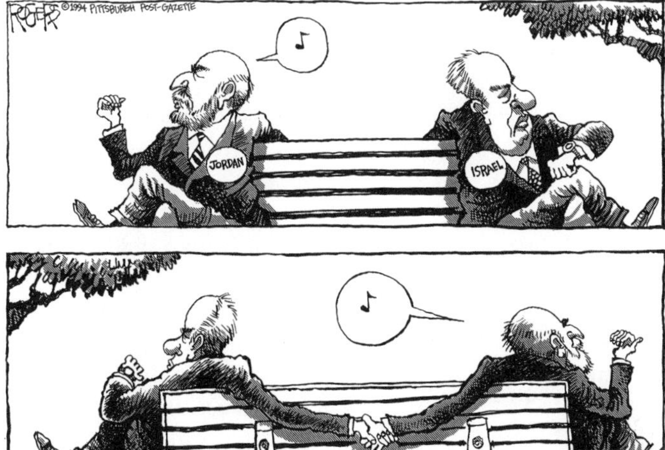

Courtesy of Rob Rogers, *Pittsburgh Post Gazette*

among the élites, that had developed from years of tacit alliance, clandestine cooperation, and informal agreements reached and kept. Intermittent contact between Jordanians and Israelis had been maintained not only at the highest levels, but between the king himself and a small number of top Israeli leaders, lending a sense of continuity and stability to the relationship and an element of trust completely lacking between Israel and any other Arab partner.[4] Meeting at the White House, Yitzhak Rabin and King Hussein admitted to a curious President Bill Clinton that they enjoyed a friendship of some twenty years' duration.[5]

In this scenario, "wealth of experience" very accurately describes the rich relationship between the two nations' leaderships. Despite the general proposition that a history of frequent encounters does not necessarily enhance the prospects for a successfully negotiated settlement, it is likely that the trust and stability created by the unique nature of long-term Jordanian-Israeli relations did contribute to the achievement of a formal peace treaty, once the two parties decided to go public. The question, then, is, if Jordan and Israel were enjoying a quiet, mutually satisfying relationship, what motivated them to come out of the shadows and into the light?

PURPOSES AND MOTIVES

Israel was born a pariah in the Middle East, and it has always been Israeli policy to try to normalize Arab-Israeli relations through bilateral peace accords with its neighbors. Since the Mandate period, Zionist leaders had fantasized about the economic potential of an open Middle East market; more recently, economists have speculated about the potential financial rewards of jointly developing commercial and tourist facilities at the Dead Sea and at the twin cities of Eilat (Israel) and Aqaba (Jordan). A formal accord with Jordan was a necessary stepping-stone along the path of mutual fiscal gain. Beyond the economics of peace, however, security-conscious Israel clearly appreciated that peace with Jordan would constitute significant closure along its long eastern front, and a buffer between it and Iraqi troops who could only march on Jerusalem via Amman.

A dalliance with Hussein was acceptable policy across Israel's highly factionalized political spectrum. Peace with Jordan was a long-cherished goal, dating from the interrupted agreement with King Hussein's grandfather, Abdallah. After capturing the West Bank from Jordan in the 1967 war, many Israelis touted the "Jordanian option" as a way to trade that territory for a separate peace, without the trauma of having to deal with the Palestinians or the PLO. Despite the recent breakthrough to direct Israeli-PLO dealings, the popularity of the accord with Hussein reflects the traditional Israeli preference for dealing with non-Palestinian Arab state leaders and the long-standing predominance of "Jordan-firsters" over "Palestine-firsters" within the Israeli foreign-policy establishment.[6] Enthusiasm for the treaty with Jordan was also an expression of relief at having found a counterweight to, or insurance policy against, Arafat's still-to-be-proven ability to "deliver the goods."

The king shared many of Israel's motivations in finally concluding a formal peace, and his thinking had similarly evolved to the point where the question was not "whether" peace was possible, but "when" and on what specific terms. Concerned that successive Israeli-PLO agreements would leave him sidelined, Hussein was anxious to maintain Jordanian influence in the West Bank. His own declaration of 31 July 1988[7] had reduced Jordanian responsibility for West Bank Palestinian affairs; any new PLO-Israeli security or economic measures established there would obviously have a huge impact on Jordan, however, and Hussein wanted to put Jordan in the best position to shape developments to its advantage.

In making peace with Israel and removing even the small risk of war there, Hussein extricated Jordan from military dependence upon Iraq. This served two interrelated Jordanian goals: reconstitution of the friendship with the United States, and economic recovery. Pressured by his vast Palestinian population to side with Iraq in the 1991 Gulf War, the king found himself estranged from his traditional US and Gulf Arab benefactors. Palestinian refugees from Kuwait and Saudi Arabia poured into Jordan, further straining its already meager resources. The fledgling Palestinian autonomy envisaged in the 13 September 1993 Israeli-Palestinian Declaration of Principles (DOP)[8] also threatened to divert potential West Bank investment from Jordanian to newly autonomous Palestinian hands.

Although the United States rewarded Jordan's participation in the Madrid conference with a resumption of military assistance, Amman's worsening economy required massive foreign intervention, including US forgiveness of Jordan's $700–million foreign debt. Nothing short of a historic, open declaration of peace with Israel could have brought such a handsome reward, and Secretary of State Warren Christopher acknowledged that, in this situation, "the economics of it may be driving the politics of it."[9] Peace with Israel served the Jordanian goal of political rehabilitation in the eyes of the United States, and promised an economic boon in terms of US aid and debt forgiveness, as well as in terms of a new economic relationship with Israel itself.

TIMING

As suggested previously, it was no surprise that Jordan and Israel shared so many common or overlapping aims, and the question is not why they were able to reach an agreement, but why *at this time?* The old expression comes to mind: "If it ain't broke, don't fix it." What gave Jordan and Israel the impetus to formalize a private and low-key relationship that was already working well?

Many of the key timing elements have already emerged in the preceding discussion. The Gulf War left Jordan's economy stagnating in its wake and prompted Hussein to consider dramatic action. The end of the Cold War and the demise of the Arab states' Soviet sponsor dictated some degree of Arab accommodation with the sole remaining superpower, which in turn required Arab reconciliation with Israel. With the PLO and Syria now talking to the United States, Jordan could not afford the remaining strains in its own relationship with the United States. Peace with Israel would help vault Hussein back into the comfort of a US partnership.[10]

The Israeli-PLO Oslo and Cairo agreements also served to force the king's hand. Jordan's on-again, off-again relationship with the PLO, and the state of conflict between Israel and the PLO, both constrained and motivated Jordanian interaction with Israel. Mindful of the sensibilities of the huge Palestinian component of his constituency, King Hussein had always been hesitant to effect a formal peace with Israel without the PLO's endorsement or prior to a resolution of the Palestinian problem. The suddenly very real prospect of an Israeli withdrawal from parts of the West Bank, the establishment of a Palestinian self-governing authority there, and Israeli-PLO negotiations about Jerusalem in the not-so-distant future persuaded Hussein that he had better move quickly to protect Jordan's interests and influence in those areas. For example, once the PLO and Israel began negotiating openly in the autumn of 1993, the PLO goal to make Jerusalem the capital of an independent Palestine challenged Jordan's self-stated responsibility for the Islamic holy sites in the city. Article 9 of the Israeli-Jordanian treaty recognizes Jordan's special role there, potentially allowing the king to outflank Arafat on Jerusalem. Reflecting again the Israeli preference for Hussein over Arafat, Rabin was only too happy to facilitate this maneuver.

Even more important was the fact that the PLO's agreements with

Israel removed the almost sacrosanct taboo against breaking pan-Arab ranks and dealing openly with Israel. Once Arafat began negotiations with Israel, he freed Hussein from any responsibility for the Palestinian cause. Under no obligation to be more Catholic than the Pope (or more Palestinian than Arafat), King Hussein finally signed a year-old draft peace agenda with Israel on 14 September 1993, the very day after the signing of the Palestinian-Israeli DOP.

Domestic considerations provided yet another timing factor that encouraged the king in his diplomacy with Israel. In the months leading up to the 8 November 1993 Jordanian elections (the first multiparty general elections since 1957), the Islamic Action Front campaigned on a platform of no peace with Israel. But the electoral results favored the conservative, tribal, and independent blocs loyal to the king, confirming Hussein's estimation that the time was ripe for an open Jordanian-Israeli peace and reinforcing his determination to make the process succeed. Hussein thus faced a rare moment when a settlement with Israel was simultaneously "mutually beneficial on the Israeli-Jordanian bilateral level, acceptable on the Jordanian-Palestinian level, and possible on the inter-Arab level."[11]

In responding to external events and economic pressures with overtures to one another, Jordan and Israel repeated some of the traditional Arab-Israeli negotiating patterns. But, unlike the historical paradigm in which ulterior motives were usually limited to maintaining the status quo and subverting the other party's position, this time the two parties independently concluded that their multiple purposes could be best served by actually seeing the negotiations through to a successful end. Both Jordan and Israel responded to timing considerations in the 1990s in a proactive sense, seeing an open window of opportunity and reaching through it toward one another with the positive goal of ending their dispute through peaceful accommodation.

STATUS OF THE NEGOTIATORS

Post-Madrid Israeli-Jordanian negotiations benefited from sustained, symmetrical, high-level interaction between the two sides. Like Sadat and Begin after Camp David and in sharp contrast to pre-1948 precedents and the failed Lebanese-Israeli negotiations of 1983, both King Hussein and Prime Minister Rabin commanded sufficient popularity and power at home to be able to make good on their promises. Rabin enjoyed a particularly strong position domestically. Even the right-wing opponents of his dealings with the PLO endorsed peace with Jordan, dubbed by one observer a "risk-free" policy, "a local equivalent to mom and apple pie."[12] Fondness for the king and the strong historical preference for dealing with him, as opposed to Arafat, meant that Israeli negotiators went into the Jordanian meetings with an unprecedented amount of public trust and support for an accord. King Hussein, for his part, faced opposition from both Islamic fundamentalists and leftist forces, not insignificant elements in the Jordanian parliament. But by closely monitoring the shifting balance of power among Jordan's domestic forces, the careful king of four decades prevailed.

Again departing from the historical pattern, Jordanians and Israelis kept their negotiations restricted to the very highest leaders and a small coterie of their most trusted advisers. The third document in the Israeli-Jordanian package, the Washington Declaration, was actually drafted by Hussein and Rabin themselves in a year-long series of secret, dusk-to-dawn meetings. The king perhaps captured the unique dynamic of this process best, saying to Rabin at their pivotal 19 May 1994 meeting in London, "You know, Yitzhak, you and I have been at this a long time."[13] Over the next few hours they worked out the basis for that July's Declaration in Washington.

Unlike most Arab and Israeli would-be negotiators, Hussein and Rabin were remarkably unplagued by errant or unofficial representatives. Shimon Peres's role in the 1993–94 agreements with Jordan stands in sharp relief against his earlier negotiations with the king, which produced the failed London Document of 1987. That accord died when then–Prime Minister Shamir flatly rejected the policy of Foreign Minister Peres. Despite a bitter, decades-long rivalry between themselves, Rabin and Peres joined forces after 1993, successfully shepherding Israeli-Jordanian relations to a full peace. At the treaty-signing ceremony in the Arava desert on 26 October 1994, the two Labor Party rivals went out of their way to praise each other for their diplomatic contributions; it was not clear whether the sharper hatchet being buried there was the one between Jordan and Israel or the one between Rabin and Peres.

Breaking the traditional pattern that had undermined the agreement of 1987, the 1993–94 Jordanian-Israeli accords thus benefited from direct and well-focused attention by strong leaders in control of their governments and well-served by trusted aides. Success was also facilitated by the fact that the high-level officials entrusted with the ongoing negotiations between the periodic meetings by their political bosses developed smooth and pleasant interpersonal relations. After their first encounters under the Madrid / Washington format, the delegations became effective in hammering out details and developing the substance of the principles enunciated by Israeli leaders and by King Hussein, who were recalled by their legal and military advisers and draftsmen only when the time was ripe to narrow remaining gaps and finalize agreed texts.

THIRD-PARTY CONSIDERATIONS

In the 1993–94 Israeli-Jordanian talks, the United States again assumed the traditional role of an external Great Power whom both sides, particularly the Jordanians, were eager to impress. US support, money, and arms were, after all, an important motivating factor for the king in declaring an open peace with Israel. Aharon Klieman cautions, however, against blindly accepting the conventional wisdom that full US participation is "absolutely essential; or, alternatively, that this involvement is both necessary and decisive at every single stage."[14] He reminds us that the "Israel-Jordan breakthrough achieved in the first half of 1994 . . . testifies to the ability of the protagonists to pursue direct channels on their own," with the definitive negotiations taking place in Amman and London between the king and Peres (November 1993) and the king and Rabin (May 1994), before direct US involvement began. A more accurate, although unconventional analysis holds that individual peace initiatives have often begun independent of the United States (e.g., Hussein-Peres in 1986–87 and the 1993 PLO-Israeli talks in Oslo), and sometimes even in opposition to US policy preferences (e.g., Sadat's 1977 overture to Israel and journey to Jerusalem). Klieman notes that the critical American contribution has been in the later stages of the diplomatic process, when the United States acted as facilitator and guarantor, keeping the negotiators on track and enticing them to persevere until they reached an accord.[15]

When the United States demonstrated the persistence and commitment to see negotiations through to a successful conclusion, it deviated dramatically from the historic pattern of third-party involvement in Arab-Israeli peacemaking efforts. The importance of the US "bandwagoning"[16] an indigenous Middle East initiative—that is, endorsing, facilitating, and underwriting a process that has already begun—is evident in the different fates of the Jordanian-Israeli initiative of the late eighties and that of the early nineties. In contrast to the American hesitancy that undermined the prospects of the 1987 accord, the United States energetically supported the later attempts at a separate Jordanian-Israeli peace. When Jordanian-Israeli negotiations at the State Department under the Madrid formula stalled, the administration applied its best diplomatic resources to the problem. Secretary of State Christopher shuttled repeatedly to the Middle East, and President Bill Clinton received the king, his brother Crown Prince Hassan, Foreign Minister Peres, and Prime Minister Rabin in Washington, DC.

In another happy departure from the historical pattern, the United States enjoyed the trust and friendship of both parties in nearly equal measure after Madrid; neither expected the Americans to impose a lopsided settlement on the other. Israelis and Jordanians regularly included American negotiators in their meetings, principally Martin Indyk (then chief Middle East specialist at the White House) and Dennis Ross (chief American negotiator for the Middle East). In the month immediately preceding the Washington Declaration, "triangular talks" among senior diplomats from the three countries occurred on an almost daily basis in Washington, DC. In another example of the sometimes surreal nature of Arab-Israeli peacemaking in the 1990s, these talks were often dominated by Israeli efforts to persuade the Americans to grant the Jordanians the financial incentives that the king needed before he could go ahead with an open reconciliation.[17]

The July 1994 Washington Declaration epitomized Jordanian and Israeli desires for an American stamp of approval for their bilateral agreements. Although the bulk of the document was drafted by Hussein and Rabin in London, both men jumped at Clinton's invitation to unveil their accord at the White House. The language of the Declaration specifically identifies it as the "initiative of President William J. Clinton," and pays tribute to the American president in four of the five introductory sentences and again in all three of the concluding sentences.[18] The word "initiative" misrepresents the US contribution to this negotiating process, but clearly reflects both parties' need to cloak themselves in American armor in revealing and defending their accord. The October 1994 Peace Treaty incorporates and elaborates upon the Washington Declaration, which is cited twice in the preamble.

There is no doubt, however, that Jordanian-Israeli efforts benefited from serious and sustained US attention throughout 1993 and 1994. Although the peace treaty was signed at a site on the Israeli-Jordanian border, President Clinton sat with the leaders on the dais and put his signature on the document as the primary witness. Perhaps most indicative of the importance both parties attached to a US endorsement of their accord was the decision to schedule the desert ceremony for 1:00 P.M., when the sun was most punishing: it may have been siesta time in the Middle East, but on the American East Coast, the morning news programs were just beginning their broadcasts.

PROPOSED TERMS OF AGREEMENT

As the parties moved through the successive stages of their peace process, the terms of agreement increased in both breadth and depth. The culmination of a four-part process that evolved over twenty-four months, the Jordanian-Israeli accords terminated the state of war between the two countries, established a full and formal peace, and went on to outline quite specific and concrete steps in many areas. The treaty's thirty articles and five annexes cover an extensive array of cooperative measures in fields including border demarcations and crossings, security, water sharing, cultural and scientific exchanges, tourism, transportation, crime, economics and trade, aviation, the environment, postal and telecommunications, energy, health, and agriculture. An interesting innovation in the treaty is its purely bilateral security clauses and the absence of any third-party or UN presence or guarantees in this domain.[19]

In contrast to the historical pattern characterized by maximum demands and minimum movement toward a compromise agreement, Hussein and Rabin and their aides prioritized Jordanian and Israeli interests, identified where they overlapped, and strove to reach a mutually accommodating agreement. Despite the clear desire of both sides to reach an accord, however, there still existed a number of issues that were not easily resolved. Competition over scarce water resources and conflicting claims to several areas along the ill-defined Arava/Araba border posed formidable obstacles. A creative agreement to swap former Jordanian territory, which had been developed and cultivated by Israelis since 1967, for an equal amount of empty Israeli territory elsewhere along the border, testified to the parties' skill and determination in finding solutions to their problems.[20]

PSYCHOLOGICAL FACTORS

A Darwinian take on pre-1977 Arab-Israeli negotiation patterns suggests that the exigencies of prolonged conflict encouraged the "survival of the most cautious" in peacemaking, if not in war. Political élites came to power by virtue of their ultranationalist credentials and remained in power by playing upon patriotic themes. Those tempted to pursue negotiations proved incapable of overcoming the opponents of a compromise solution.

Here the firm leadership of Hussein and Rabin, as previously cited, deviated from the historical norm. Rabin had the easier task, since selling Israelis on peace with Jordan was essentially preaching to the converted. He used the momentum with Jordan, however, to justify his more controversial dealings with the PLO, arguing that the former could not have come about without the latter. Rabin attempted to persuade the Israeli public that his was truly a broad policy aimed at winning peace for Israel with *all* its Arab neighbors—a program of which the distasteful partnership with the PLO was a necessary component. When Israeli and Jordanian diplomats abandoned the conference rooms of Washington to meet for the first time at their common border in mid-July 1994, the Rabin government portrayed the "change of venue [as] a triumph, signaling another step toward full acceptance [of Israel] by its Arab neighbors."[21]

Commitment to pan-Arab consensus among the general population and a large Palestinian constituency required that the king work considerably harder to prepare his people for peace with Israel and the renunciation of all hostile claims against it. On 9 July 1994, Hussein warned his parliament that without superpower support Jordan could not withstand the economic and political pressures it faced, adding that he would meet with Rabin if that would bring relief in the form of renewed US support for the kingdom. The July border meeting, and the Washington Declaration and joint address to Congress by Hussein and Rabin later that month, were all broadcast live by Jordanian state television, signaling clearly the end of the era of sub-rosa Israeli-Jordanian contacts and the régime's new policy of open relations and normalization.

Abba Eban has stated that "the task of leadership is not to follow public opinion blindly, but to lead public opinion."[22] Here again, Arab and Israeli leaders stepped out of the traditional pattern. In launching concerted campaigns in support of compromise, trust, and peace with the other, each leader sought to persuade his society that in suing for peace he was not abandoning cherished national interests, but rather securing them in the best way possible.

Having concluded simultaneously that peace between their nations was achievable and worth pursuing, Hussein and Rabin had to subject their leadership to the test of public opinion. This required the overcoming of a legacy of mistrust, fear, and hatred and replacing it, at the popular level, with a belief that accommodation with the other side was possible and would even enhance their respective national interests.

The Israeli public had significantly less ground to cover in terms of trusting Hussein and taking a leap of faith into a Jordanian-Israeli peace. Especially when compared to Arafat and the PLO—names that many Israelis uttered in a tone reserved for Hitler and the Nazis[23]—King Hussein was not feared as a vicious enemy but rather seen as a gallant opponent.

The Jordanian public was decidedly more skeptical, particularly those of Palestinian descent, and especially the refugees of 1967 and their families. Against a backdrop of generally unfriendly images of Jews, Israelis, and Zionism,[24] Jordanians had been exposed to decades of news coverage of harsh Israeli actions in the occupied territories, and shared in the general Arab perception of Israeli aggressiveness and aspirations to regional economic hegemony. These factors gave many Jordanians pause as to the nature of their new partner in peace. While Israelis had little to lose in making peace with Jordan and embraced the idea almost instantly, Jordanians needed time and persuading to consider that the benefits of peace with Israel would outweigh any possible damage to their interests at home, in the Arab world, and vis-à-vis the Palestinian cause.[25]

The 1993 Israeli-Jordanian Common Agenda and the 1994 Washington Declaration set into motion measures for dismantling both pragmatic and psychological barriers between Jordanians and Israelis. The rapidity with which the treaty's requirements have been fulfilled and the early crush of border crossings by both dignitaries and ordinary citizens, albeit disproportionately from west to east, indicate that perhaps the leaders have succeeded in beginning to break down some of the psychological barriers between their peoples. As a Jordanian border guard observed, "It is much better to be invaded by tourists than soldiers."[26]

One journalist opened her coverage of the Washington Declaration with a saying from the Talmud to the effect that the Messiah will come when he is no longer needed, adding that "peace between Jordan and Israel is coming because it already exists."[27] But we must not belittle the reality of the Jordanian-Israeli conflict, or the importance of its official resolution. Jordanians and Israelis died in battle against one another;

gunmen penetrated the border on occasion with lethal results. Partly in response to these difficulties, however, Jordanian and Israeli leaders identified areas of common concern early on, and quietly cooperated in securing their shared border and accommodating mutual interests.

The ultimate evolution of a full Jordanian-Israeli peace appears to validate Klieman's reflections on the inherent shortcomings of the former clandestine relations. He found "something disquieting" about those ties: not only the "furtive manner by which they [were] conducted," but also the fact they did "not go quite far enough, neither resolving the outstanding political differences that remain[ed] nor actually bringing about peace." Over time, the co-conspirators may have broken from their comfortable status quo when they realized that it had become "converted into something it was neither intended nor designed to be: a hiding place from decision; a quasi-permanent structure."[28]

Once the timing elements clicked into place, the Israeli and Jordanian leaders chose to decide in favor of an above-board relationship. Having done so, they found the groundwork uniquely prepared for a Jordanian-Israeli treaty—the uniquely positive consequence of a process that deviated dramatically in virtually every respect from the historical pattern of failed Arab-Israeli negotiations.

NOTES

1. Preceding the October 1994 treaty are a draft agenda for peace, a product of the Washington talks of October 1992; a Common Agenda of 14 September 1993; and the Washington Declaration of 25 July 1994, which formally ended the state of war between the two countries. The text of the 1993 Common Agenda is reproduced in Institute for Palestine Studies, *The Palestinian-Israeli Peace Agreement: A Documentary Record,* 2nd ed., Washington, DC: Institute for Palestine Studies, 1994, 147–48, and that of the 1994 Washington Declaration (given as the "Washington Agreement") is in *The Israel-Arab Reader: A Documentary History of the Middle East Conflict,* 5th rev. and updated ed., eds. Walter Laqueur and Barry Rubin, New York: Penguin, 1995, 655–57. Most of the preceding documents may also be obtained from the Israel Ministry of Foreign Affairs (MFA), http://www.israel-mfa.gov.il or http://www.israel.org/peace, or by e-mail from ask@israel-info.gov.il.

2. Thomas L. Friedman, "Another Wall Is Tumbling Down as Israel and Jordan Meet in US," *NYT,* 2 October 1993, p. A1.

3. Aharon Klieman, *Statecraft in the Dark: Israel's Practice of Quiet Diplomacy,* Jerusalem: Jerusalem Post and Boulder, CO: Westview Press, for Jaffee Center for Strategic Studies, Tel Aviv University, 1988, 94.

4. "No Arab leader understands as well as Hussein the intricacies of Israel's domestic politics, none has spent as much time talking candidly with senior Israeli leaders." Samuel W. Lewis, "Israel: The Peres Era and Its Legacy," *Foreign Affairs* 65:3 (1987), 601, quoted in Klieman, *Statecraft,* 111.

5. Elaine Sciolino with Thomas Friedman, "Amid Debt, Doubt and Secrecy, Hussein and Rabin Made Peace," *NYT,* 31 July 1994, p. A1.

6. For discussions of these two orientations, see: Avi Shlaim, *Collusion across the*

Jordan: King Abdullah, the Zionist Movement, and the Partition of Palestine, Oxford: Clarendon Press, 1988, chap. 16; Ilan Pappé, "Moshe Sharett, David Ben-Gurion and the 'Palestine Option,' 1948–1956," *Studies in Zionism* 7:1 (Spring 1986), 77–96; Itamar Rabinovich, *The Road Not Taken: Early Arab-Israeli Negotiations,* New York and Oxford: Oxford University Press, 1991, 60; Aharon S. Klieman, *Israel and the World after 40 Years,* Washington, DC: Pergamon-Brassey's International Defense Publishers, 1990, 213–32.

7. Text in *The Israeli-Palestinian Conflict: A Documentary Record, 1967–1990,* ed. Yehuda Lukacs, Cambridge and New York: Cambridge University Press, 1992, 520–25.

8. Appendix, Document 13; discussed in Chapter 6.

9. Quoted in Douglas Jehl, "Jordan and Israel Join in Pact," *NYT,* 26 July 1994, p. 1. Cf. Marwan Muasher, "Jordanian Attitudes to the Peace Process," lecture by the Ambassador of Jordan to Israel, Tel Aviv University: Moshe Dayan Center for Middle Eastern and African Studies, 12 June 1995.

10. See Stephen Zunes, "The Israeli-Jordanian Agreement: Peace or Pax Americana?" *Middle East Policy* 3:4 (April 1995), 57.

11. Dan Schueftan, "Jordan's 'Israeli Option,'" in *Jordan in the Middle East: The Making of a Pivotal State,* eds. Joseph Nevo and Ilan Pappé, London: Frank Cass, 1994, 265.

12. Clyde Haberman, "Israel-Jordan Handshake," *NYT,* 16 July 1994, p. 5. The bipartisan appeal of peace with Jordan is reflected not only in the personal diplomacy of Likud leader Benjamin Netanyahu, but also in the summer 1987 rumors of secret meetings between Prime Minister Yitzhak Shamir and King Hussein. See, e.g., Klieman, *Statecraft,* 102.

13. Sciolino with Friedman.

14. Aharon Klieman, "Approaching the Finish Line: The United States in Post-Oslo Peace Making," Ramat Gan: Begin-Sadat Center for Strategic Studies, Bar-Ilan University, 1995 (Security and Policy Studies, No. 22, June 1995), 18. Cf. Ilana Kass and Bard O'Neill, *The Deadly Embrace: The Impact of Israeli and Palestinian Rejectionism on the Peace Process,* Lanham, MD: University Press of America, 1997, 319–20.

15. Klieman, "Approaching," 16–18.

16. Ibid., 17.

17. Sciolino with Friedman.

18. Jordanian-Israeli Washington Declaration, 25 July 1994, Laqueur and Rubin, 655–57.

19. Elyakim Rubinstein, "The Israel-Jordan Peace Treaty," lecture (in Hebrew) to Middle East course, Israel Ministry of Foreign Affairs, 26 February 1995, p. 11. Ambassador Rubinstein served as the defense ministry's legal adviser and special assistant to the prime minister under both Yitzhak Shamir and Yitzhak Rabin, headed the Israeli delegation in talks with Jordanians and Palestinians after the Madrid Conference, and was one of the chief architects of the treaty.

20. Some forty square kilometers were exchanged in this way. The persevering Israeli and Jordanian negotiators based themselves on precedents for resolving frontier disputes along the Jordanian-Saudi and Iraqi-Jordanian borders. Ibid., 8–9.

21. Clyde Haberman, "Israelis and Jordanians Meet in Public," *NYT,* 19 July 1994, p. A1. Cf. Elyakim Rubinstein remarks, Israel-Jordan Peace Talks (Ein Avrona), 18 July 1994; Peres address, 5th session of the Trilateral Talks (Dead Sea Spa Hotel, Jordan), 20 July 1994, MFA.

22. Quoted in Hedges.

23. See, e.g., Joseph Alpher, "Why Israel Should Recognize the PLO and Invite

Arafat to Jerusalem," *Moment*, July-August 1988, 12. Cf. Harold H. Saunders, *The Other Walls: The Arab-Israeli Peace Process in a Global Perspective*, rev. ed., Princeton: Princeton University Press, 1991, 47–48.

24. For an exposé of disturbing antisemitic themes in Jordanian publications, see Victor Nahmias, "Israel in Jordanian Eyes," *JPI*, w/e 25 January 1986, p. 15.

25. Marwan Muasher, "Jordanian Attitudes to the Peace Process,"; Stephanie Genkin, "Not Quite Normal," *JR*, 7 September 1995, pp. 22–25; Hirsh Goodman, "The Mirage of Peace," *JR*, 5 October 1995, p. 72; Michele Chabin, "Jordanians Skeptical of Peace," *Pittsburgh Jewish Chronicle*, 2 November 1995, p. 7; Zunes, 57–68.

26. Chris Hedges, "On Road to Peace, a Gate Is Opened," *NYT*, 10 August 1994, p. A4.

27. Elaine Sciolino, "Two Neighbors Agree," *NYT*, 26 July 1994, p. A4.

28. Klieman, *Statecraft*, 94, 111.

Chapter 6

JUDGMENT OF SOLOMON

THE ISRAELI-PALESTINIAN PEACE PROCESS, 1993–1996

The stunning revelation of a secret Israeli-PLO agreement in September 1993 completely recast the anatomy of the Arab-Israeli peace process. The fact of direct PLO-Israeli negotiations was startling enough; even more surprising was the "diplomatic equivalent of a 'blitzkrieg'"[1] that unfolded in the following months, beginning with the signing of the 13 September Declaration of Principles on Interim Self-Government Arrangements (DOP, also known as the Oslo Accord; Appendix, Document 13). Following it were the 1994 Cairo Agreement, the 1995 "Oslo II" Agreement, and smaller agreements negotiated along the way to implementing these major accords.[2]

Despite this apparently successful trail of historic documents, serious differences between the Palestinians and Israel remained unresolved. The gravity of the domestic opposition that the PLO and Israeli leaderships faced within their own communities was driven home in November 1995 with the assassination of Prime Minister Yitzhak Rabin by a young Israeli Jew fanatically opposed to Israel's relinquishing its biblical claim to the occupied territories. Rabin's assassination, the first-ever murder of a prime minister in Israel's history, demonstrated the huge gap between the Rabin-Peres government's commitment to trading land for peace and the fervent rejection of that policy by those on the far right.[3] Palestinian society was similarly torn between those who supported the peace process and those who would destroy it.

In this final case study we shall focus on the breakthrough achieved by the Rabin government and the PLO in 1993 and the negotiated agreements which followed. An Epilogue (page 144ff.) sketches out the beginning of an application of our negotiating paradigm to the Palestinian-Israeli peace process in the first eight months following the mid-1996 election of Benjamin Netanyahu as Israel's prime minister.

PREVIOUS EXPERIENCE

Fruitless Zionist-Palestinian negotiations during the Mandate period left Jewish Agency officials with a decided preference for working toward an accommodation over Palestine through pan-Arab leaders beyond its borders. Israel's post-1948 inclination to deal with individual Arab states rather than with Palestinian groups reflected a continuation of this pattern. The creation of the Palestine Liberation Organization in 1964 signaled the emergence of a new generation of Palestinian leaders and the reawakening and radicalization of the dispersed Palestinian community. The PLO's National Covenant (1968)[4] declared a perpetual armed struggle aimed at destroying the Zionist state, explicitly ruling out a diplomatic solution. By the time the 1974 Rabat Arab summit crowned the PLO the "sole legitimate representative" of the Palestinian people,[5] most Israelis and Palestinians had no inclination to pursue direct contacts with one another.

From the late 1960s until the mid-1980s, the "non-dialogue" between Israelis and Palestinians consisted of parallel efforts to delegitimize each other in the eyes of the international community. The PLO highlighted Israel's harsh treatment of Palestinians under military occupation in the West Bank and Gaza, while Israel could point to a series of horrific PLO terrorist attacks, including the murder of Israeli athletes at the 1972 Olympics in Munich. In 1975 Israel obtained an American promise not to recognize or talk with the PLO until it formally accepted UN Resolution 242's implied recognition of the Jewish state.[6] For its part, the PLO successfully imposed a ban against Palestinian contacts with Israel, largely observed by other Arab actors as well. Israel resorted to the familiar pre-1948 tactic of dealing with non-Palestinian leaders like King Hussein (in secret) and President Sadat (openly), while fostering rival Palestinian organizations, such as the West Bank "Village Leagues," to challenge the authority of the PLO.[7]

In the years after 1948, only a handful of Israeli and Palestinian mavericks dared to talk to the enemy and had little or no impact on mainstream opinion or official policy.[8] Ideological purists in the Palestinian camp attempted to enforce the boycott against dealing with Israelis by ostracism and assassination.[9] Israel sharpened its longstanding discouragement of contact with the PLO in August 1986 when Prime Minister Yitzhak Shamir's government amended its Prevention of Terror law to make such encounters illegal. Yet, breaches of the mutual boycott were common during the 1980s, especially among intellectuals and academics working or traveling in Europe and North America.[10] But these rare and always top-secret meetings between Palestinians and Israelis were hardly enough to challenge the century-long history of avoidance and antagonism that characterized the two people's shared experiences.

This lack of contact did not mean, however, that Israel and the PLO were uninformed as to each other's goals; here was no conflict based on misunderstood intentions that needed only straightforward talks to clear the air. Given each party's familiarity with the other's objectives, the dearth of contact cannot serve as an explanation for the ferocity of the conflict between them. It did, however, contribute substantially to the easy demonization of the other, creating a psychological obstacle to peace of tremendous import.

PURPOSES AND MOTIVES

Historically, ulterior motives—rather than the quest for a peaceful accommodation—brought Zionists (and later, Israelis) together with Palestinian Arabs for futile encounters. Breaking with the pattern of a century of mutual evasion and enmity, veteran soldier-diplomat-politician Yitzhak Rabin won the June 1992 Israeli elections on a platform built on two interrelated goals: normalization of relations with the Arab world, and an agreement with the Palestinians in the occupied territories. Despite Rabin's reputation as a hard-liner on security issues, he and his former rival, now Foreign Minister Shimon Peres, applied themselves diligently to the various Arab-Israeli talks taking place in Washington under the Madrid peace process. The Rabin government quickly showed greater flexibility than its predecessor, particularly in accepting the evolution of the Jordanian-Palestinian talks into separate Jordanian and Palestinian negotiating tracks.

Israeli aims under the Rabin-Peres team included terminating the occupation of Gaza and much of the West Bank, and reaching an accommodation with the Palestinians that would diminish terrorism, end the *Intifada,* and allow for normal interstate Arab-Israel relations. Yitzhak Rabin, the military man, came to realize that only the PLO had the manpower and legitimacy to police the Palestinian population and control residual anti-Israel violence in the wake of a future Israeli withdrawal. Recognizing and cooperating with the hated PLO was a decidedly hard pill for most Israelis to swallow; Rabin hoped to sweeten it with the promise that a Palestinian deal would open the doors to the long-term Israeli goal of achieving normal relations with the rest of the Arab world, bringing about the full integration of Israel into a politically and economically stable region. Peres laid out his own sweeping vision of Rabin's pragmatic goals in a book entitled *The New Middle East.*[11]

Mainstream PLO intentions had evolved from the original goal of destroying Israel to proposals for coexisting with it. Technically excluded from the Palestinian portion of the joint Jordan-Palestinian delegation to Madrid, the PLO gave its nod of approval to Palestinian participation in

Courtesy of Rob Rogers, *Pittsburgh Post Gazette*

the conference and follow-up negotiations and worked hard to control the Palestinian agenda from behind the scenes.[12] From the shadows of Madrid, the PLO moved to secret direct talks with Israel in the shadows of Oslo.

The PLO's goal in these negotiations was a comprehensive resolution of the Palestinian plight, with the short-term aims of:

- an immediate Israeli withdrawal from some occupied Palestinian land, an accomplishment with which to turn back the growing popularity of Hamas, the Palestinian Islamic movement based in Gaza;
- recognition by Israel;
- recognition by, diplomatic relations with, and economic support from the United States; and
- an Israeli commitment to future pullbacks from additional land in the occupied territories.

The long-term goal was the establishment of an independent Palestinian state under PLO leadership. To achieve all this, Arafat—like Rabin—would also have to play his "recognition" card.

TIMING

By the fall of 1992, a wide range of events converged to convince both Israeli and PLO leaders that their interests might best be served by a Palestinian-Israeli compromise, something that neither had been prepared to accept before. Why now?

The 1991 Madrid Conference had broken the historic taboo against direct Arab-Israeli talks and had set into motion follow-up bilateral and multilateral talks in Washington and other world capitals. Yitzhak Rabin took office in June 1992 keenly aware that he would be judged by history—and the Israeli electorate—on his ability to use those negotiations to fulfil his campaign promises to deliver a quick agreement with the Palestinians and normal relations with the Arab states. Early in Rabin's tenure, however, domestic Israeli politics, independent of the peace process, threatened the viability of his Labor coalition. The government needed something as spectacular as a Palestinian peace deal to pull itself above the internal political fray and to enhance its chances of making good on the most difficult of its campaign promises. Once it became clear that the Palestinians in DC—hamstrung by the need for repeated under-the-table consultations with the PLO in Tunis—could not deliver what Israel needed from them, Rabin came to believe that he had no choice but to go directly to the PLO.

The timing was such that the PLO was now equally prepared for direct talks with Israel. Both the suffering and renewed self-esteem connected with the *Intifada* activated a new constituency within the Palestinian movement—the leadership within the occupied territories—that was "anxious to see progress on the diplomatic front that would make their sacrifice worthwhile."[13] For his part, Arafat was struggling to maintain a minimum level of PLO services to his far-flung Palestinian constituency. The fall of the Soviet Union had stripped the PLO of a large source of its diplomatic and military support. Angry at Arafat's support of Iraq during the Gulf War, the PLO's wealthy Gulf state patrons instituted a "financial siege" that forced reductions in essential Palestinian social, educational, medical, and cultural programs, with devastating repercussions for both Palestinian society and the PLO's leadership role within it. With the Palestinian condition deteriorating and the PLO estranged from many of its natural Arab supporters, Arafat knew that a growing number of Palestinians were finding the PLO increasingly bankrupt, politically and financially. Hence Arafat's desperate need to produce tangible results on the ground.[14]

The rise in popularity and power of Hamas further caused Arafat and Rabin to look upon each other through new eyes.[15] Hamas emerged during the *Intifada* as an Islamic alternative to the PLO, and its covenant added a fundamentalist imperative to existing Palestinian demands, calling for the destruction of Israel and the establishment of an Islamic Palestinian state in its place.[16] Arafat feared that a militant Hamas would soon rival and perhaps overtake the PLO as the object of the people's loyalty and the standard-bearer of their cause. After more than a quarter of a century, the PLO had liberated not one centimeter of Palestine; compared to the young, hard-bitten Hamas militants, Arafat and his companions looked tired and old, their energy and their treasury depleted. Arafat gambled that if he could negotiate an Israeli withdrawal from the occupied territories, popular support would swing dramatically in his favor.

The timing was indeed "ripe,"[17] as the Israeli government was coming to the same conclusion at the same time, and finding it in Israel's own interest.[18] Hamas also created for the Israeli government a new sense of urgency for settling the Palestinian problem. As Richard Bulliet has suggested, an "instinctive feeling that suicidal religious fanatics are more dangerous than suicidal secular fanatics" led to an Israeli estimation that "the prospect of being marooned in a sea of militant Islamic enemies seemed more horrifying than the longstanding reality of being marooned in a sea of militant secular enemies."[19] Absolutely rejecting any Israeli-Palestinian compromise, Hamas unwittingly pushed the PLO and Israel into an awkward embrace. Rabin and his advisers calculated that, between Arafat and Hamas, Arafat was clearly the lesser of two evils. The time had come to strike a deal with Arafat, while he was still inclined to deal, and before he had become irrelevant.

In a major departure from the historical model, Israel and the PLO simultaneously came to perceive immediate benefits with acceptable costs in a preliminary negotiated settlement between them.[20] Both the PLO and Israel hoped that a deal between them that allowed Arafat to claim responsibility for an initial Israeli withdrawal would pull the rug out from under Hamas and pave the way for a mutually acceptable resolution to their conflict. Arafat calculated that the PLO's recovery of some land from Israeli control, along with Israeli and American legitimization of his organization, would counter the anticipated backlash from those Palestinian quarters that had consistently rejected any compromise with Israel. For his part, Rabin believed that a deal with the PLO could be tolerated if quickly followed by the palliative of open and positive relations between Israel and the Arab world.

This confluence of conditions—the rise of an Israeli government specifically committed to a negotiated settlement with the Palestinians, the impotence of the Palestinian negotiating team in Washington, the financial woes of a PLO desperately in need of a tangible victory, and the increasing power of a mutually threatening common enemy in Hamas—combined to create a unique moment in Palestinian-Israeli history. Veteran Egyptian analyst Mohamed Heikal contends that the momentum in Norway was such that, by the end of May 1993,

> Rabin was on the road to acceptance of the tentative Oslo deal, Peres was full of excitement, and Arafat wanted to press ahead as soon as possible. The negotiations had reached a point where it was less difficult for the parties to go ahead than to turn back.[21]

Veering sharply from the historical pattern, sworn enemies simultaneously realized that, without the other's cooperation, each lacked both the power to impose its own solution against the other's objections and the wherewithal to overcome internal opponents.

THIRD-PARTY CONSIDERATIONS

Given their mutual non-recognition policies, the PLO and Israel had long relied on third parties to exchange what little communication passed between them. Traveling journalists and academics from many countries transmitted messages back and forth; the Jordanians, Egyptians, and Moroccans played postman on occasion as well. In the era of Madrid-style talks, however, everyone assumed that the United States held the preeminent third-party position. Surprise at the September 1993 announcement that secret Israeli-PLO negotiations had produced an accord was compounded by the revelation that Norway—rather than America—had played the critical third-party role.

Although in late 1992 the Clinton administration "inherited the most promising Arab-Israel diplomatic initiative since the Camp David Accords of 1978,"[22] the Madrid process had already begun to falter at the end of George Bush's term, due in part to a lapse in US attention. Soviet Premier Mikhail Gorbachev's problems and the dissolution of the USSR distracted American foreign policymakers. Furthermore, Secretary of State Baker was suddenly called away from the State Department to manage the struggling Bush presidential campaign. Although President Bill Clinton kept on those diplomats responsible for US Middle East policy, the new administration had priorities besides the languishing Israeli-Palestinian effort in Washington.[23] This electoral hiatus in US activity thus contributed unwittingly to the determination of the conspirators in Oslo to forge ahead.

The Norwegian option developed from contacts in the spring of 1992 between Yossi Beilin, then an opposition member of the Knesset, and Terje Rød Larsen, a Norwegian academic conducting research in the occupied territories. After Labor's June 1992 electoral victory, Norwegian diplomat Jan Egeland proposed to introduce Beilin (then deputy foreign minister) to some of Larsen's senior PLO acquaintances, principal among them PLO treasurer Ahmad Qurei (Abu Alaa), and offered Norway as the venue for secret talks. In fifteen sessions over an eight-month period, beginning in January 1993, the negotiators in Oslo succeeded where their counterparts in the parallel negotiations in Washington, DC failed.[24]

Reflecting back on the clandestine meetings, one of the Israeli participants, Haifa University professor Yair Hirschfeld, suggested four elements in the Oslo talks that had enhanced their chances of success: (1) absolute secrecy, (2) excellent working conditions, (3) personal chemistry among individuals involved, and (4) a sense of realism.[25] All of these can be credited, in different degrees, to the unique Norwegian factor, a judgment echoed by the accolades offered by Palestinian participants as well.[26] Norway, a "middle" rather than a "great" power, off the beaten track of international diplomatic activity, contributed to the peacemaking effort in ways that differed from the usual patterns of third-party involvement. The hush-hush nature of the Oslo talks offered a sharp contrast to the talks in DC, which came under the daily scrutiny of the mass media. Away from the public eye, Israeli and PLO negotiators could float trial balloons and dispense with dramatic posturing.

Terje Rød Larsen and Norwegian Foreign Affairs Minister Johan Jørgen Holst facilitated the second and third of Hirschfeld's four conditions, personal chemistry and positive working conditions, by serving "as generous hosts and gentle mediators,"[27] providing comfortable and expansive accommodations in various homes and estates. In a series of mini-Camp David-like escapes, Israelis, Palestinians, and Norwegians stayed together at the same site, taking meals together and augmenting formal negotiations with informal late-night discussions. Subsequent marathon negotiating sessions in Taba and Eilat tried to duplicate the intimate sequestration model used with success in Oslo.[28]

Norway satisfied the fourth condition, a sense of realism, by breaking with the historical pattern by which a powerful third party inadvertently perpetuated the conflict by permitting one or both sides to maintain unrealistic hopes of having its preferred solution imposed on the other by an outside arbitrator. With no expectations whatsoever that the government of Norway would dictate a one-sided accord, Israelis, Palestinians, and their Norwegian facilitators got down to the business of driving hard, but ultimately workable, bargains among themselves.

Norway and Israel apprised the United States of the secret talks, but when Peres met with Warren Christopher in late August 1993 to brief him on the impending accord, the American secretary of state registered surprise that the talks in Norway "had become a decision-making channel."[29] The US assumption was clearly that if there were to be a Palestinian-Israeli breakthrough, it would be born of the process to which the United States had played midwife in Madrid and under whose aegis the talks in Washington were taking place. Immediately following the announcement of the DOP, the United States reverted to its accustomed third-party role. The document was signed, not at the Norwegian parliament, but on the White House lawn. By shaking hands in Washington, Prime Minister Rabin and Chairman Arafat signaled to their respective constituencies that the fragile accord between them enjoyed the backing of the United States, which they could expect to be manifest in material, economic, and diplomatic forms. Throughout the complex follow-up negotiations leading to the Cairo Agreement of May 1994 and the Oslo II pact of September 1995, the role of the United States as interested third party remained crucial.[30] "There are so many pitfalls en route to . . . the final status settlement," observed Michael Hudson, "that the behavior of the 'Only Remaining Superpower' can either facilitate or destroy the negotiations."[31]

PROPOSED TERMS OF AGREEMENT

Measured against the historical record, the DOP and Cairo and Oslo II agreements suggest that both sides dramatically scaled back previously irreconcilable demands. Immediately preceding the DOP, and proving that sometimes the fewest words speak volumes, two brief letters of mutual recognition effectively swept away decades of mutual denial (Appendix, Document 12).[32] That correspondence paved the way for the September 1993 DOP, which framed new terms of agreement for a preliminary accommodation, based on:

- immediate Palestinian self-rule in Gaza and Jericho;
- redeployment of Israeli troops away from Palestinian population centers;
- Palestinian elections in those areas;
- a PLO renunciation of violence, and recognition of the Jewish state;
- Israeli recognition of the PLO as the representative of the Palestinians;
- economic cooperation between the two parties; and
- scheduled "permanent-status" negotiations to resolve the most tendentious matters in dispute: Jerusalem, refugees, Jewish settlers, security arrangements, borders, and the final settlement.

Eight more months of difficult negotiations produced the Cairo Agreement, a hefty document including almost 300 pages of annexes dealing solely with the "Gaza-Jericho-first" provision of the DOP. The Agreement provided for the withdrawal of the Israeli Defense Forces (IDF) from virtually the entire Gaza Strip and the West Bank Palestinian Arab town of Jericho, and for the transfer of two dozen spheres of administration in those regions to a Palestinian Authority (PA). By including Jericho, the negotiators signaled that Palestinian self-governance would not be limited to the impoverished Gaza Strip but would eventually extend to areas of the West Bank.[33]

In September 1995, after continued frustrations and missed deadlines, Arafat and Peres signed the Oslo II Agreement, weighing in at almost 400 pages and including seven annexes. Oslo II sought to broaden Palestinian self-government in the West Bank through Palestinian elections and

- further Israeli withdrawal from 456 Palestinian cities, towns, and villages;
- the creation of areas "A," "B," and "C" to be under Palestinian, Israeli, or joint jurisdiction;
- the transfer of further administrative powers to the PA;
- a PA pledge to act vigorously against anti-Israel violence emanating from within its domain; and

- a PLO commitment to convene the Palestinian National Council to change the 1968 Palestinian Covenant within two months of the Palestinian elections.

The last item reflected Israel's insistence that the many articles that delegitimized Jewish nationhood and called for the destruction of Israel starkly contradicted the Arafat-Rabin mutual recognition letters of September 1993, and constituted an obstacle to continued bargaining in good faith.[34]

In assessing the new terms of agreement, one finds both encouraging deviations from and worrisome repetitions of traditional patterns. A strikingly new feature is, of course, that PLO and Israeli leaders agreed on anything at all. Oxford Historian Avi Shlaim termed the DOP "the triumph of pragmatism on both sides."

> After a hundred years of conflict and bloodshed, the two principal protagonists have put behind them the ideological dispute as to who is the rightful owner of Palestine and turned to addressing the practical problem of how to share the small piece of territory on which they are doomed to live together.[35]

Implicitly, the DOP recognized the basic principle of partitioning the Land of Israel/Palestine between Jews and Arabs.[36] Partition of the original Palestine Mandate into an Arab state and a Jewish state had been a frequently suggested and rejected solution to the conflict since the 1930s. Palestinian Arab opinion categorically opposed partition recommendations by the Peel Commission (1937) and the UN Special Committee on Palestine (1947). The Zionist leadership accepted the UN partition plan, but Israel's first government declared the plan to have been superseded by the ensuing war, for which it held the Arab states responsible.

The distance between the 1968 Covenant's demand for the liberation of all of Mandatory Palestine (comprising contemporary Israel and Jordan) and the 1993 DOP's recognition of the Jewish state is vast, and it is remarkable that the PLO survived as an organization, with Arafat as its leader, throughout this hotly contested metamorphosis of ends and means. This transformation did not happen overnight, but was accompanied by subtle policy shifts, contradictory public and whispered statements, and deep schisms over the intervening twenty-five years.[37] The Palestinian Declaration of Independence proclaimed during the November 1988 Palestine National Council meeting in Algiers retained the lofty and militant rhetoric of the late 1960s; the PNC Political Communiqué following the same meeting was replete with similar sentiments, but also included references to the PLO's commitment to "peaceful coexistence" and the "settlement of regional and international disputes by peaceful means."[38] A series of carefully crafted PLO speeches and press statements the next month[39] led some observers to believe that the PLO goal had become an independent Palestinian state in Gaza and the West Bank, coexisting with both Jordan and Israel. Five years later, Arafat's letter to Rabin and his signature on the DOP made those inferences explicit.

The Rabin government also evinced an appreciable scaling back of traditional Israeli maximalist demands. Many early Zionists had aspired to a Jewish state in all of Mandatory Palestine, including both banks of the River Jordan. In 1969, Labor Prime Minister Golda Meir argued that "there was no such thing as Palestinians."[40] Nine years later at Camp David, her Likud counterpart, Menachem Begin, proposed personal autonomy for the "inhabitants of Judea, Samaria and the Gaza district"[41] (skirting the issue of Palestinian peoplehood), but insisted on preserving Israel's control over "Greater Israel" within its biblical boundaries, including "Judea and Samaria" (the West Bank); the succeeding Shamir government firmly adhered to this goal. It was Yitzhak Rabin who focused on the one million Arabs living in the occupied territories, insisting that a democratic Israel could not rule over another people. Rabin actually declared Oslo II "a mighty blow to the delusion of Greater Israel."[42] His government was the first to recognize the Palestinian people, with the PLO as its representative, and pledge an Israeli withdrawal from the territories and peaceful coexistence with some type of Palestinian entity there.

For the first time, the parties' respective definitions of their national goals seemed to allow for some common ground between two conflicting sets of terms of agreement. In coming full circle to the partition concept, the DOP was "a powerful testimony to the limits of perversity in politics. . . . [B]oth the Palestinian leadership and Israel had tried and exhausted every other alternative, including stalemate, and had been left with nothing but what might be called the default option of their history."[43]

The successive Cairo and Oslo II accords addressed many of the issues and concessions in "stunning . . . detail and scope,"[44] but even "seemingly innocuous phrases often conceal a powerful clash of principles."[45] Each agreement proved significantly more difficult to negotiate than the one before. Yet, whatever the outcome of the peace process, in endorsing the concept of partition and beginning to implement it between the Israeli and Palestinian peoples, the DOP and Cairo and Oslo II agreements represent important departures from the historical record of mutually exclusive Zionist and Arab claims to the land.

STATUS OF THE NEGOTIATORS

Unlike the historical pattern in which only mavericks or dissidents dared to make contact with the other side, the Oslo talks took place with the knowledge and blessing of Israeli and Palestinian leaders of the highest echelon. It was shortly after Labor's June 1992 victory that Yossi Beilin secured Foreign Minister Peres's permission to contact the Norwegians who had earlier offered to introduce him to senior PLO officials. At the later stages of the process, Israeli academics Yair Hirschfeld and Ron Pundak were joined by Uri Savir, Director-General of the Foreign Ministry, and Joel Singer, Peres's legal adviser. The last important Israeli passenger to board the "PLO Express" toward the accord was the prime minister himself.[46] Of all the Israelis in the know, Rabin clung the longest to the formal position of avoiding the PLO, hoping to reach a settlement with the (technically non-PLO) Palestinian negotiators in Washington. Once convinced, however, that the DC negotiating team simply could not make grand decisions without Arafat, Rabin ordered stepped-up negotiations with the PLO itself via the Norwegian back-channel.[47]

This triumvirate of high Israeli officials (Beilin, Peres, and Rabin) prepared to negotiate with the PLO deviated dramatically from Israel's long-standing strategies of seeking out non-Palestinian interlocutors and talking only with so-called "moderate" (i.e., non-PLO) Palestinians. Once Rabin endorsed the talks with the PLO, the Israeli negotiators in Oslo were fully empowered to make difficult compromises that no Israeli representatives had ever been ready or able to make before. Rabin and Peres also offered a particularly strong team for selling those compromises to the Israeli public. Peres had diplomatic vision, but lacked public popularity and support; Rabin was dogmatic, but his tough reputation meant that more Israelis were willing to trust him not to sign a deal endangering the nation's security.

The equally surprising willingness of the PLO to negotiate directly with Israel constituted another important step in overcoming the historic futility of only lower-status representatives negotiating with the other side. The conditions that brought PLO chairman Arafat to the table have been discussed above. After conferring with his associate Mahmoud Abbas (Abu Mazen), an expert on Israel and a veteran of many clandestine meetings with Israelis, Arafat dispatched trusted senior associates Hasan Asfour, PLO treasurer Abu Alaa, and the latter's former economic advisor, Maher al-Kurd, to meet the Israelis in Oslo. For the first time ever, the Palestinian case was presented directly to the Israelis by a popular and authentic Palestinian leadership.[48]

A comparison of the parallel Palestinian-Israeli negotiations—the lower-level Israelis and supposedly non-PLO Palestinians meeting in Washington versus the high-level Israeli and PLO delegates meeting in Norway—reveals some striking, even counter-intuitive findings. Both the Israeli and PLO teams in Norway proved more flexible in their positions and more willing to compromise than their counterparts in Washington, who were laboring under old priorities, the Madrid constraints, and the media's constant glare. The secret Oslo talks also proved more crisis-resistant than the public ones in Washington: Rabin's expulsion to Lebanon of 400 Hamas activists in December 1992 caused a four-month suspension of the DC negotiations, whereas the Oslo talks began in January 1993 while the Hamas members still languished on a snowy hillside in Lebanon.

Interestingly, both parties kept their official negotiators in Washington in the dark about the more serious encounters underway in Oslo, while allowing their secret negotiators in Norway to draw upon the strengths and learn from the weaknesses of the effort in the United States. Hasan Asfour, who drafted much of the DOP, was also the secretary of the PLO follow-up committee to the Washington negotiations, and borrowed freely from the DC documents to which he had full access.[49] Nabil Shaath, a close Arafat advisor and supervisor of the Palestinian-Israeli talks in Washington, insists that the difference between the failure in DC and the success in Oslo was not a matter of texts and terms, but rather a difference "in the political will on the part of the two parties to strike a deal. . . . And this could only happen once the Israelis decided to negotiate directly with the PLO."[50]

The unusually high status of the Israeli and Palestinian parties to the DOP was a drastic deviation from the historical pattern and can partially explain their success at reaching an agreement. Difficulties and delays in implementing parts of the accord, however, indicated that even support from the highest political echelons was no guarantee that each side would be able to "deliver the goods" indefinitely. And as Rabin's assassination attested, high status offered no immunity against attacks by determined domestic opponents.

PSYCHOLOGICAL FACTORS

Mutual recognition between Israel and the PLO had, in the words of veteran journalist Thomas L. Friedman, "fundamentally alter[ed] both the political and psychological maps of the region. It may not bring peace tomorrow or the day after," he predicted, "but it will reshape the Middle East more than any other single event since the establishment of Israel in 1948."[51] The greatest significance of the 1993–96 PLO-Israeli rapprochement lay within the psychological realm. Even the most cynical of seasoned Middle East watchers caught their breath when Rabin and Arafat clasped hands on that day in September 1993.[52]

As individuals, Rabin and Arafat and the circle of élites around them reluctantly made the difficult psychological transformation that led them down the avenues of mutual recognition and diplomacy. But by negotiating an end to their conflict in secret and then springing it suddenly upon their people, PLO and Israeli leaders made the already Herculean task of persuading their constituents to make the necessary, abrupt psychological about-face that much more difficult.[53] In the wake of the successive Oslo accords, each leader faced a daunting domestic spectrum of critics, running from skeptics to fanatics. Appeals to each other's constituencies proved similarly futile. Despite Rabin's stinging condemnation of the massacre of Palestinians at prayer by a Jewish settler in Hebron[54] and Arafat's ringing condemnation of multiple Hamas suicide bombings and his expression of deep sorrow at Rabin's murder, large numbers of Pales-

Courtesy of Jimmy Margulies, *The Record*

tinians and Israelis still held the erstwhile enemy leader suspect: Rabin as the defense minister who issued the order to "break the bones" of Palestinian rioters during the *Intifada* and Arafat as the personification of terrorism. Even those who accepted the sincerity of their post-Oslo sentiments worried that they did not truly reflect the will of their people.

Without advance preparations of their public opinion for the new realities of mutual recognition, PLO and Israeli officials scrambled to capitalize on the surprise and euphoria that swept through much of both camps immediately after the DOP signing in September 1993. Using television, radio, and print interviews, PLO officials appealed directly to the Israeli people, insisting upon the sincerity of their commitment to coexist peacefully with the Jewish state. They were seconded by Rabin government officials who testified as to Arafat's credibility and to the good working relationship between them and their PLO counterparts. Israel appealed to the Palestinians with goodwill gestures such as the immediate redeployment of IDF troops away from Palestinian population centers, the repatriation of Hamas deportees from Lebanon, and the release of Palestinian prisoners from Israeli jails. Arafat's lieutenants emphasized to the Palestinian population their conviction that diplomacy would lead to a full satisfaction of Palestinian rights, and that their negotiating experience had convinced them that Rabin's people could be trusted.

That early euphoria was soon replaced by disenchantment, stemming from a failure of the PLO and Israeli leadership to communicate to their people realistic expectations of what had been accomplished. The initial announcement that an agreement had been reached sent thousands of Palestinians and tens of thousands of Israelis into the streets in jubilation. But, as Mark Heller pointed out, there was some question as to what they were celebrating.

> In Israel, the accord was often referred to as a peace agreement, rather than simply as an agreement on a process that might ultimately culminate in peace. Among Palestinians, there was a widespread perception, which the leadership did not try very vigorously to dispel, that this was an agreement on Palestinian independence, rather than simply an agreement on a process that might fulfil that aspiration.[55]

Implementation of the agreements quickly revealed these and other discrepancies, and both camps experienced the growth of popular disappointment and extremist opposition. Arafat's opponents came from a wide spectrum within the Palestinian constituency. Opposition from Hamas, and from its even more radical offshoot, Islamic Jihad, was of course anticipated. Less expected was evidence of the limits of Arafat's ability to win over the Palestinian street. Although revered for his years as the unchallenged leader and symbol of the Palestinian national resistance, Arafat's transition from revolutionary to statesman and governor did not impress important segments of his community. Despite his election as president in the January 1996 Palestinian elections, the Palestinian Authority under his control was highly undemocratic and staffed largely with personal cronies from Tunis. In passing over qualified administrators from Gaza and the West Bank, Arafat alienated those Palestinians who were most supportive of his deal with Israel, most eager to participate in shaping the Palestinian future, and who had the most to gain from its success. His dismissal of several of his closest aides, such as Mahmoud Abbas (Abu Mazen) and Bassam Abu-Sharif, pointmen in the negotiations with Israel and architects of Palestinian self-rule, sent confusing signals.[56] Opposition to the entire Oslo program by mainstream PLO members and supporters such as Farouk Qaddumi, Hanan Ashrawi, Raja Shehadeh, and Edward Said, and the dissatisfaction of local heroes like Haydar Abd al-Shafi, head of the Palestinian delegation to Madrid, called into question Arafat's continued command of broad Palestinian loyalty.[57]

Muhammad Muslih has argued that once Arafat compromised with Israel and accepted the imperfect reality of something less than an independent Palestinian state in less than all of Palestine, his status was necessarily reduced to smaller dimensions:

> The relationship with the masses that the charismatic Arafat had enjoyed during the bright youthful days of Amman and Beirut was diminished by the concessions he made to Israel. Arafat would stand at the helm not as a revolutionary resister, but as a subdued figure.[58]

Ordinary Palestinians initially prepared to give this peace a chance also found cause for concern as the Oslo process unfolded in fits and starts. In late 1994, Eyad Elsarraj, a Gazan psychiatrist and former delegate to the Washington talks, expressed the increasing Palestinian perception that the DOP and Cairo Agreement were signed by "two unequal parties."

> Israel has in effect dictated the terms of the Agreement to the Palestinians, whose leadership entered the negotiations from a position of inner weakness edging on total collapse, thus giving grounds for a big measure of submission. There is a growing consensus among the Palestinians that the peace accords have devastated their dream of liberation, reduced the size of Palestine even further and the PLO leadership to a ghetto life. . . . [The] sensation of loss is bewildering and overwhelming, making the road to peace replete with potential hazards.[59]

Elation at the withdrawal of IDF troops from one Palestinian town after another was tempered by restrictions on the movement of Palestinians among these islands of PA authority, continued Israeli land confiscations in the Jerusalem environs, and the perpetuation of special privileges for Jewish settlers in the West Bank. Retaliatory closures of the "green-line" borders after Palestinian bombings inside Israel and the replacement of Palestinian labor with workers from Europe and Asia reassured many Israelis who worried about terrorists coming from the territories, but angered Palestinians who saw this as unfair collective punishment and a serious blow to their fledgling economy. The February 1994 suicidal rampage by settler Baruch Goldstein in Hebron's al-Ibrahimi mosque killed twenty-nine Muslims at prayer and dealt a staggering blow to Palestinian faith in a post-Oslo reconciliation. The assassinations (apparently by the Israeli Mossad) of Islamic Jihad leader Fathi Shikaki in October 1995 and of Hamas bomb-maker Yahya Ayyash in January 1996 further angered Palestinians, who accused Israel of taking Arafat's cooperation as a license to kill.

Contrary to the expectations expressed by both sides in Oslo, Israeli withdrawals from Gaza and most of the Palestinian population centers in the West Bank did not sap the strength of the Islamic extremists. Categorically opposed to the existence of the Jewish state and any compromise with it, Hamas and Islamic Jihad responded to each new phase of the Oslo agreements with an upsurge in murderous attacks directed at civilians within Israel proper, as well as at Jewish settlers and soldiers in the occupied territories. By the second anniversary of the DOP, 149 Israelis had been killed in terrorist attacks, compared to 86 in the preceding two years, leading many to question a peace that was proving more lethal than the former state of war.[60] Hamas suicide strikes hardened mainstream Israeli public opinion against further concessions, and reinforced Israeli fears that the interim stage of Palestinian self-governance might be only the first step in a long-suspected Palestinian plan for the elimination of Israel by "stages."[61] The PA's reluctance or inability to crush Hamas and its refusal to extradite Palestinian fugitives to Israel confirmed for many Israelis their presumption that Arafat could not be trusted.[62] After a series of spectacular suicide bus bombings perpetrated by Hamas within Israel in mid-1995, acting Prime Minister Shimon Peres spoke candidly "about

Courtesy of Tim Menees, *Pittsburgh Post Gazette*

the political hazards of peacemaking, [admitting] 'We are winning historically, but losing politically.'"[63] After a similar round of terrorist attacks in the spring of 1996, his pro-Oslo camp lost the election.

The terrorist attacks that exhausted ordinary Israeli confidence in the peace process also galvanized the forces of the most committed opponents of the land-for-peace approach: the Jewish settlers in Gaza and the West Bank, who were but a small percentage of the electorate but whose "concerns and actions resonate[d] with Israelis in the ideological hinterland on the right of the national political spectrum."[64] During the summer and fall of 1995, after several devastating bus bombings by Hamas, nationwide demonstrations undertaken by an alliance of religious and nationalist opponents of Oslo threatened a massive campaign of civil disobedience and potential civil war. Prime Minister Rabin further incensed "Greater Israel" adherents by bluntly dismissing them as "crybabies" and ridiculing their concerns.[65]

In an unprecedented challenge to the democratically elected civil authority, a group of rabbis, led by former chief rabbi Avraham Shapira, adopted a religious ruling in July 1995 prohibiting the "uprooting of IDF bases" in the West Bank and urged religious soldiers to disobey such orders.[66] Rabin's secular opponents made common cause with the rabbis and religious extremists, who castigated him for violating God's will by

Courtesy of Rob Rogers, *Pittsburgh Post Gazette*

his willingness to relinquish parts of the West Bank to Palestinian control. Immediately preceding his assassination, the vitriolic debate between those opposed to and supportive of the government reached unprecedented heights of viciousness. One right-wing rally depicted Yitzhak Rabin, in Nazi uniform, hung in effigy; elsewhere he was routinely portrayed in either Nazi or Arab garb. It was from this hysterical atmosphere that Rabin's killer, Yigal Amir, emerged.[67] In his first appearance before an Israeli court, Amir's brief statements to reporters constituted

> a virtual inventory of the basic tenets of the far-right—the belief that the Government was surrendering the biblical heritage of the Jews and betraying settlers in the West Bank, and that the new Palestinian autonomy taking shape in once-occupied lands put Israel in mortal danger.[68]

After Rabin's murder, security forces moved quickly against members of the unrepentant radical right, and Peres's caretaker government announced harsh new laws against political incitement.[69] Although the vast majority of Israelis suddenly united in horror at the lethal excess to which their political differences had led, the basic issues dividing them—trust in Arafat and continued withdrawal from most of the West Bank—remained.

There is no doubt that the DOP and follow-up accords constituted a tremendous deviation from the historical Palestinian-Israeli record. But time, terror, and tragedy led even Israeli and Palestinian supporters of the process to greet each successive agreement in the DOP–Cairo–Oslo II package with increasing caution. Whereas the first PLO-Israeli agreement was hailed as a marriage of Israeli and Palestinian interests, the third of the accords was more of a "divorce agreement"; observers described the signing ceremony in Washington as decidedly less stirring.[70]

Arafat, Rabin, and Peres became political bedfellows in challenging the dynamics of deadlock that plagued the Palestinian-Israeli conflict, but significant portions of their constituencies—proportionately higher among the Palestinians—resisted the new call to diplomatic arms.[71] Nevertheless, the highly visible presence of King Hussein, President Mubarak, and representatives from Oman, Qatar, and Arafat's PA at Rabin's funeral—in Jerusalem, no less—testified to the vast sea change in Arab-Israeli relations that followed the Oslo I, Cairo, and Oslo II Accords. After the February and March bus bombings in 1996, Israel joined twenty-seven nations, including Saudi Arabia and other Arab states, at an anti-terrorism conference in Sharm el-Sheikh, Egypt, convened in support of Israel's struggle against Hamas attacks.[72] By late May, however, circumstances arising from the assassination and those bus attacks combined with traditional problems regarding the leaders' ability to implement their agreements against vehement opposition, the remaining gulf between their stated terms of agreement, and a continuing crisis in popular psychological perceptions to leave the unfinished reconciliation process in a weak and precarious state. Middle East watchers retreated from depictions of a newly functioning peace process to gloomily familiar predictions of "a violent peace," "meltdown," and "years of disillusionment."[73]

NOTES

1. Aharon Klieman, "Approaching the Finish Line: The United States in Post-Oslo Peace Making," Ramat Gan: Begin-Sadat Center for Strategic Studies, Bar-Ilan University, (Security and Policy Studies, No. 22), June 1995, 13.

2. Israel-PLO Cairo Agreement, 4 May 1994, text in Institute for Palestine Studies, *The Palestinian-Israeli Peace Agreement: A Documentary Record,* 2nd ed., Washington, DC: Institute for Palestine Studies, 1994, Document C.6, 161–69; Israel-Palestinian Interim Agreement on the West Bank and the Gaza Strip [Oslo II], 28 September 1995; Protocol Concerning the Redeployment in Hebron (as initialed on 15 January 1997). Most of the preceding documents may also be obtained from the Israel Ministry of Foreign Affairs (MFA), http://www.israel-mfa.gov.il or http://www.israel.org/peace, or by e-mail from ask@israel-info.gov.il. For an official Israeli summary of the early stages of the Israel-PLO negotiations, see *The Middle East Peace Process: An Overview,* Jerusalem: Israel Ministry of Foreign Affairs, December 1995, 13–29.

For an early and forceful Palestinian critique of the Oslo Accords, see Burhan Dajani, "The September 1993 Israeli-PLO Documents: A Textual Analysis," *JPS* 23:3 (Spring 1994), 5–23.

For an excellent journalistic treatment of the whole process until late 1996, see Connie Bruck, "The Wounds of Peace," *New Yorker,* 14 October 1996, 64–91; see also Mark A. Heller, "Rabin and Arafat: Alone, Together," *Current History,* 94:591 (January 1995), 28–32.

3. Rabin was not, however, Israel's first "peace" victim. Thirteen years earlier, right-wing counter-demonstrators tossed a grenade into a "Peace Now" rally protesting the war in Lebanon, killing peace activist Emil Grunzweig.

4. Text of the Palestinian National Covenant, July 1968, in *The Israeli-Palestinian Conflict: A Documentary Record, 1967–1990,* ed. Yehuda Lukacs, Cambridge: Cambridge University Press, 1992, 291–95. For assessments of this document, see

Yehoshafat Harkabi, *The Palestinian Covenant and Its Meaning,* London: Valentine Mitchell, 1979; Helena Cobban, *The Palestine Liberation Organization: People, Power and Politics,* London: Cambridge University Press, 1984, 43–44; Muhammad Muslih, "Towards Coexistence: An Analysis of the Resolutions of the Palestine National Council," *JPS* 19:4 (Summer 1990), 7–12. See also Aaron David Miller, *The PLO and the Politics of Survival,* New York: Praeger (The Washington Papers 99), published for the Center for Strategic and International Studies, Georgetown University, 1983.

5. Text of the Arab League Summit Conference Communiqué, Rabat, 29 October 1974, in Lukacs, 464.

6. Washington's commitment was made as part of a package leading to the 1975 Israeli-Egyptian disengagement in Sinai. See Steven L. Spiegel, *The Other Arab-Israeli Conflict: Making America's Middle East Policy, from Truman to Reagan,* Chicago: University of Chicago Press, 1985, 300–303. For a critical assessment of this US commitment to Israel, see Donald Neff, "Nixon's Middle East Policy: From Balance to Bias," in *US Policy on Palestine from Wilson to Clinton,* ed. Michael W. Suleiman, Normal, IL: AAUG Press, 1995, 156.

7. For a critical look at the Village Leagues, see Salim Tamari, "In League with Zion: Israel's Search for a Native Pillar," *JPS* 12:4 (Summer 1983), 41–56. For historical precedents of Zionists fostering friendly groups within the Palestinian-Arab community during the 1920s, see Neil Caplan, *Palestine Jewry and the Arab Question, 1917–1925,* London: Frank Cass, 1978, chap. 7.

8. See, e.g., Simha Flapan, ed., *When Enemies Dare to Talk: An Israeli-Palestinian Debate (5/6 September 1978),* London: Croom Helm, 1979; Uri Avnery, *My Friend, the Enemy,* Westport, CT: Lawrence Hill, 1986; Mohamed Heikal, *Secret Channels: The Inside Story of Arab-Israeli Peace Negotiations,* London: HarperCollins, 1996, 321–25, 343–51.

9. Mahmoud Abbas (Abu Mazen), *Through Secret Channels: The Road to Oslo: Senior PLO Leader Abu Mazen's Revealing Story of the Negotiations with Israel,* Concord, MA: Paul (Reading: Garnet), 1995, 13; Heikal, 343–44.

10. For an account of several Israeli-Palestinian dialogue projects (some of which were indirectly connected to attempts to foster a US-PLO dialogue) during the 1980s, see Mohamed Rabie, *US-PLO Dialogue: Secret Diplomacy and Conflict Resolution,* Gainesville: University Press of Florida, 1995, chaps. 3, 8, 12. See also Bassam Abu-Sharif, "Prospects of a Palestinian-Israeli Settlement," Algiers, 7 June 1988, reproduced [dated 18 June] in Lukacs, 397–99; the Abu-Sharif document is also reproduced, along with "Response by Prominent American Jews to the Abu Sharif document," 30 June 1988, in *JPS* 18:1 (Autumn 1988), 272–75, 302–303; Bassam Abu-Sharif and Uzi Mahnaimi, *Best of Enemies: The Memoirs of Bassam Abu-Sharif and Uzi Mahnaimi,* Boston: Little, Brown, 1995, 257–62; David Makovsky, *Making Peace with the PLO: The Rabin Government's Road to the Oslo Accord,* Boulder, CO: Westview Press, 1996, 17; Abbas, 4–8, 13–18; Heikal, 343–51.

11. Shimon Peres, *The New Middle East,* New York: Henry Holt, 1993. For an excellent overview of the evolution in Rabin's thinking on the Palestinian issue and Middle East peace, see Yoram Peri, "Afterword" [trans. Maxine Kaufmann Nunn] in Yitzhak Rabin, *The Rabin Memoirs,* expanded edition [trans. Dov Goldstein], Berkeley: University of California Press, 1996, 339–380. See also David Horowitz, ed., and the Jerusalem Report Staff, *Shalom Friend: The Life and Legacy of Yitzhak Rabin,* New York: New Market Press, 1996.

12. Abbas, chap. 6.

13. Efraim Karsh, "Peace Not Love: Toward a Comprehensive Arab-Israeli Settlement," *Washington Quarterly* 17:2 (Spring 1994), 149.

14. Rashid Khalidi, "A Palestinian View of the Accord with Israel," *Current*

History 93:580 (February 1994), 64–65; Camille Mansour, "The Palestinian-Israeli Peace Negotiations: An Overview and Assessment," *JPS* 22:3 (Spring 1993), 5–7, 30–31; Ziad Abu-Amr, "Palestinian-Israeli Negotiations: A Palestinian Perspective," in *The Arab-Israeli Search for Peace,* ed. Steven L. Spiegel, Boulder and London: Lynne Rienner, 1992, 27.

15. Ziad Abu-Amr, "Hamas: A Historical and Political Background," *JPS* 22:4 (Summer 1993), 5–19; Ilana Kass and Bard O'Neill, *The Deadly Embrace: The Impact of Israeli and Palestinian Rejectionism on the Peace Process,* Lanham, MD: University Press of America, 1997, chap. 4.

16. Extracts of the Covenant of Hamas, 18 August 1988, in Lukacs, 400–403. Regarding the Palestinian *Intifada* (uprising), see Ze'ev Schiff and Ehud Ya'ari, *Intifada: The Palestinian Uprising—Israel's Third Front,* New York: Simon and Schuster, 1990; Yossi Melman and Dan Raviv, *Beyond the Uprising: Israelis, Jordanians and Palestinians,* New York: Greenwood Press, 1989; F. Robert Hunter, *The Palestinian Uprising: A War by Other Means,* 2nd ed., Berkeley: University of California Press, 1993; Robert O. Freedman, ed., *The Intifada: Its Impact on Israel, the Arab World, and the Superpowers,* Gainesville: University Presses of Florida, 1991.

17. I. William Zartman, "The Negotiation Process in the Middle East," in *The Arab-Israeli Search for Peace,* ed. Steven L. Spiegel, Boulder and London: Lynne Rienner, 1992, 66, defined a diplomatically "ripe" moment as "a mutually hurting stalemate, optimally marked by a recent or looming catastrophe (sticks), a way out (carrots), and valid spokespersons for all parties." See also Richard N. Haass, *Conflicts Unending: The United States and Regional Disputes,* New Haven and London: Yale University Press, 1990.

18. Makovsky, 53, 96, 113–14.

19. Richard W. Bulliet, "The Future of the Islamic Movement: The Israeli-PLO Accord," *Foreign Affairs* 72:5 (November-December 1993), 41. Israel had initially viewed the emergence of Hamas with equanimity, pleased to see an alternative to Arafat that might sap the appeal of the PLO. Obviously, no one anticipated the rapid expansion of genuine Hamas power.

20. Mark A. Heller, "The Israeli-Palestinian Accord: An Israeli View," *Current History* 93:580 (February 1994), 58.

21. Heikal, 445.

22. Michael Hudson, "The Clinton Administration and the Middle East: Squandering the Inheritance?" *Current History* 93:580 (February 1994), 51.

23. Aharon Klieman discusses the problems of broken continuity in "Approaching," 16–21. Middle East policymakers who did continue under Clinton were Samuel Lewis, Edward Djerejian, Martin Indyk, and Dennis Ross.

24. For an account of the genesis and evolution of PLO-Israeli talks in Norway, see Avi Shlaim, "The Oslo Accord," *JPS* 23:3 (Spring 1994), 24–40; Abbas, chap. 8; Makovsky, chap. 1; Heikal, 433–70. Cf. Harold Saunders's prescient suggestions for preparing a breakthrough in this way. Harold H. Saunders, *The Other Walls: The Arab-Israeli Peace Process in a Global Perspective,* rev. ed., Princeton: Princeton University Press, 1991, 133–34.

25. Hirschfeld, quoted in Shlaim, "Olso Accord," 33.

26. Abbas, chaps. 7, 11.

27. Shlaim, "Oslo Accord," 30.

28. Serge Schmemann, "Negotiators, Arab and Israeli, Built Friendship from Mistrust," *NYT,* 28 September 1995, p. A1.

29. Hudson, "Clinton Administration," 52.

30. When the Taba talks in September 1995 between Arafat and Peres verged on collapse, for example, the Israelis placed a middle-of-the-night emergency phone call to Dennis Ross, the Clinton administration's chief Middle East negotiator, at

home in Bethesda, Maryland. Ross's "shuttle diplomacy by telephone" throughout the night guided and cajoled the Palestinian and Israeli teams toward the conclusion of Oslo II by dawn. Steven Greenhouse, "Mideast Shuttle's New Twist: US Aide Mediated by Phone," *NYT,* 25 September 1995, p. A1. See also Glenn Frankel, *Beyond the Promised Land: Jews and Arabs on the Hard Road to a New Israel,* New York: Simon and Schuster/Touchstone, 1996, 356–59, 387.

31. Hudson, 53. Ironically, by the time the Oslo II pact was ready to be signed, the Washington venue had become a burden on Rabin and Arafat, further incensing their opponents, but a gift from them to President Clinton, whose lackluster approval rating sorely needed a foreign policy victory. See R. W. Apple, Jr., "Score One for Clinton," *NYT,* 29 September 1995, p. A1.

32. Includes a letter from Arafat to the Norwegian Foreign Minister.

33. Abbas, 200–204; Makovsky, 34–38.

34. Targeted for modification were those articles (2, 5, 6, 9, 10, 15, 19, 20, 22, and 23) that delegitimized Jewish nationhood, the Zionist movement, and the Jewish connection to Palestine; rejected the legality of the establishment of the State of Israel; and called for the destruction of Israel by violent means. For the text of the Palestine National Covenant, see Lukacs, 291–95. For a controversial Israeli argument that the PLO Covenant was already a dead letter, long before Oslo, see Uri Avnery, "Should the Palestinians Change the Charter?" *New Outlook* 23:2 (March 1980), 19–23; and 23:3 (April 1980), 26–31.

35. Shlaim, "Prelude to the Accord: Likud, Labour, and the Palestinians," *JPS* 23:2 (Winter 1994), 19.

36. Heller, "Israeli View," 56; Thomas L. Friedman, "Partition of Palestine," *NYT,* 9 July 1995, p. E15.

37. Milestones along the way included the twelfth PNC platform (June 1974), which called for the establishment of a "Palestinian national authority" in any *part* of liberated Palestine and the PLO's endorsement of the August 1981 Fahd peace plan, which went further than any other Arab declaration in "affirming the right of all countries in the region to live in peace" and which was largely echoed by the Arab League Summit resolutions at Fez (September 1982). Many Israelis saw these as modifications of means, but not ends. See Lukacs, 307–12, 477–79; Muslih. Cf. Saunders, chap. 4 ("Palestinians: Moving toward a New Pragmatism"); Rabie, 63–64, 83–87; Ann M. Lesch, "The Reagan Administration's Policy toward the Palestinians," in *US Policy on Palestine from Wilson to Clinton,* ed. Michael W. Suleiman, Normal, IL: AAUG Press, 1995, 175–76, 189–90; Valerie Yorke, "Domestic Politics and the Prospects for an Arab-Israeli Peace," *JPS* 17:4 (Summer 1988), 11.

38. Text of the Palestinian Declaration of Independence, Algiers, 15 November 1988, in Lukacs, 411–15; Palestine National Council, Political Communiqué, Algiers, 15 November 1988, excerpts in ibid., 415–20.

39. Especially Arafat address to UN General Assembly, Geneva, 13 December 1988; Arafat press statement, Geneva, 15 December 1988; reprinted in Lukacs, 420–34. See also ibid., 397–99, 403–11, 438–41, 449–53; Saunders, 203–34; see multiple PLO documents in *JPS* 18:2 (Winter 1989), 213–23 and 18:3 (Spring 1989), 161–71, 176–81; Lesch 175–76, 189–90; Abu-Sharif and Mahnaimi, 257–62, 272–73; Heikal, 388–99.

40. Quoted in the *Sunday Times,* London, 15 June 1969; Baruch Kimmerling and Joel S. Migdal, *Palestinians: The Making of a People,* New York: Free Press, 1993, xvi.

41. Autonomy Plan of 28 December 1977, in Lukacs, 153–55.

42. David Makovsky and Michal Yudelman, "PM: Oslo II Is 'Blow to Greater Israel,'" *JPI,* w/e 26 August 1995, p. 1; Herb Keinon, "Massive Oslo 2 Protest Floods Zion Square," *JPI,* w/e 14 October 1995, p. 3.

43. Heller, "Israeli View," 56.

44. Hirsh Goodman, "Oslo II: Can It Work?" *Jerusalem Report,* 19 October 1995, p. 58.

45. Serge Schmemann, "Beyond the Details, a Sketch of Peace," *NYT,* 1 October 1995, section 4, p. 4.

46. Although it never became public knowledge, Yitzhak Rabin, as defense minister in Yitzhak Shamir's National Unity Government, had allegedly initiated several secret overtures, starting in February 1988, to the PLO in search of a face-saving formula to end the *Intifada*. See Rabie, 9–12, 106, 142–43.

47. Leslie Susser, "What Next?!" *JR,* 7 October 1993, p. 18.

48. Abbas, 114–41, which contain what Abbas claims are minutes from the first and subsequent Oslo meetings; Heikal, 436–42.

49. "The Oslo Agreement: An Interview with Nabil Shaath," 9 September 1993, *JPS* 23:1 (Autumn 1993), 8–9.

50. Ibid., 9. Cf. David McDowall, *The Palestinians: The Road to Nationhood,* Concord: Paul, 1995, 120.

51. Thomas Friedman, "The Brave New Middle East," *NYT,* 10 September 1993, p. A1.

52. The handshake constituted a stunning photo opportunity and an excellent case study in body language. Whereas Arafat's eager handshake indicated how much he relished his new-found legitimacy and his place on stage with Israeli and US leaders, Rabin reached toward the Palestinian leader with a gesture clearly radiating discomfort and reluctance. Afterward Rabin admitted publicly that the prospect of shaking Arafat's hand had given him "butterflies in the stomach"; privately he confided that it had made him want to "retch." Leslie Susser, "What Next?!" *JR,* 7 October 1993, p. 18; Clyde Haberman, "Ambivalent Rabin Reflects Israel's Wary View of Peace," *NYT,* 7 July 1995, p. A1; Haberman, "Recalling a Realist Peacemaker, Not a Dove," *NYT,* 6 November 1995, p. A1. For Rabin's own reflections on the handshake, see Yitzhak Rabin, "On the Road to Peace" (December 1993) in Rabin, *The Rabin Memoirs,* Appendix G. See also Frankel, 183.

53. For thoughtful analyses, written by peace proponents from both camps, of the psychological difficulties inherent in a Palestinian-Israeli reconciliation, see "Psychological Dimensions of the Conflict," *Palestine-Israel Journal of Politics, Economics and Culture* I:4 (Autumn 1994).

54. Rabin's public pillorying of Baruch Goldstein is translated in Kass and O'Neill, 61.

55. Heller, "Israeli View," 59. Cf. McDowall, 118–19.

56. Youssef M. Ibrahim, "Ousted Arafat Aide Assesses Future of the PLO," *NYT,* 28 May 1995, p. A3.

57. Edward W. Said, "Projecting Jerusalem," and Haydar Abd al-Shafi "Interview with Haydar Abd al-Shafi" in *JPS* 25:1 (Autumn 1995), 5–14 and 76–85; E. W. Said, "The Mirage of Peace," *Nation,* 16 October 1995, 413–20; "Symbols vs. Substance: A Year after the Declaration of Principles, An Interview with Edward Said," *JPS* 24:2 (Winter 1995), 60–72; Edward W. Said, *Peace and Its Discontents: Essays on Palestine in the Middle East Peace Process,* New York: Vintage, 1995; Naseer H. Aruri, *The Obstruction of Peace: The US, Israel and the Palestinians,* Monroe, ME: Common Courage Press, 1995; McDowall, 119, 124; Naseer H. Aruri, "Palestine: How to Redress the Wrongs of Oslo?" *Middle East International,* no. 536, 25 October 1996, 18–19.

58. Muhammad Muslih, "Arafat's Dilemma," *Current History* 94:591 (January 1995), 24. Cf. David Hirst, "A Movement Withering on the Inside," *Guardian,* 17 April 1995, p. 7.

59. Eyad Elsarraj, "Shaping a Culture of Peace," *Palestine-Israel Journal of Politics, Economics and Culture* I:4 (Autumn 1994), 59.

60. Figures compiled by the monitoring group "Peace Watch," cited in Jon Immanuel, "Riding a Peace Jalopy," and Herb Keinon, "Peace Watch: 83 Israelis Killed in Past Year, 66 in Previous Year," both in *JPI,* w/e 23 September 1995, pp. 8, 32.

61. This is how many Israelis interpreted the PNC Platform of June 1974 and even the Palestinian Declaration of Independence of November 1988. Cf. FBIS Analysis Report, "PLO Statements on the Middle East: Speaking with a Forked Tongue?" Washington, DC, 26 July 1989, reproduced in *JPS* 19:3 (Spring 1990), 171–78.

62. David Horowitz, "Beyond the Law," *JR,* 21 September 1995, p. 26; Herb Keinon, "Extradition: Politics before Justice," *JPI,* w/e 23 September 1995, p. 3. McDowall, 124.

63. David Makovsky, "Shortsighted Visionaries," *JPI,* w/e 5 August 1995, p. 14.

64. Heller, "Israeli View," 59. For discussions of Israel's populist, radical-right movements, beginning with the *Gush Emunim* (Bloc of the Faithful) founded in 1974, see Yehoshafat Harkabi, *Israel's Fateful Hour,* New York: Harper and Row, 1988; Ian Lustick, *For the Land and the Lord: Jewish Fundamentalism in Israel,* New York: Council on Foreign Relations, 1988; Ehud Sprinzak, *The Ascendance of Israel's Radical Right,* New York: Oxford University Press, 1991; Kass and O'Neill.

65. Clyde Haberman, "Settlers Fight Next Step in West Bank Transfer," *NYT,* 15 June 1995, p. A3; Chaim Herzog, "Divide the Land, Not the People," *JR,* 10 August 1995, p. 60; Abba Eban, "Tyranny of the Few," *JPI,* w/e 19 August 1995, p. 12; Serge Schmemann, "Bus Bombing Kills Five in Jerusalem; 100 Are Wounded," *NYT,* 22 August 1995; Herb Keinon, "1,000 Reservists say they will refuse to uproot settlements," *JPI,* w/e 16 September 1995, pp. 1–2; Joel Greenberg, "Settlers Angrily Protest Accord in Hebron," *NYT,* 29 September 1995, p. A1; Sarah Honig, "Opposition Stages Its Own Signing, Declares Loyalty to Land of Israel," *JPI,* w/e 7 October 1995, p. 4; A. M. Rosenthal, "For Peace in Israel," *NYT,* 7 November 1995, p. A15.

66. Herb Keinon, "Rabbis: Halacha Forbids Moving Army Bases from Judea, Samaria," *JPI,* w/e 22 July 1995, p.1; Yossi Klein Halevi, "Torn between God and Country," *JR,* 10 August 1995, pp. 12–17; Ehud Ya'ari, "A Jewish Fatwa," *JR,* 10 August 1995, p. 35; Herzog, 60.

67. Serge Schmemann, "Israel's Leader Declines to Call Early Elections," *NYT,* 8 November 1995, p. A1; Thomas Friedman, "How About You?" *NYT,* 8 November 1995, p. A15; Ze'ev Chafets, "Israel's Quiet Anger," *NYT,* 7 November 1995, p. A15; A. M. Rosenthal, "For Peace in Israel;" S. Schmemann, "The Political Finger-Pointing Begins," *NYT,* 10 November 1995, p. A6; Frankel, 388–89, 391–93.

68. Serge Schmemann, "Rabin Is Laid to Rest, Mourned by Israel and the World," *NYT,* 7 November 1995, p. 1.

69. John Kifner, "Israelis Investigate Far Right; May Crack Down on Speech," *NYT,* 8 November 1995, p. A1; Alan Cowell, "Among Hard-Liners in Hebron, Ambivalence and Brooding but Little Grief," *NYT,* 7 November 1995, p. A10.

70. Serge Schmemann, "Living Apart in Mideast," *NYT,* 26 September 1995, p. A1; Alison Mitchell, "A Less Stirring Moment than Last Time," *NYT,* 29 September 1995, p. A1. Cf. Clyde Haberman, "No More Magic in the Middle East," *NYT,* 14 May 1995, p. E3.

71. For a cultural analysis of domestic political influences on the process of reversing long-standing popular Israeli objections to dealing with the PLO, see Myron J. Aronoff and Yael S. Aronoff, "A Cultural Approach to Explaining Domestic Influences on Current Israeli Foreign Policy: The Peace Negotiations," *Brown Journal of World Affairs* 3:2 (Summer-Fall 1996), 83–101.

72. Summit of Peacemakers, Final Statement Issued by Co-Chairmen, Egyptian President Hosni Mubarak and US President Bill Clinton, Sharm el-Sheikh, 13 March 1996, MFA.

73. See, e.g., Heikal, 508–54; Leslie Susser and Isabel Kershner, "Meltdown," *JR* 9 January 1997, pp. 14–18.

Conclusion

PEACE IN THE MAKING

> Peace is never made but is always in the making. Like other human relationships, peace must be constantly tended, nurtured and developed.[1]

PEACE AS A PROCESS

One of the most misused phrases in the lexicon of the Arab-Israeli conflict is "peace process." For years it has been used to describe every American foray into Arab-Israeli affairs and every non-battlefield encounter between the two sides, regardless of purpose or outcome. But was "peace" really the common objective? And how often was a "process"—a series of actions or operations leading toward a particular result—really underway?

Writing in 1988, fully ten years after Camp David but in the absence of any subsequent diplomatic accomplishments, Irving Kristol insisted that "there really is no such thing as a Middle East peace process. What there is, and has been since 1973, is a cold war between Israel and the Arabs, interrupted occasionally by bursts of violence."[2] The passage of yet another decade of diplomatic activity coupled with continued struggle and bloodshed provoked Edward Said's critical reference to "the wanton murder of language evident in the phrase 'peace process.'"[3]

Our readers will appreciate that we do not share this cynicism. Recent evidence, particularly since 1991, indicates a real, albeit halting, momentum toward the diplomatic resolution of the interlocking disputes collectively known as the "Arab-Israeli conflict." There is a history of futile negotiation experiences that runs parallel to the history of Jewish-Arab conflict in the Middle East. It is only since leaders began to diverge from the historical patterns characteristic of those unsuccessful diplomatic encounters, we believe, that one can speak of a genuine peace process.

Our review of six cases suggests two important aspects of the process: the importance of *gradualism,* and the sometimes useful, sometimes dangerous, role of *ambiguity,* or what William Quandt has called "constructive obfuscation."[4] In the debate over the efficacy of a grand comprehensive solution versus partial ones arrived at step by step, the long-term success of Camp David makes a persuasive case in favor of the latter. Despite the fashion among academics and analysts to pooh-pooh Camp David's narrow bilateral accomplishments and lament its larger shortcomings, the Egyptian-Israeli agreement nevertheless stands as the first concrete evidence that peace between Arabs and Israelis is not impossible. Its cluster of three documents set an important precedent by separating bilateral, regional, and local-Palestinian issues. Building on the Camp David model, the Madrid planners, in their turn, envisioned a series of interdependent relationships, sequentially timed to allow for confidence-building measures along the way. Recognizing the problems of profound outstanding differences on the terms of a final settlement and popular skepticism as to the other side's motives, the peace process begun at Oslo similarly postponed the "final-status" decisions in favor of a succession of agreements leading to negotiations on the final settlement.

Those impatient to see the current Israel-PLO agreements produce definitive results all at once—whether Israelis expecting a total halt to terror attacks, or Palestinians anxious for full and immediate independence—may find the merits of this "gradualist" or "incremental" approach unconvincing. But, as Abba Eban observed, "When descending to earth from an exceptionally tall ladder, it is often prudent to use the intervening rungs, rather than seek posthumous glory by a single leap."[5] Israeli-Arab enmity has soared to terrible heights, both during and outside periods of diplomatic activity. Camp David constituted the uppermost rung of what is a very tall ladder and a long way down indeed.

The same logic that applies to the wider Arab-Israeli conflict applies as well to the specific Palestinian-Israeli dimension of the dispute. The utter lack of trust between the two sides and the depth of their enmity dictate against the wisdom of a single all-encompassing solution. The September 1993 Declaration of Principles adopted a classic step-by-step approach to peacemaking in which the overall problem was broken down "into negotiable pieces, evolving agreements that would build confidence and would change the political environment."[6] Sometimes, in the name of building mutual confidence, negotiators "agree to disagree" or otherwise fudge remaining disagreements on some matters so as not to derail emerging consensus on others, as happened at Camp David.

In Oslo, Israeli and Palestinian leaders encountered both the opportunities and the pitfalls historically associated with deliberately ambiguous agreements. The DOP endorsed the premise of Israel and the Palestinians sharing the land between them. Ambiguity in this case concerned the final parameters of a settlement. It was no secret that the Palestinians' ultimate goal was an independent Palestinian state throughout Gaza and the West Bank, with Arab East Jerusalem as its capital. Israel's declared goal, on the other hand, was coexistence with a less-than-sovereign Palestinian entity in Gaza and most of the West Bank, with united Jerusalem as the capital of the state of Israel. From the moment the DOP was announced, Rabin and Arafat proceeded to regale their followers with conflicting assertions as to the inviolability of unified Jerusalem as Israel's capital versus the destiny of East Jerusalem as the capital of a Palestinian state[7]—anything but good omens for the success of their mutual peace venture.

How can both parties continue to espouse such radically contradictory goals? Is it dangerous if ambiguities allow each side to believe that the accord will eventually satisfy its full demands? An optimistic answer to these questions is that popular support, the passage of time, and a successful trial run at coexistence might produce revised demands that are more flexible than current possibilities, ultimately allowing for compromise. A pessimistic interpretation suggests that such ambiguity permits unrealizable expectations to fester, and that sooner or later the process will implode when the signed accord is shown merely to have papered over an unbridgeable chasm between the two sides. Oslo's architects banked their agreement on the belief that, if the parties demonstrate their ability to uphold their interim-agreement bargains faithfully, subsequent negotiations will see both sides better prepared to consider—or reconsider—their positions, unblocking the way to acceptable solutions.

Economic interdependence, geographic imperatives, and demographic intersections rule out hermetic separation. Contemporary peacemakers have resurrected creative strategies reminiscent of those devised and rejected in the 1930s, in the forms of autonomy, interim periods, a self-governing authority, phased solutions, confederations, and lease-back options. As we observed earlier, it is likely that the eventual resolution of the Arab-Israeli and Palestinian-Israel conflicts will incorporate one or more proposals suggested and spurned as unworkable in earlier periods.

BREAKING THE PATTERNS

Successfully negotiated settlements since 1977 demonstrated changes in virtually all of the seven elements—previous experience interacting, dubious purposes and ulterior motives, timing difficulties, the problematic status of negotiating partners, generally negative third-party involvement, a gulf between proposed terms of agreement, and psychological obstacles—of our model of failed Arab-Israeli dialogue. Some of these changes were more far-reaching than others, but there is strong evidence that, by the close of the century, Arab-Israel diplomacy will have deviated dramatically from the earlier patterns of futile negotiations in a number of ways, including:

- parties coming together with the genuine intention of resolving their conflict;
- parties recognizing and negotiating with one another's chosen leadership;
- parties scaling back their minimum demands from a zero-sum to a mutual-accommodation approach;
- parties looking to third-party mediators to facilitate or underwrite a compromise rather than impose a unilateral solution; and
- the growing perception among Arabs, Israelis, and Palestinians that coexistence and peace are possible and worthy of risks and sacrifices.

Just as peace is always in the making, so too is deviation from complex negative historical patterns a subtle and ever-incomplete affair—with inevitable regressions and relatively few clear-cut or all-at-once departures to magically transform failures into successes.

PREVIOUS NEGOTIATING EXPERIENCE

Reviewing each of our seven elements in turn, we find the wealth (or dearth) of experience to be perhaps the least influential in determining the outcome of negotiations. Extensive contacts, whether secret or open, and even positive, could not guarantee positive results at the bargaining table, as in Israeli-Lebanese and Israeli-Jordanian negotiations in 1983 and 1987. Our findings caution against expecting the increase in the volume of direct Arab-Israeli talks since Madrid, ipso facto, to enhance the prospects for peace. On the other hand, a century of purposeful avoidance did not obstruct agreement once Israel and the PLO formally introduced themselves in Oslo in 1993.

STATUS OF THE NEGOTIATORS

The status of the negotiators, however, emerged as one of the most critical elements in influencing an initiative's success or failure. The best-intentioned of negotiators might have shattered the precedent in terms of flexibility, moderation, and psychological reorientation; but if he could not persuade his peers and people to follow him down his chosen path, his signature on a dotted line was worthless. The archives of pre-1948 Zionist diplomacy contain dozens of such agreements. Amin Gemayel's fragile position greatly contributed to the impotence of the 1983 Israeli-Lebanese accord. A hamstrung Shimon Peres, to his own chagrin, created a similarly inoperative document in his 1987 negotiations with King Hussein. Alternatively, leaders firmly and formally in power have been able to implement agreements despite opposition from domestic or regional rivals and hesitancy on the part of their people, as with Camp David, the 1994 Israel-Jordan Treaty, and significant portions of the DOP and its successor agreements.

Status-of-the-negotiator issues figured prominently in the fledgling Israeli-Palestinian rapprochement. Ironically, it was the Shamir government's insistence upon the non-PLO status of the Palestinian delegates at Madrid that eventually led the frustrated Rabin government to seek out genuine PLO leadership. Yet, even then, the status of the leaders wavered on the edge of the classic precipice. Splits between the official spokespersons and their well-supported opponents were evident in both communities. Prime Minister Rabin fell victim to a religiously motivated ultranationalist, and his assassin's ideological cohorts continued to press their allies in the Netanyahu government to halt further concessions to the PLO. Netanyahu's ability to "deliver the goods" in his unwanted Oslo inheritance was diminished by opposition from the radical right, which had originally supported his candidacy with the expectation that he would reverse the whole process.

Despite his preeminent status as PA President, Arafat's capability to carry out the existing agreements and forge ahead with the next round is threatened by radical Islamic opposition and secular activists and intellectuals disenchanted with his leadership. Historical patterns associated with the status dilemma raise the possibility that the former "radical" and "freedom-fighter" may be transformed into a "moderate" unable to hold up his end of the bargain. For example, Arafat's midnight trip to Tel Aviv to pay a condolence call to Leah Rabin may have heartened those who had been skeptical of the guerilla leader's political transformation; but the more Israelis and their friends warm to him, the greater the distance between him and mainstream Palestinian sentiment grows. Conversely, Arafat's harsh condemnations of Netanyahu and more militant rhetoric are welcomed by the bulk of the Palestinian constituency but are cited by Israelis as further evidence of his untrustworthiness.

Finally, the status component of the unfinished Israel-PLO negotiations is also problematic because the identity of Arafat's successor is unclear. Does Arafat have the staying power, or his replacement the status, to effect the peaceful transfer of most of the West Bank to an authentic and popular Palestinian authority? Are the institutions in place to maintain a peaceful coexistence afterward?

PROPOSED TERMS OF AGREEMENT

We have argued that attempts to resolve the various Arab-Israeli conflicts have not failed for a lack of fresh, new formulae. For decades an unbridgeable gap separated the minimal acceptable Arab and Israeli terms for agreement. This reflected the unwillingness of one or both of the combatants to compromise at different times, combined with a determined refusal to allow the other side to realize at least part of its aspirations.

Egypt and Israel were the first to transcend this obstacle by adopting a full-peace, full-withdrawal program; fifteen years later, Jordan and Israel followed a similar course. By contrast, the case of the failed Israel-Lebanon

Courtesy of Rob Rogers, *Pittsburgh Post Gazette*

Agreement of 17 May 1983 illustrated what can result when a militarily dominant party seeks to dictate a unilaterally pleasing outcome to the vanquished party. But as Egyptian, Jordanian, and Palestinian talks with Israel demonstrated, once factors combined to launch a diplomatic initiative, the lack of immediately attractive terms of agreement did not necessarily doom the negotiations. History has shown that "yesterday's rejected ideas" may become "tomorrow's accepted plan," following a pattern of "recycling" proposals dating back to the Mandate period.[8]

It is one of the ironies of Arab-Israeli negotiation that the complex and laborious Oslo process resulted in a form of Palestinian autonomy that had already been on the table—rejected as unacceptable by the Arab states and the Palestinians and accepted without enthusiasm by the Israelis—during the post–Camp David autonomy negotiations (1979–82). Some observers classify this as a "missed opportunity" for peace, and assail Palestinian or Israeli leaders for the grief and spilled blood of the intervening decades. Our assessment, which is reality-based and not hindsight-driven, views this phenomenon rather as a vivid illustration of the interplay of the terms of agreement and timing factors.

A consistent feature of the struggle between Palestinians and Israelis has been their zero-sum mentality. The architects of the PLO-Israeli accords deviated significantly from that unhelpful historical pattern in abandoning that mentality and agreeing to share Mandatory Palestine between their peoples. Rabin's insistence that his ultranationalist opponents relinquish their vision of Greater Israel and Arafat's appeal to his far-flung constituents that they forgo Jaffa and Galilee in favor of the reality of a Palestinian state-in-the-making in Nablus, Hebron, Ramallah, and Gaza represented important deviations from the model. This situation offers an interesting reversal of the pre-1948 pattern, in which the recognized leaders proved consistently less generous and accommodating than unofficial activists among their people. Post-1948 peace overtures have seen Sadat, Begin, Peres, Hussein, Rabin, Arafat, and most recently Netanyahu trying to sell compromise to domestic rivals who would limit the pace and scope of the peace process, if not halt it entirely.

TIMING

Timing emerged as something of a wild-card factor in the launching and outcome of diplomatic initiatives. Encompassing as it does the unpredictable actions of lone fanatics and unstable rulers in the global community, timing is perhaps the least controllable of all the elements in our negotiation paradigm. The complexity and longevity of the Palestinian-Israeli conflict left many fearing that a propitious moment for a negotiated settlement might never materialize. Some worried that it arrived too late: that the Israeli settlements and their supporters had passed a point of no return, and that Hamas would make Arafat obsolete. Others bemoaned the fact that the agreement was announced prematurely, before the negotiators had resolved all the details, thus squandering the euphoria so soon with contentious post-handshake wrangling. Some of our case studies offer positive indications of how people with good intentions and strong leadership abilities have either created or seized the moment to move the peace process forward; Anwar Sadat leaps immediately to mind.

One repetition of the historical pattern saw Sadat and Begin, as well as Rabin and Arafat, enter into direct negotiations to circumvent imminent threats coming from elsewhere, namely, the US-Soviet intention to convene a new Geneva conference in late 1977 and the deteriorating Palestinian-Israeli talks in Washington in mid-1993, respectively. The timing of other encounters was in varying degrees a byproduct of wars, such as the 1983 Israel-Lebanon Agreement which followed Israel's 1982 invasion of Lebanon, and the Madrid conference and Jordanian-Israeli peace accord which came in the wake of the 1991 Gulf War. Further examples include the impact on negotiation prospects of electoral cycles (at home and abroad) and the perceived weakening or strengthening of various leaders, as was the case for the 1987 London Document and the PLO-Israeli reconciliation.

We should also reconsider briefly the familiar notion of time as healer. Writing in 1978, John Stoessinger observed that

> when people of good will despair of finding a solution, they tend to find solace in time as the great healer of wounds. This confidence in the power of time has not been warranted by the experience of the [many] wars between the Arab states and Israel.[9]

Stoessinger was correct to argue that the passage of time had not served to diminish Arab-Israeli hatred. Yet, paradoxically, it may have enhanced progress toward peace to the extent that "conflict fatigue" set in among leaders and significant portions of their people, particularly within the Israeli and Palestinian camps. The constant and cumulative drain of protracted strife has the power to exhaust protagonists on both sides and leave them with no options more attractive than compromise.

PURPOSES AND MOTIVES

Intimately linked with timing and terms of agreement—and equally crucial—are the purposes and motives with which each party enters into negotiation. Traditionally, Arabs and Israelis engaged one another in discussion when their true aim was posturing rather than reaching a fairly negotiated settlement. The Lebanon-Israel Agreement of 17 May 1983 constituted a perfect example of the old dubious-purposes, ulterior-motives charade. The traditional desire for third-party (American) approval and tangible rewards figured as a persuasive incentive in bringing the various parties together at the 1991 Madrid conference. Once there, Syria (and Lebanon) and Israel under Shamir scarcely disguised their ulterior motives for attending, took their seats at the table, but resisted all pressures to move beyond minimum correct formalities.

But those actors willing to take risks with the genuine aim of resolving their differences ended up taking advantage of the Madrid mechanism and momentum. Jordan and Israel under Rabin followed through all the way to their 1994 peace treaty, while the Palestinians/PLO and Israel finally emerged from recurrent deadlocks with the DOP and its offshoots. Given the long history of mutual antagonism and official boycott, the shift in Palestinian and Israeli purposes and motives was nothing short of revolutionary.

Nevertheless, the DOP and its sister agreements suffered because significant constituencies on each side remained suspicious of the other's true intentions. Even accepting the integrity of each party's stated goal of terminating the conflict by allowing for Palestinian self-governance, the end of Israel's occupation of territory captured in the 1967 war, and peaceful Palestinian-Israeli coexistence, there remains the terms-of-agreement obstacle. It is almost impossible to imagine a mutually acceptable formula that will satisfy both the Palestinians' demand that they be fully sovereign and Israeli insistence that they not. Good intentions are a great improvement on the past record but cannot, by themselves, resolve the conflict.

THIRD-PARTY CONSIDERATIONS

The third-party contribution was often critical to the success or failure of negotiation efforts. Most recently, Norway used its unusual low-key approach and moderate resources to excellent advantage in providing Palestinians and Israelis with the inducements to reach an agreement. More often, however, it is a strong outside actor, typically the United States, that can advance the process by offering material incentives, political support, and military guarantees necessary for persuading Arabs and Israelis to take risks for peace. This was the *modus operandi* by which President Carter achieved success at Camp David and President Bush presided over a full complement of guests in Madrid.

It was Henry Kissinger's shuttle diplomacy in the 1970s that heralded the emergence of the United States as the sole Middle East peace broker, a role reinforced by the dissolution of the Soviet Union in the early 1990s. All of the case studies showed evidence of Arabs and Israelis lobbying the United States to shape peace agreements conducive to their respective interests, and looking to the United States to mediate, endorse, and guarantee diplomatic initiatives. Some observers draw from Camp David a lesson that direct negotiations, without American involvement, have little chance of success.

Another legacy of the Kissinger era was the expectation of Middle Eastern leaders that effective US involvement necessarily entails personal commitment at the very highest level of government.[10] The recent and important contributions of Norway notwithstanding, almost every major peace initiative since Camp David can be linked with an American president or secretary of state, and in those cases where actual US mediation was minimal, as with the DOP and in many respects the Jordanian-Israeli treaty, the parties still found it necessary to sign their agreements in the presence of the American president and with his full and public support. The reciprocal American enthusiasm for presiding over these ceremonies reflected both the classic interest in asserting US superpower primacy, and the tendency of each administration, particularly those "under siege (Nixon, Carter, Bush, and . . . Clinton) . . . [to] become almost fixated with registering a dramatic achievement on the Arab-Israel front, thereby redeeming themselves politically."[11]

Here we must recall Aharon Klieman's important cautionary alert against the blithe assumption of US indispensability to the Arab-Israeli peace process.[12] There are enough examples of independent, bilateral Arab-Israeli initiatives—the initialed treaty between Abdallah and Israel, Jordanian-Israeli cooperative measures throughout the years, Sadat's journey to Jerusalem, the Hussein-Peres London Document, and the secret PLO-Israeli agreement negotiated in the Oslo back-channel—to argue that much of Middle East diplomacy has unfolded independent of direction from Washington. Nevertheless, one wonders if the more successful of these efforts would have survived to full fruition without US intervention at some point during negotiations.

Klieman poses fresh and important corrective questions about the US role in Middle East peacemaking, but evidence based on our case studies concludes that successful negotiations have required both bilateral Arab-

Israeli talks *as well as* creative and consistent American facilitation.[13] Indeed, the simultaneous availability of *both* direct channels and third-party mediation contributed heavily to the Camp David Accords, the Israeli-Palestinian agreements, and the Israel-Jordan peace treaty. In the last case, success reflected a rare balance between the desire of the Jordanians and Israelis to make peace, and the efforts of the United States to help them along. Despite extended haggling over the prenuptial agreement, this was no shotgun wedding; Hussein and Rabin went willingly to the altar, under the beaming countenance of their American best man.

One of the main features of the pattern for failed Arab-Israeli negotiations was that, historically, third parties have meddled more than they mediated, often unwittingly discouraging leaders from making the difficult compromises successful negotiation demands. As useful as American activity was at Camp David, in Madrid, and with the 1994 Jordanian-Israeli effort, misguided American pressure to conclude the Agreement of 17 May 1983 encountered a complex Israeli-Lebanese situation and took it from bad to worse. Uncertain American support for the London Document of 1987 made King Hussein hesitant to pursue the agreement and denied Shimon Peres important ammunition needed to prevail over Prime Minister Shamir's dissent. The remaining Syrian-Israeli and Lebanese-Israeli impasses and difficulties in operationalizing the Palestinian-Israeli accords offer the United States a continued, high-profile, intermediary role, which our survey of case studies shows it can either use or abuse.

THE PSYCHOLOGY OF PEACEMAKING

No other single factor outweighs the psychological element as a determinant in the ultimate success of negotiations to produce an accord and of leaders to make it work. In this book, we have considered the psychological dimension of peacemaking in terms of leaders choosing diplomacy over war and people choosing to give the new approach a chance.

A successful experiment in peacemaking requires, first and foremost, the psychological conversion of the élites, by which Arab and Israeli leaders conclude simultaneously that peace between their nations is both desirable and achievable. The dynamics-of-deadlock factor is the test of their leadership abilities in persuading their people of the same thing, namely, to overcome generations of mistrust, fear, and hatred, and to embrace instead a cautious faith in accommodation, compromise, and the mutual satisfaction of many—but not all—of the aspirations of each party.

Israelis quickly gave Anwar Sadat and King Hussein their trust; they were more reserved in their feelings for their everyday Egyptian and Jordanian counterparts. Whatever the quality of personal relations between Arafat's entourage and Israeli leadership circles, animosity between ordinary Palestinians and Israelis still runs deep. For years, Israelis considered Arafat terrorism personified, and he remains highly suspect in the minds of many. The Holocaust experience is still a convincing reminder to many Israelis that nothing is so terrible that it cannot come true. After narrowly escaping attempted genocide, Jews and Israelis regard classical Palestinian demands for politicide—the destruction of the Zionist state—as more than rhetoric and all too plausible; they find less believable the vision of a world in which Arab leaders and their people are prepared to coexist with the Jewish state.

Arabs throughout the Middle East have grown up with Palestinian refugees in their midst, and know by heart their story of displacement and disenfranchisement. Palestinians see Israelis as their historical oppressors, rather than as fellow victims of circumstance or of world powers. The harsh conditions of the decades-long military occupation of the West Bank and Gaza brought average Palestinians into extended, frequent, and almost always negative contact with Israelis. They remember Yitzhak Rabin as the defense minister who in 1987 ordered his troops to break the bones of Palestinian protesters during the *Intifada*. And they simply do not trust his successor, Benjamin Netanyahu, who campaigned relentlessly against the Oslo process, against Arafat, against further Israeli withdrawals in the occupied territories, and against a Palestinian state.

Even after the advent of formal peace treaties signed between Israel and their governments, Egyptians and Jordanians still look askance at Israelis, their leaders, and the relatively high-powered Israeli economy. The economic benefits of peace to the Arab economies have been slow to materialize. Some Arabs perceive the eagerness that Israeli companies and entrepreneurs display toward extending business dealings across Israel's borders as "typical" Israeli aggressiveness in a new fiscal form, and invoke the old Arabic saying, "He left by the door but came back through the window." In other words, many Jordanians, Egyptians, and Palestinians fear that Israeli military domination may be ending, only to be replaced by economic domination of the region.

Our case studies illustrate that leaders who opted *for* the diplomatic route had to fight against being held hostage to the very same sentiments they had previously used to rally public opinion *against* concessions to the enemy. Held accountable to the extremist, religiously fundamentalist, and ultranationalist wings of their constituencies, both Arab and Israeli leaders struggled to maintain their legitimacy and still engage each other in diplomatic discourse. A review of the dynamics-of-deadlock factor suggests that relatively hard-line leaders can persuade the majority of their highly skeptical and suspicious people to accept great risks for the sake of peace. The 1973 war is widely seen as the baptism by fire that Anwar Sadat needed to prove he could make war with Israel before he could make peace. Menachem Begin, nationalist credentials firmly in place, pulled off Camp David. Yasir Arafat would have been unable to negotiate the Oslo compromise without his credentials as a veteran freedom fighter in the Palestinian armed struggle. Unlike Shimon Peres, who was seen as too eager to make peace with the Arabs, Yitzhak Rabin, the tough and dour military man, commanded sufficient public trust to make the peace gamble.[14] Those who place great stock in this phenomenon insist that the hard-line Benjamin Netanyahu may yet take his place in the roll call of unlikely warmakers-turned-peacemakers.

Leaders who pursued the peace option have often paid the supreme price for breaking with the dynamics of deadlock and forcing their followers to confront and reverse deeply ingrained fears and prejudices. One long-time diplomat ruefully observed that "the diplomat is the bearer of a view of the world which his fellow citizens cannot always accept."[15] Sadly, political assassination is a peacemaking risk well within the historical parameters of our model. King Abdallah, President Sadat, President-elect Bashir Gemayel, and Prime Minister Rabin paid with their lives for having dared to negotiate with the enemy. They joined Issam Sartawi, an early Palestinian proponent of PLO-Israeli dialogue, felled by a Palestinian hard-liner's bullet in Lisbon, and Peace Now activist Emil Grunzweig, victim of a right-winger's grenade in Jerusalem, both of whom died in 1983.[16]

But despite the precedents for assassination along the tortured trail of Arab-Israeli relations, the murder of Yitzhak Rabin in November of 1995 stunned observers around the world, Arabs and Israelis no less. The assumption had always been that the threat to Rabin was electoral in nature, and that Arafat was the more likely of the two to be struck down by one of his own. The often raw and riotous Israeli political scene had been remarkably free of violence,[17] and even those following the increasing radicalization of the ultra-religious opposition to Rabin's peace policies did not anticipate the lethal lengths to which its adherents would go.[18] The war against terrorism meant a war against Hamas, not fellow Israelis.

The willingness of radical Arab and Jewish opponents of peaceful compromise to engage in violent opposition to the nascent reconciliation effort is its most serious threat. Despite the bloodshed, terrorism is first and foremost a psychological weapon, and one used with devastating results against wary people whose leaders are asking them to trust the enemy and the eventual outcome of an untried and risky policy. It was the PLO that introduced terrorism as the preferred Palestinian weapon against Israeli civilians; Hamas, with its suicide bombers and multiple bus attacks, raised the art form to new heights. Ultranationalist Israelis created a network of cells they called "terror against terror," but their murderous operations were few in number and never commanded a broad range of support within their own society.

However, recent right-wing veneration of Baruch Goldstein and sympathy for Yigal Amir, coupled with the continued popularity of Hamas in significant Palestinian quarters, constitute a grotesque convergence of interests between Palestinian and Israeli militants who count on recurrent terror to harden public opinion against continuing the current agenda of compromise and coexistence. Ilana Kass and Bard O'Neill end their scholarly and sober comparison of the extremist phenomenon in both camps with an unexpectedly emotional warning:

> Unlike novelists, we cannot end on a happy note. The right policy choices are likely to reduce the impact of self-righteousness and hatred. Paradoxically, however, the desperation will remain, if not deepen. Brooding in their own, self-imposed darkness, the last rejectionists might emerge as a modern incarnation of the four horsemen of the apocalypse, to inflict untold suffering on their own communities, if not on the world at large. Thus, what the peacemakers are confronting is not just a set of political problems and alternative courses of action. Rather, they are engaged in an epic struggle against evil itself.[19]

Having made their own psychological conversion in favor of a negotiated compromise, leaders hoping to make those right policy choices must tend to and develop the *psychology* of peacemaking as closely as the *politics* of peacemaking. This means using gestures and words to nurture a realistic reappraisal of an acceptable resolution to the conflict among their people, and acting mercilessly to restrain those incapable of making the change and determined to use violence to prevent others from doing so. Yitzhak Rabin had made that personal psychological transformation, and on the night he died he gave a speech designed to accomplish precisely those two tasks, vigorously urging his fellow citizens to stay the difficult diplomatic course, and condemning those who would resort to violence. Breaking the dynamics of deadlock requires that a leader imbue his people with a strong sense of mission: Rabin used the word "peace" twenty-five times in his brief remarks, and declared in his usual direct way:

> I was a military man for 27 years. I fought so long as there was no chance for peace. I believe there is now a chance for peace, a great chance. . . . I want to say bluntly, that we have found a partner for peace among the Palestinians as well: the PLO, which was an enemy, and has now ceased to engage in terrorism. Without partners for peace there can be no peace. We will demand that they do their part for peace, just as we will do our part for peace, in order to solve the most complicated, prolonged and emotionally charged aspect of the Arab-Israeli conflict: the Palestinian-Israeli conflict.[20]

Yasir Arafat, the PLO leader whom Rabin openly pronounced his "partner for peace," apparently made that difficult psychological transformation himself, although his credibility is still tentative, particularly in the west. Upon the signing of the 1994 Cairo Agreement, Arafat spoke in favor of the olive branch and announced that the Palestinian people

> extends its hand to the Israeli people to start this era and end the whirlpool of violence for the sake of our real interests today, and the interests of the coming generations. Coexistence is possible. It is inevitable. It is our common fate to live together as neighbors governed by the rules of justice, democracy, and national and human dignity. . . . [O]ur peace is a peace for the Arab nation. It is a peace for Israel, for the Middle East region, for the whole world. Yes, it is a peace for the whole world.[21]

These noble sentiments mark a radical departure from Arafat's historic position and bespeak a new commitment to the means of diplomacy and the ends of peace; yet his penchant for more militant Arabic speeches, away from Western microphones, contributes to the suspicion among many that his conversion is not yet complete.

There is no question but that King Hussein made the necessary psychological transformation. Echoing the word "peace" thirteen times at Rabin's funeral, he delivered a moving eulogy to the slain Israeli premier which spoke frankly of the affection and respect he and Rabin had developed over the years, calling Rabin

> a brother, colleague, and a friend, a man, a soldier who met us on the opposite side of a divide, whom we respected, as he respected us. A man I came to know because I realized, as he did, that we have to cross over the divide, establish a dialogue, get to know each other and strive to leave for those who follow us a legacy that is worthy of them. And so we did. And so we became brethren and friends. (Appendix, Document 15)

After years of clandestine meetings and furtive diplomatic probes, the quiet king declared, "I believe it is time for all of us to come out openly and to speak our peace. . . . Let us not keep silent." Rising to the challenge of leadership, he urged his audience to follow him all the way across the vast psychological divide, while warning the religious extremists who resorted to violence that the peace camp had reclaimed God and would not let them prevail in their perverse reading of God's will.

Yitzhak Rabin's funeral constituted as surreal an event as the September 1993 handshake with which we began our study. One should not underestimate the symbolic importance of the scene on Mount Herzl on 6 November 1995: slain by a Jewish assassin's bullets, an Israeli prime minister was eulogized in Jerusalem by an Egyptian president and a Jordanian king in the presence of high-ranking Moroccan, Omani, Qatari, and Palestinian dignitaries.[22] It was a stunning illustration of how far the peace process had come. Yet vocal, vigorous, and violent rejectionists still agitate within the Arab and Israeli communities. Clinging to their absolutist visions of complete victory, these people rail against the imperfect realities of negotiated compromise. They are not without regional allies who have vested interests in preventing an Arab-Israeli reconciliation.[23]

Matt Davies, courtesy Gannett Suburban Newspapers, United Feature Syndicate

One does not need a crystal ball to know that more innocent lives will be lost before the Arab-Israeli and Palestinian-Israeli conflicts are resolved, and that the Rabin state funeral may not be the last.

We close by returning to the three "p" words in the subtitle of this book. Our research has indeed identified a specific pattern that characterizes both early and recent failed negotiation attempts, and that serves as a checklist of obstacles over which successful negotiators must prevail. When contemporary efforts at negotiating Middle East solutions have faltered or failed, the problems have invariably been among those described in our paradigm. Apparent successes, beginning with Camp David and expressed most recently by limited Palestinian-Israeli and Jordanian-Israeli accomplishments, suggest the possibility that deviations from the historical pattern can allow for productive negotiations.

Arab-Israeli negotiations since Oslo have made headlines, but have they made history? To the extent to which they deviated from the historical pattern, the answer is affirmative. Although Arab-Israeli hostility remains a constant feature of the Middle East, the existence of Arab and Israeli leaders making compromise and reconciliation national policy, the achievement of several agreements, and ongoing negotiations toward others are all fresh and welcome changes in the dismal history of the conflict. Roughly fifty years after the first Arab-Israeli war, it does not seem as impossible as it once did to imagine that the region may be inching closer to that day when disputes that were once inflamed by the argument of force may be settled by the force of argument.

NOTES

1. Harold H. Saunders, *The Other Walls: The Arab-Israeli Peace Process in a Global Perspective,* rev. ed., Princeton: Princeton University Press, 1991, 37.

2. Irving Kristol, "There's No 'Peace Process' in Mideast," *Wall Street Journal,* 19 February 1988, p. 18.

3. Edward W. Said, "The Mirage of Peace,"*Nation,* 16 October 1995, p. 416.

4. William B. Quandt, *Camp David: Peacemaking and Politics,* Washington, DC: The Brookings Institution, 1986, 118.

5. Abba Eban, "Camp David: The Unfinished Business," *Foreign Affairs* 57 (Winter 1978–79), 348.

6. Saunders, *Other Walls,* 36.

7. Arafat's Johannesburg Mosque speech, 10 May 1994 (extracts quoted in the *Jerusalem Post,* 18 May 1994); Evelyn Gordon, "Labor MK: Arafat's Speeches Violate Accord," *JPI,* w/e 12 August 1995, p. 4. See also Joel Greenberg, "Plans to Celebrate Past Divide Jerusalem Anew," *NYT,* 28 May 1995, p. A8; Helen Kaye and Bill Hutman, "Rabin: Undivided Jerusalem is Ours," *JPI,* w/e 16 September 1995, pp. 1–2.

8. Kenneth W. Stein and Samuel W. Lewis (with Sheryl J. Brown), *Making Peace among Arabs and Israelis: Lessons from Fifty Years of Negotiating Experience,* Washington, DC: United States Institute of Peace, October 1991, 25–26.

9. John G. Stoessinger, *Why Nations Go to War,* New York: St. Martin's, 1978, 216. Cf. Klieman, "Approaching the Finish Line: The United States in Post-Oslo Peace Making," Ramat Gan: Begin-Sadat Center for Strategic Studies, Bar-Ilan University (Security and Policy Studies, No. 22), June 1995, 27–28.

10. Stein and Lewis, 8–11.

11. Klieman, 9.

12. Ibid., 5–6, 15–16.

13. Ibid., 17–21, 23–25, 30, 36–38, 42. Cf. Stein and Lewis, v–viii.

14. "There is historic irony in the fact that it took a leader of Rabin's known hawkishness on security to bring the Labor party back to the path of political moderation." Avi Shlaim, "Prelude to the Accord; Likud, Labour and the Palestinians," *JPS* 23:2 (Winter 1994), 18.

15. Abba Eban, "A Diplomatic Reality," *JPI,* w/e 22 February 1997, p. 10.

16. Mohamed Heikal, *Secret Channels: The Inside Story of Arab-Israeli Peace Negotiations,* London: HarperCollins, 1996, 343–44; Uri Avnery, *My Friend, the Enemy,* Westport, CT: Lawrence Hill, 1986, 117–294; "Eyewitness," in Shulamith Hareven, *The Vocabulary of Peace: Life, Culture and Politics in the Middle East,* San Francisco: Mercury House, 1995, 157–63.

17. There are at least two historical precedents for political assassination in the pre-1948 Jewish community in Palestine: the killing of an outspoken anti-Zionist Dutch Jew, Jacob de Haan, in East Jerusalem in 1924, and the gunning down of the young labor leader and political secretary of the Jewish Agency Executive, Dr. Chaim Arlosoroff, on the Tel Aviv beach in 1933. The assassins, in both cases, were never definitively identified. In the former case, de Haan's supporters suspected an agent of the Zionist Executive or the Histadrut Labor Federation. In the latter case, Labor Party activists believed that the culprits were right-wing Revisionists. In both cases, there was conflicting evidence that the assailants might have been Arabs.

18. Ehud Sprinzak, an Israeli academic and a leading authority on the religious right, revealed that "only a week before the shooting he met with top security officials to discuss 'the very real possibility' of a Jewish plot to assassinate Israeli leaders. But, he added, 'we just couldn't bring ourselves to really believe it.'" John

Kifner, "Zeal of Rabin's Assassin Springs from Rabbis of Religious Right," *NYT,* 12 November 1995, p. A1.

19. Ilana Kass and Bard O'Neill, *The Deadly Embrace: The Impact of Israeli and Palestinian Rejectionism on the Peace Process,* Lanham, MD: University Press of America, 1997, 337.

20. Remarks by Prime Minister Yitzhak Rabin at the Tel Aviv Peace Rally, 4 November 1995. Information Division, Israel Ministry of Foreign Affairs (MFA), http://www.israel-mfa.gov.il or http://www.israel.org/peace or by e-mail at ask@israel-info.gov.il; reprinted in Yitzhak Rabin, *The Rabin Memoirs,* expanded ed., trans. Dov Goldstein, Berkeley: University of California Press, 1996, Appendix J.

21. Yasir Arafat, speech at the signing of the Cairo Agreement, 4 March 1994, in *The Israel-Arab Reader: A Documentary History of the Middle East Conflict,* eds. Walter Laqueur and Barry Rubin, 5th rev. and updated ed., New York: Penguin, 1995, 644–47.

22. Shortly thereafter, Yasir Arafat, accompanied by Oslo architects Abu Mazen and Abu Alaa, paid a surprise visit to Rabin's widow in Tel Aviv and praised the fallen Israeli leader as "a hero of peace" and a "personal friend." Joel Greenberg, "Arafat Visits Israel to Give Condolences to Leah Rabin," *NYT,* 10 November 1995, p. A6.

23. Kass and O'Neill are not alone among scholars speculating about potentially catastrophic failures of the peace process. See, e.g., Anthony H. Cordesman, *Perilous Prospects: The Peace Process and the Arab-Israeli Military Balance,* Boulder, CO: Westview Press, 1996.

Epilogue

THE BEGINNING OF THE NETANYAHU-ARAFAT ERA

JUNE 1996–JANUARY 1997

Historians generally enjoy the luxury of pursuing their work unfettered by the hazards of current events. The thesis of this book, however, is that an application of our historical model to ongoing (and future) Arab-Israeli negotiations will clarify the forces at work behind the headlines. Obviously the new dimensions of Palestinian-Israeli relations that have emerged since the election of Israeli Prime Minister Benjamin Netanyahu in May 1996 will require a case study of their own. At this writing, however, the Arafat-Netanyahu era of Palestinian-Israeli peacemaking has been relatively brief, primary sources are few, and scholarly secondary sources are generally not yet available. We offer here only a sketch of how the traditional pattern of Arab-Israeli negotiations may correspond to current behavior; readers persuaded of the validity of our thesis are encouraged to apply it more rigorously to the larger picture that will have emerged between the writing and publication of this book. By the same token, future developments along the unfinished Syrian-(Lebanese-)Israeli tracks will also provide excellent opportunities for a further application of our model.

The Oslo process was very much the personal property of three men: Yasir Arafat, Yitzhak Rabin, and Shimon Peres. The loss of two of them,

Rabin by bullet in November 1995 and Peres by ballot in May 1996, was bound to have tremendous ramifications for the ongoing business of Palestinian-Israeli rapprochement; their replacement by Benjamin ("Bibi") Netanyahu from the rival Likud Party deepened the impact. When Israeli and Palestinian negotiators finally resumed activity in the summer of 1996, most of the seven negotiating elements we have been examining had changed since the Oslo architects had inaugurated the process.

Netanyahu was not an immediately obvious successor to the peacemaker role played by Rabin and Peres. Peres had supported the reconciliation with the PLO enthusiastically; Rabin had come reluctantly to the conclusion that it was the only game in town. These two elder statesmen broke the classic dynamics of deadlock. Tackling the formidable *psychological obstacles*, they promoted an entirely new attitude by which a strong Israel could recognize the enemy, talk to him directly, and risk the compromises inherent in any negotiated settlement. Ironically, the election of the younger man, Netanyahu, constituted the return of the old "adversary paradigm,"[1] by which a constantly besieged Israel trusts no one, dares not take risks for an unguaranteed peace, and insists that its only choices are to overcome or be overcome.

Netanyahu ran on a platform explicitly denouncing the Oslo Accords and vowing to reverse them. His allies in the campaign were the ultranationalists and ultraorthodox adamantly opposed to an Israeli withdrawal from the West Bank, and the settlers committed to expanding Jewish settlements there. At the time of her husband's death, Leah Rabin publicly blamed Netanyahu for encouraging the climate of hysteria and hatred that produced the assassin. The new Netanyahu government quickly adopted the expected positions that it would forbid the establishment of a Palestinian state, that it would encourage the expansion of Jewish settlements in the West Bank, that Jerusalem was non-negotiable, and that Israel would never come down from the Golan Heights.

These principles constituted a major change in the *terms of agreement* that had produced the Oslo Accords and that were the presumably unalterable precepts driving the subsequent talks leading to a final settlement. In April 1996 the Labor Party dropped the clause in its campaign platform rejecting the possibility of coexistence with a Palestinian state; after the election, rumors developed that, anticipating a Labor victory, the Peres government and Arafat had actually agreed upon a blueprint for a two-state solution, with East Jerusalem as the nominal Palestinian capital.[2] Netanyahu's win and his reassertion of hard-line pre-Oslo positions meant that the terms of agreement had become a more serious obstacle in further negotiations than they had been since Oslo.

Although Netanyahu tried to calm jittery pro-peace Israelis, Arabs, and westerners with firm declarations that his government would abide by all existing agreements, he insisted on re-opening negotiations concerning an IDF withdrawal from the last major Arab city in the West Bank, Hebron. Palestinian negotiators protested fiercely against re-negotiating an agreement to which the Labor government had already committed Israel, but which had been delayed by the slew of bloody Hamas suicide bus bombings in the spring of 1996. Reflecting the unequal power balance between the PA and Israel, however, all parties eventually returned to the table, where it took almost seven months, many crises, and intense American mediation before a deal on Hebron was finally signed on 15 January 1997.

The bitter re-negotiation of Hebron cut both ways as an indicator of terms of agreement issues. The easy conclusion is that the difficult agreement on a new Hebron withdrawal plan indicated that the gaps that had been narrowed between the PA and the Labor government had yawned wide once again when the Likud Party took power. Netanyahu's people defended the Hebron agreement to their dismayed right-wing supporters—who had lobbied for continued IDF control of the town—as a vast improvement over the Labor version, with substantial new security guarantees for the enclave of 450 Jews dug in among 150,000 Palestinian Arabs. In actuality, the differences between the Netanyahu agreement and the earlier one were largely symbolic or insignificant, and the Israeli withdrawal finally went off without a hitch within a week of the mid-January 1997 signing. The only real difference lay in the acrimony, distrust, and bad faith that distinguished these tortuous negotiations from the original ones. While boding ill for the *psychological element* in our model, the end result of the Hebron talks suggested that, despite its firmly stated *terms of agreement*, this government could be moved away from its hard-line positions.[3]

The West Bank rabbis who had challenged the Rabin government with a religious ruling forbidding the withdrawal of the IDF from Judea and Samaria weighed in on the Hebron debate with another religious injunction,[4] this one specifically forbidding a pull-back from Hebron, site of Jewish biblical history and the resting place of the Jewish patriarchs and matriarchs. As if in response, two weeks prior to the agreement, an unstable orthodox IDF soldier opened fire in the Hebron market, wounding several Palestinians. Roundly criticized by Oslo supporters for his rigid and uncompromising stance toward Israel's Palestinian peace partners, the right-wing prime minister also faced the same opponents, even further to his right, who had censured his predecessor. The announcement of the Hebron Accord was met with cautious relief by the peace camp, many of whom were angry at the new government for squandering so much political capital to achieve virtually the same agreement previously concluded. The ultranationalist camp immediately denounced Netanyahu for abandoning his principles and his campaign promises, not to mention the Jewish settlers in Hebron. Promises by the government to open the coffers and borders for increased Jewish settlements only partly appeased the suspicious hard-liners, and embittered those Palestinians and Israelis who wanted to see the Oslo process continue.

The leadership dimension, what we have called the "dynamics-of-deadlock" element, is very much in evidence here. With roughly half of the nation backing them, Rabin and Peres struggled mightily to persuade the other half to give their new peace gambit a chance. Their inability to overcome the resistance of that other half of the nation served as a brake on the speed and scope of further Palestinian-Israeli negotiations. The task of retaining the confidence of one's supporters while simultaneously earning the confidence of one's opponents may be even harder for a Netanyahu government whose natural nationalist principles are in conflict with both internal and external pressures to allow the peace process to advance.

The *status-of-negotiator* factor shifted wildly, several times, early in Netanyahu's tenure. We have mentioned above the issue of the prime minister's own standing and command within a sharply polarized Israeli public. The initial impression, provoking dismay among his opponents and joy among his supporters, was that a prime minister of Netanyahu's right-wing ideological predilections would use his considerable power to halt the process of concessions and compromises that marked the Oslo vision of, and path to, a final settlement. But the example of the Hebron Agreement highlights a phenomenon observed elsewhere in the historical pattern that has occasionally worked to the advantage of peacemakers: namely, the special ability of hard-line leaders to sell diplomatic solutions to people primed for military ones. Menachem Begin, hailing from the same "Greater Israel" branch of the Likud Party, presents a possible model for Netanyahu. Begin relinquished the entire Sinai but held fast to Judea and Samaria; some note wryly that, having presided over the withdrawal from Hebron on the West Bank, Netanyahu has already surpassed his Likud mentor for generosity to the Palestinians. But sometimes a hard-liner remains exactly that, and another potential model for Netanyahu could be the immovable Yitzhak Shamir. Netanyahu's early months in office were characterized by vacillation between gestures to pacify the Israeli and international pro-Oslo crowd and gestures to reassure his own nationalist, anti-Oslo camp. In January 1997, it was too early to tell which direction would prevail.

The more important status-of-negotiator issue concerned Netanyahu's relations with the PA and its elected president, Yasir Arafat. Netanyahu's campaign speeches had pilloried the Palestinian leader as the quintessential and unrepentant terrorist. Once in power, Netanyahu's refusal to meet personally with Arafat revived the historic status-of-negotiator obstacle in which one or both sides refused to meet with the other's recognized leadership. Netanyahu's determination *not* to shake Arafat's hand carried as much symbolism and as serious implications as Rabin's historic decision to do so three years earlier.

In accepting Arafat as a negotiating partner, Rabin helped catapult his former enemy to a higher level of legitimacy and power than he had ever commanded before; in the intervening three years, Arafat had cemented his status as the internationally recognized spokesman for the Palestinian people, a role confirmed by his 1996 election as PA president in the first Palestinian elections. By avoiding a meeting with Arafat, Netanyahu not only reverted to the pre-Oslo status quo but also delivered a deliberate slap to his face. This and other humiliations of the Palestinian leader recall the historical pattern (repeated a decade and a half earlier in Menachem Begin's derisive and demanding attitude toward Bashir Gemayel) by which the stronger party assumed it could use its greater strength to impose an uneven resolution upon its weaker opponent.

Whether born of psychological factors, the arrogance of power, ideological precepts, or misjudged negotiating tactics, Netanyahu's early insistence upon avoiding the Palestinian leader was so strong that, when crises necessitated serious Israeli-PA consultation, the Netanyahu government insisted upon secret "dark channel" talks[5]. The first high-level, clandestine meetings took place in August 1996.[6] In an era where direct discussion between Israeli prime ministers and the PA president had become commonplace, these sub rosa meetings were a step backward and signaled the return of the status of negotiator obstacle in Arab-Israeli negotiations.

Another example was even more telling. When full-blown violence erupted between Israelis and Palestinians in September 1996, including firefights between Israeli and Palestinian troops, Netanyahu's first response was to place an emergency call to Hosni Mubarak, requesting his assistance in restoring calm.[7] The incredulous Egyptian president responded that in the post-Oslo age, the Israeli prime minister should pick up the phone and call Arafat instead. The phone call to Egypt is clearly reminiscent of the traditional Israeli preference for dealing with the Palestinians via non-Palestinian Arab interlocutors. Public pressure from Israeli president Ezer Weizman, who had censured Netanyahu for allowing the relationship with the Palestinians to deteriorate by refusing to meet with Arafat,[8] finally provoked the prime minister to issue a statement of intention to meet the PA president. The gravity of the September disturbances finally, belatedly, persuaded him that the meeting could not be delayed any longer. The pretext of "security" necessities provided an alibi against right-wing critics.

The Arafat-Netanyahu handshake came at the Erez checkpoint between Israel and the Gaza Strip in late September 1996. Several observers noted that, when Arafat grasped hands with Rabin, he had shaken hands with half of Israel; in greeting Netanyahu, he shook hands with much of the other half.[9] An old saying holds that you make peace with your enemies, not your friends. The Labor government, whose leaders became fond of quoting this dictum, had become Arafat's closest friend. Perhaps the peace process could go no further until Likud had at least broken the handshake barrier.

In subsequent meetings, Bibi and Yasir took publicly to referring to one another as "friends" and "partners," partially correcting the old status obstacle. Meetings between top Israeli and Palestinian officials again became routine. Stepped-up cooperation speaks to the *experience* issue, allowing the parties to capitalize on the surge of intensive PLO-Israeli interactions that had taken place since Oslo.

In addition to highlighting the problems associated with status and leadership, the violent outbursts of September 1996 also demonstrated the centrality and vulnerability of the *psychological* element of the peace process. Against the backdrop of Netanyahu's non-recognition of Arafat and non-movement on the Oslo track, his decision to open a new entrance to an ancient Jerusalem tunnel ignited massive Palestinian protest. The tunnel emerged at the Wailing Wall, a holy Jewish site within the Old City of Jerusalem, and at the base of the Dome of the Rock, a holy Muslim site directly above. Of negligible import in and of itself, the new tunnel gate was for Palestinians a symbolic and psychological affront to their claim to the Old City and represented a defiant Israeli violation of the pledge to resolve the Jerusalem problem through negotiations, not via the fait accompli. In scenes reminiscent of the *Intifada,* Palestinians engaged IDF troops in running street battles in dozens of cities and outposts throughout the West Bank and in Jerusalem itself. Unlike the *Intifada,* however, this time they were accompanied by thousands of Palestinian police officers, armed and positioned as per Oslo stipulations, some of whom opened fire on their IDF counterparts. The ensuing chaos resulted in over sixty Palestinian and Israeli deaths.

Although Arafat had been increasingly critical of Netanyahu in the weeks preceding the tunnel incident, he apparently neither encouraged his security troops to open fire upon the Israelis nor anticipated their doing so. That PA soldiers turned against the IDF with weapons that Israel had allowed into their hands horrified Israelis. For some it verified the belief that, once empowered, the Palestinians could not be trusted to coexist peacefully with Israel; for others it called into question Arafat's ability to control his people and hold up his end of the peace bargain. Still others saw in the violence a new urgency to move ahead with the peace process more quickly and substantively. While some Palestinian and Israeli troops exchanged fire, others rushed to the aid of the stricken, Arab and Jew alike, mirroring the gamut of reactions to the peace process within both communities. In the immediate aftermath of the riots, PA and IDF officers drafted new measures to prevent future breakdowns in their cooperative security arrangements.

The tunnel crisis brought the mutually distrustful Netanyahu and Arafat régimes to the brink, and demonstrated the potential reversibility of some of Oslo's achievements. It showed that the psychological wounds between Jews and Arabs were still raw and quick to bleed. It pointed to vast reservoirs of distrust, fear, and hatred still readily available to both sides. But it also served as the catalyst for the Netanyahu-Arafat meeting and renewed diplomatic efforts to stabilize the situation, revealing the unpredictability of the *timing* factor in Arab-Israeli peacemaking.

Third-party intervention continued to be an important element in the adaptation of Oslo to the Arafat-Netanyahu era. In establishing the "dark channel" talks, Netanyahu's government relied on Norwegian official Terje Rød Larsen, of Oslo fame, once again to mediate secret PLO-Israeli talks, in effect reinventing the wheel. Again, however, the primacy of the US role reemerged when things got difficult, as after the tunnel mêlée. When four days of intensive US phone mediation failed to produce an agreement to assuage Palestinian grievances and Israeli fears, Arafat, Netanyahu, and King Hussein were convened in Washington for highly publicized consultations with President Clinton. Most of the traditional pressures associated with third-party intervention were present. With Clinton in the midst of a heated reelection campaign, one White House official suggested that both the Israeli and Palestinian leaders would have to be "attentive of their host's requirements" for success, a classic third-party feature that could also provide them with "political cover for compromise."[10] The Washington meeting produced the appropriate high-minded pledges of mutual cooperation and revitalized the stalled Hebron talks. It took four more months of contentious debate, along with the intensive and exhausting mediation of intrepid US negotiator Dennis Ross, to see the talks through to a resolution. US intervention proved indispensable to that success, largely because of the renewed levels of distrust that prevailed between the Palestinian and Israeli sides.

This heavy reliance on the Americans reflected a backward step in the peace process and the disintegration of the fragile mutual trust that Arafat and Rabin had tentatively established between their teams. In a remarkable testimony to both sides' view of the United States as an essential player, neither would sign the Hebron Accords until Ross drafted and appended a "Note for the Record" (Appendix, Document 16), essentially an American guarantee as to what had been agreed upon and mutually understood. The Americans departed from negative historical patterns by serving as a "reality principle, letting both sides know what was possible and what was not."[11] However, as the historic pattern often demonstrated, over-reliance on American intervention for every issue, small or large, can also encourage the unhelpful negotiation behavior of *dubious purposes and motives,* whereby the parties end up using negotiations primarily as a vehicle for advancing their own relationship with the superpower at the expense of the goals of regional peacemaking and the advancement of direct PA-Israeli contact and trust.[12]

Netanyahu's originally stated terms of agreement suggested that his government was interested in enjoying the benefits of the process without paying the price of future concessions. An examination of his principles for a final settlement—personal autonomy for Palestinians as individuals, but continued Israeli control of the land, resources, foreign policy, and security; no Palestinian state; no compromise on Jerusalem—would suggest

Courtesy of Chan Lowe, *South Florida Sun-Sentinel*, Ft. Lauderdale, Fla.

that Israel's goal was to make the interim settlement into a permanent one. If this analysis is accurate, then the *purposes and motives* with which the new government entered into the peace talks are reminiscent of the historical pattern by which parties negotiated to impress an outsider, to give the appearance of flexibility, or to wear down the opponent—but without intending to move beyond the status quo.

There was, however, a momentum to the Oslo process that made it more than the personal prerogative of a few men huddled deep in secret meetings. Once it had become part of the public domain, even negotiators with instructions to hold firm found the pressure of rising popular expectations and demands and international pressure to produce results difficult to withstand, as Netanyahu learned in Hebron. In January 1997, a bipartisan negotiating team led by Michael Eitan, Likud parliamentary whip, and Labor's Yossi Beilin released a non-binding Israeli proposal for a final settlement with the Palestinians that was more expansive than the one Netanyahu came to office championing. Negotiations are hard to begin but, once begun, difficult to control. Even reluctant participants can find the force of circumstances moving them beyond their original intentions.

Developments on the Palestinian side of the equation did not rival the 1996 upheaval within Israel in terms of drama, but presented serious ramifications nonetheless for Arafat's continued role in the peace process. His election as PA president in January 1996 added a feather to his *status* cap, but popular displeasure with his leadership and régime continued to mount throughout the year. By 1996, negotiations on general refugee issues had failed to materialize, further darkening the mood in the diaspora. Addressing neither the right of the 1948 refugees to return to homes within Israel nor compensation for their loss, the Oslo agreements did little to enhance Arafat's standing among the millions of Palestinians living outside of the West Bank and Gaza, who "were profoundly embittered by an accord that apparently consigned them to oblivion."[13] Although Arafat recognized correctly that the priority of the Palestinians in the occupied territories was the replacement of the IDF with a Palestinian National Authority, the emergence of a PA characterized by fiscal irregularities, nepotism, and secretive policymaking demoralized the elements of the population most inclined to support him. Despite the fact that virtually all Palestinians in the West Bank and Gaza now live under an elected Palestinian leadership, many describe PA rule as being as repressive as the occupation it replaced. Critics such as Edward Said have only grown more vocal and insistent in their condemnation of a régime that appears increasingly corrupt and tyrannical. Proving their point, Arafat's leadership banned the sale of Said's books in August 1995. Human rights organizations, Palestinian and international, report a long list of abuses, ranging from the torture and death of prisoners to political censorship and intimidation by any of the more than thirteen security and command structures operating in the hazy PA infrastructure under Arafat's personal control. The failure of the Oslo process tangibly to improve the standard of living of ordinary Palestinians further depletes the resiliency of many who had been ready to give peace a chance.

Palestinian peace activists pushing Arafat for reforms have allies in Israel, who use their access to Arafat to press him to open up the Palestinian system to genuine popular participation, giving ordinary Palestinians a vested interest in seeing the peace process proceed. Israeli critics see the unsavory aspects of Arafat's leadership as endemic to the man, and proof of his untrustworthiness as a peace partner. Delays in amending the PLO covenant, as called for in each of the successive Oslo agreements, fuel the skeptics' conviction that an increasingly weak Arafat either cannot or will not fulfil his end of the deal.

Discontent in Gaza and the West Bank challenges Arafat's ability to lead his people through increasingly difficult negotiations with the Netanyahu government. The *status*, *leadership*, and *psychological* elements are all heavily involved. Palestinian society never produced a large-scale equivalent of Israel's Peace Now movement, and the pro-peace camp under the Palestinian Authority remains proportionately much smaller than its Israeli counterpart. A huge January 1997 rally in Nablus celebrating the memory of slain bomb-maker Yahya Ayyash, and another at Bir Zeit University featuring an enthusiastic reenactment of a suicide bus bombing, provoked not a word of reproach or censure from a régime not particularly enamored of free speech. These mass expressions of support for terrorism had an obviously negative impact on the Israeli psyche, as does the veneration by some extremist settlers of Hebron mosque murderer Baruch Goldstein on the Palestinian psyche. But popular demonstrations such as those in Nablus and Bir Zeit also question Arafat's post-Oslo success in changing Palestinian psychology about and accommodation with Israel, and his ability to make good on the Palestinian end of future Israeli-PA bargains. In February 1997 Arafat succeeded in convening a Palestinian "national dialogue" conference to plan strategy for the final-status talks. The participation of Islamic and leftist groups critical of Oslo indicated that Arafat still exercised considerable leadership skills and that he understood the need for more broadly based Palestinian support in his negotiations with Israel.

Even under the best of circumstances, it would be difficult for the celebrated guerilla leader to maintain his unchallenged leadership position in a more traditional political arena. Having long used his ability to appear to be all things to all people, Arafat must now settle for the unambiguous role of peacemaker. The strength of Camp David as a precedent for the PLO-Israeli agreement cuts both ways, with the PA president being compared to the late Egyptian leader "both by those who revere Sadat as a statesman and those who revile him as an opportunistic traitor to the Palestinian and Arab cause."[14] Most Palestinians are torn between hopes that the indignities of statelessness are finally ending, and fears that they may end up with nothing more than "a corrupt and dictatorial Palestinian Bantustan under Israeli domination."[15] Ironically, polls suggest that a growing number of Israelis are resigning themselves to the inevitability of an independent Palestinian state, while Palestinian confidence in the same increasingly wanes.

Since mid-1996, the Palestinian-Israeli peace process has threatened to become locked into a novel vicious circle, replacing the traditional dynamics of deadlock. Israel's leaders have minimal public support for making concessions to Arafat unless he demonstrates that he can govern his people and make good on his promises. Arafat, meanwhile, needs continuing concessions from Israel in order to secure his role as the popular leader who can deliver what his followers are seeking. Should it continue, Netanyahu's early tendency to accompany any pro-Oslo gesture with another designed to appease the far right will likely produce more flashpoints of the Jerusalem tunnel variety. If Arafat proves unwilling or unable to halt Hamas terrorism, the peace process will further disintegrate.

A brief review of the situation since June 1996 reveals that many of the historical obstacles overcome or diminished during the 1993–96 period have reasserted themselves in traditionally more negative ways. Can the Israeli and Palestinian societies accomplish a reversal of deeply ingrained hatreds, or will those elements unable to make the psychological turnabout derail the process of reconciliation? Have Israelis and Palestinians finally come to sit together at the table, only to have it collapse under the weight of a century's worth of ingrained hatred and unproductive negotiating techniques? Or will new approaches triumph over old habits? At the time of this writing, we must leave the answers to those questions to future historians.

NOTES

1. Gordon Fellman, "The Struggle toward a Peace Culture: Rabin's Career, the Assassination, and Paradigm Shift," paper presented at the Association for Israel Studies Annual Conference, Boston, 1–3 June 1996.

2. Evelyn Gordon, "Israel was ready to accept a Palestinian State," *JPI*, w/e 1 August 1996, p. 32; "A Would-Be Palestinian Pact: Rabin Aide Discloses Details," *NYT*, 30 July 1996, p. A8.

3. Adding to this impression was the highly unpopular February 1997 release from Israeli jails of 30 Palestinian women prisoners, some convicted murderers of Israelis, as obligated by the Oslo II and Hebron accords.

4. "Rabbis Warn against Hebron Redeployment," *JR*, 12 December 1996, p. 6.

5. David Makovsky, "A Peek into the Dark Channel Talks," *JPI*, w/e 14 September 1996, p. 1.

6. Those involved in undercover contacts were Netanyahu's diplomatic advisor, Dore Gold; his intelligence aide, Colonel Shimon Shapiro; Arafat's Oslo negotiator, Mahmoud Abbas (Abu Mazen); and the head of PA preventive security, Muhammad Dahlan.

7. Thomas L. Friedman, "Bibi's Moment of Truth," *NYT*, 29 September 1996, section 4, p. 15.

8. The maverick Israeli president threatened to upstage the prime minister by sitting down with the Palestinian leader himself.

9. Herb Keinon, "A Meeting with Destiny," *JPI*, w/e 14 September 1996, p. 3; Hirsh Goodman, "Crossing the Rubicon," *JR*, 3 October 1996, p. 64.

10. Quoted in Steven Erlanger, "Clinton's Choice: Chaos or Diplomacy," *NYT*, 30 September 1996, p. A1.

11. Thomas L. Friedman, "Pickle in the Middle," *NYT*, 26 January 1997, p. E13.

12. Ibid.; Barry Rubin, "Stuck with the US," *JPI*, w/e 1 February 1997, p. 9.

13. David McDowall, *The Palestinians: The Road to Nationhood*, Concord: Paul, 1995, 119.

14. Michael Hudson, "The Clinton Administration and the Middle East: Squandering the Inheritance?" *Current History* 93:580 (February 1994), 54.

15. "Bantustan" was the derisive term used to refer to each of the pseudo-independent African homelands created and controlled by the apartheid régime in South Africa. Muhammad Ali Khalidi, "A First Visit to Palestine," *JPS* 24:3 (Spring 1995), 79. Cf. Edward Said, "The Mirage of Peace," *Nation*, 16 October 1995, p. 413; McDowall, 119; Serge Schmemann, "For Gazans, Joy of Freedom Has Its Borders," *NYT*, 25 August 1995, p. A1; David Hirst, "The Axe Is Sharpened for Arafat," *The Guardian*, 15/16 April 1995, p. 21. David Hirst, "Shameless in Gaza," *Guardian Weekly*, 27 April 1997, p. 8; Glenn Frankel, *Beyond the Promised Land: Jews and Arabs on the Hard Road to a New Israel*, New York: Simon and Schuster/Touchstone, 1996, 380.

APPENDIX: DOCUMENTS

See list of Abbreviations and Bibliography for full source citations.

1. UN SECURITY COUNCIL RESOLUTION 242, 22 NOVEMBER 1967

The Security Council,

Expressing its continuing concern with the grave situation in the Middle East,

Emphasizing the inadmissibility of the acquisition of territory by war and the need to work for a just and lasting peace in which every State in the area can live in security,

Emphasizing further that all Member States in their acceptance of the Charter of the United Nations have undertaken a commitment to act in accordance with Article 2 of the Charter,

1. *Affirms* that the fulfillment of Charter principles requires the establishment of a just and lasting peace in the Middle East which should include the application of both the following principles:

(i) Withdrawal of Israeli armed forces from territories occupied in the recent conflict;

(ii) Termination of all claims or states of belligerency and respect for and acknowledgment of the sovereignty, territorial integrity and political independence of every State in the area and their right to live in peace within secure and recognized boundaries free from threats or acts of force;

2. *Affirms further* the necessity

(a) For guaranteeing freedom of navigation through international waterways in the area;

(b) For achieving a just settlement of the refugee problem;

(c) For guaranteeing the territorial inviolability and political independence of every State in the area, through measures including the establishment of demilitarized zones;

3. *Requests* the Secretary General to designate a Special Representative to proceed to the Middle East to establish and maintain contacts with the States concerned in order to promote agreement and assist efforts to achieve a peaceful and accepted settlement in accordance with the provisions and principles in this resolution;

4. *Requests* the Secretary-General to report to the Security Council on the progress of the efforts of the Special Representative as soon as possible.

Sources: Lukacs, 1–2; MFA.

2. STATEMENT TO THE ISRAELI KNESSET BY PRESIDENT SADAT, 20 NOVEMBER 1977

In the name of God, the Gracious and Merciful.

Mr. Speaker, Ladies and Gentlemen:

Peace and the mercy of God Almighty be upon you and may peace be for us all, God willing. Peace for us all on the Arab land, and in Israel as well, as in every part of this big world, which is so complexed by its sanguinary conflicts, disturbed by its sharp contradictions, menaced now and then by destructive wars launched by man to annihilate his fellow man. Finally, amidst the ruins of what man has built and the remains of the victims of Mankind, there emerges neither victor nor vanquished. The only vanquished remains man, God's most sublime creation, man whom God has created—as Ghandi the apostle of peace puts it: to forge ahead to mould the way of life and worship God Almighty.

I come to you today on solid ground, to shape a new life, to establish peace. We all, on this land of God; we all, Muslims, Christians, and Jews, worship God and no one but God. God's teachings and commandments are love, sincerity, purity and peace.

I do not blame all those who received my decision—when I announced it to the entire world before the Egyptian People's Assembly—with surprise and amazement. Some, gripped by the violent surprise, believed that my decision was no more than verbal juggling to cater for the world public opinion. Others, still, interpreted it as political tactics to camouflage my intention of launching a new war. I would go as far as to tell you that one of my aides at the Presidential Office contacted me at a late hour following my return home from the People's Assembly and sounded worried as he asked me: "Mr. President, what would be our reaction if Israel should actually extend an invitation to you?" I replied calmly, I will accept it immediately. I have declared that I will go to the end of the world; I will go to Israel, for I want to put before the People of Israel all the facts.

I can see the point of all those who were astounded by my decision or those who had any doubts as to the sincerity of the intentions behind the declaration of my decision. No one would have ever conceived that the President of the biggest Arab State, which bears the heaviest burden and the top responsibility pertaining to the cause of war and peace in the Middle East, could declare his readiness to go to the land of the adversary while we were still in a state of war. Rather, we all are still bearing the consequences of four fierce wars waged within thirty years. The families of the 1973 October War are still moaning under the cruel pains of widowhood and bereavement of sons, fathers and brothers.

As I have already declared, I have not consulted, as far as this decision is concerned, with any of my colleagues and brothers, the Arab Heads of State or the confrontation States. Those of them who contacted me, following the declaration of this decision, expressed their objection, because the feeling of utter suspicion and absolute lack of confidence between the Arab States and the Palestinian People on the one hand, and Israel on the other, still surges in us all. It is sufficient to say that many months in which peace could have been brought about had been wasted over many differences and fruitless discussions on the procedure for the convocation of the Geneva Conference, all showing utter suspicion and absolute lack of confidence.

But, to be absolutely frank with you, I took this decision after long thinking, knowing that it constitutes a grave risk for, if God Almighty has made it my fate to assume the responsibility on behalf of the Egyptian People and to share in the fate-determining responsibility of the Arab Nation and the Palestinian People, the main duty dictated by this responsibility is to exhaust all and every means in a bid to save my Egyptian Arab People and the entire Arab Nation the horrors of new, shocking and destructive wars, the dimensions of which are foreseen by no other than God himself.

After long thinking, I was convinced that the obligation of responsibility before God, and before the people, make it incumbent on me that I should go to the farthest corner of the world, even to Jerusalem, to address members of the Knesset, the representatives of the People of Israel, and acquaint them with all the facts surging in me. Then, I would leave you to decide for yourselves. Following this, may God Almighty determine our fate.

Ladies and Gentlemen, there are moments in the lives of nations and peoples when it is incumbent on those known for their wisdom and clarity of vision to overlook the past, with all its complexities and weighing memories, in a bold drive towards new horizons. Those who, like us, are shouldering the same responsibility entrusted to us, are the first who should have the courage to take fate-determining decisions which are in consonance with the circumstances. We must all rise above all forms of fanaticism, self-deception and obsolete theories of superiority. The most important thing is never to forget that infallibility is the prerogative of God alone.

If I said that I wanted to save all the Arab People the horrors of shocking and destructive wars, I most sincerely declare before you that I have the same feelings and bear the same responsibility towards all and every man on earth, and certainly towards the Israeli People.

Any life lost in war is a human life, irrespective of its being that of an Israeli or an Arab. A wife who becomes a widow is a human being entitled to a happy family life, whether she be an Arab or an Israeli. Innocent children who are deprived of the care and compassion of their parents are ours, be they living on Arab or Israeli land. They command our top responsibility to afford them a comfortable life today and tomorrow.

For the sake of them all, for the safeguard of the lives of all our sons and brothers, for affording our communities the opportunity to work for the progress and happiness of man and his right to a dignified life, for our responsibilities before the generations to come, for a smile on the face of every child born on our land—for all that, I have taken my decision to come to you, despite all hazards, to deliver my address.

I have shouldered the prerequisites of the historical responsibility and, therefore, I declared—on 4 February 1971, to be precise—that I was willing to sign a peace agreement with Israel. This was the first declaration made by a responsible Arab official since the outbreak of the Arab-Israeli conflict.

Motivated by all these factors dictated by the responsibilities of leadership, I called, on 16 October 1973, before the Egyptian People's Assembly, for an international conference to establish permanent peace based on justice. I was not in the position of he who was pleading for peace or asking for a ceasefire.

Motivated by all these factors dictated by duties of history and leadership, we signed the first disengagement agreement, followed by the second disengagement agreement in Sinai. Then we proceeded trying both open and closed doors in a bid to find a certain path leading to a durable and just peace. We opened our hearts to the peoples of the entire world to make them understand our motivations and objectives, and to leave them actually convinced of the fact that we are advocates of justice and peace-makers.

Motivated by all these factors, I decided to come to you with an open mind and an open heart, and with a conscious determination, so that we might establish permanent peace based on justice.

It is so fated that my trip to you, the trip of peace, should coincide with the Islamic feast, the holy Feast of Qurban Bayram, the Feast of Sacrifice when Abraham—peace be upon him—great-grandfather of the Arabs and Jews, submitted to God; I say when God Almighty ordered him, and to Him Abraham went, with dedicated sentiments, not out of weakness, but through a giant spiritual force and by a free will, to sacrifice his very own son, prompted by a firm and unshakable belief in ideals that lend life a profound significance.

This coincidence may carry a new meaning to us all, which may become a genuine aspiration heralding security and peace.

Ladies and Gentlemen, let us be frank with each other, using straightforward words and a clear conception, with no ambiguity. Let us be frank with each other today while the entire world, both East and West, follows these unparalleled moments which could prove to be a radical turning point in the history of this part of the world, if not the history of the world as a whole. Let us be frank with each other as we answer this important question: how can we achieve permanent peace based on justice?

I have come to you carrying my clear and frank answer to this big question, so that the people in Israel as well as the whole world might hear it, and so that all those whose devoted prayers ring in my ears, pleading to

God Almighty that this historic meeting may eventually lead to the results aspired to by millions, might also hear it.

Before I proclaim my answer, I wish to assure you that, in my clear and frank answer, I am basing myself on a number of facts which no one can deny.

The first fact: no one can build his happiness at the expense of the misery of others.

The second fact: never have I spoken or will I ever speak in two languages. Never have I adopted or will I adopt two policies. I never deal with anyone except in one language, one policy, and with one face.

The third fact: direct confrontation and a straight line are the nearest and most successful methods to reach a clear objective.

The fourth fact: the call for a permanent and just peace, based on respect for the United Nations resolutions, has now become the call of the whole world. It has become a clear expression of the will of the international community, whether in official capitals, where policies are made and decisions taken, or at the level of world public opinion which influences policy-making and decision-taking.

The fifth fact: and this is probably the clearest and most prominent, is that the Arab Nation, in its drive for permanent peace based on justice, does not proceed from a position of weakness or hesitation, but it has the potential of power and stability which tells of sincere will for peace. The Arab-declared intention stems from an awareness promoted by a heritage of civilization that, to avoid an inevitable disaster that will befall us, you and the entire world, there is no alternative to the establishment of permanent peace based on justice—peace that is not shaken by storms, swayed by suspicion, or jeopardized by ill intentions.

In light of these facts which I meant to place before you the way I see them, I would also wish to warn you in all sincerity; I warn you against some thoughts that could cross your minds; frankness makes it incumbent upon me to tell you the following:

First: I have not come here for a separate agreement between Egypt and Israel. This is not part of the policy of Egypt. The problem is not that of Egypt and Israel. Any separate peace between Egypt and Israel, or between any Arab confrontation State and Israel, will not bring permanent peace based on justice in the entire region. Rather, even if peace between all the confrontation States and Israel were achieved, in the absence of a just solution to the Palestinian problem, never will there be that durable and just peace upon which the entire world insists today.

Second: I have not come to you to seek a partial peace, namely to terminate the state of belligerency at this stage, and put off the entire problem to a subsequent stage. This is not the radical solution that would steer us to permanent peace.

Equally, I have not come to you for a third disengagement agreement in Sinai, or in the Golan and the West Bank. For this would mean that we are lacking the courage to confront peace, that we are too weak to shoulder the burdens and responsibilities of a durable peace based on justice.

I have come to you so that together we might build a durable peace based on justice, to avoid the shedding of one single drop of blood from an Arab or an Israeli. It is for this reason that I have proclaimed my readiness to go to the farthest corner of the world.

Here, I would go back to the answer to the big question: how can we achieve a durable peace based on justice?

In my opinion, and I declare it to the whole world from this forum, the answer is neither difficult nor impossible, despite long years of feud, blood vengeance, spite and hatred, and breeding generations on concepts of total rift and deep-rooted animosity. The answer is not difficult, nor is it impossible, if we sincerely and faithfully follow a straight line.

You want to live with us in this part of the world. In all sincerity, I tell you, we welcome you among us, with full security and safety. This, in itself, is a tremendous turning point; one of the landmarks of a decisive historical change.

We used to reject you. We had our reasons and our claims, yes. We used to brand you as "so-called" Israel, yes. We were together in international conferences and organizations and our representatives did not, and still do not, exchange greetings, yes. This has happened and is still happening.

It is also true that we used to set, as a precondition for any negotiations with you, a mediator who would meet separately with each party. Through this procedure, the talks of the first and second disengagement agreements took place.

Our delegates met in the first Geneva Conference without exchanging a direct word. Yes, this has happened.

Yet, today I tell you, and declare it to the whole world, that we accept to live with you in permanent peace based on justice. We do not want to encircle you or be encircled ourselves by destructive missiles ready for launching, nor by the shells of grudges and hatred. I have announced on more than one occasion that Israel had become *fait accompli*, recognized by the world, and that the two superpowers have undertaken the responsibility of its security and the defence of its existence.

As we really and truly seek peace, we really and truly welcome you to live among us in peace and security.

There was a huge wall between us which you tried to build up over a quarter of a century, but it was destroyed in 1973. It was a wall of a continuously inflammable and escalating psychological warfare. It was a wall of fear of the force that could sweep the entire Arab Nation. It was a wall of propaganda, that we were a Nation reduced to a motionless corpse. Rather, some of you had gone as far as to say that, even after 50 years, the Arabs would not regain any strength. It was a wall that threatened always with the long arm that could reach and strike anywhere. It was a wall that warned us against extermination and annihilation if we tried to use our legitimate right to liberate the occupied territories. Together we have to admit that that wall fell and collapsed in 1973.

Yet, there remained another wall. This wall constitutes a psychological barrier between us. A barrier of suspicion. A barrier of rejection. A barrier of fear of deception. A barrier of hallucinations around any action, deed or decision. A barrier of cautious and erroneous interpretations of all and every event or statement. It is this psychological barrier which I described in official statements as representing 70 percent of the whole problem.

Today through my visit to you, I ask you: why don't we stretch out our hands with faith and sincerity so that, together, we might destroy this barrier? Why shouldn't our and your will meet with faith and sincerity, so that together we might remove all suspicion of fear, betrayal and ill intentions? Why don't we stand together with the bravery of men and the boldness of heros who dedicate themselves to a sublime objective? Why don't we stand together with the same courage and boldness to erect a huge edifice of peace that builds and does not destroy? An edifice that is a beacon for generations to come—the human message for construction, development and the dignity of man? Why should we bequeath to the coming generations the plight of bloodshed, death, orphans, widowhood, family disintegration, and the wailing of victims?

Why don't we believe in the wisdom of God conveyed to us by the Proverbs of Solomon:

"Deceit is in the heart of them that imagine evil; but to the counsellors of peace is joy. Better is a dry morsel, and quietness therewith, than a house full of sacrifices with strife."

Why don't we repeat together from the Psalms of David:

"Hear the voice of my supplications, when I cry unto thee, when I lift up my hands towards the holy oracle. Draw me not away with the wicked, and with the workers of iniquity, which speak peace to their neighbors, but mischief is in their hearts. Give them according to their deeds, and according to the wickedness of their endeavours."

To tell you the truth, peace cannot be worth its name unless it is based on justice, and not on the occupation of the land of others. It would not be appropriate for you to demand for yourselves what you deny others. With all frankness, and with the spirit that has prompted me to come to you today, I tell you: you have to give up, once and for all, the dreams of conquest, and give up the belief that force is the best method for dealing with the Arabs. You should clearly understand and assimilate the lesson of confrontation between you and us.

Expansion does not pay. To speak frankly, our land does not yield itself to bargaining. It is not even open to argument. To us, the national soil is equal to the holy valley where God Almighty spoke to Moses—peace be upon him. None of us can, or accept to, cede one inch of it, or accept the principle of debating or bargaining over it.

I sincerely tell you that before us lies the appropriate chance for peace, if we are really serious in our endeavours for peace. It is a chance that time cannot afford once again. It is a chance that, if lost or wasted, the plotter against it will bear the curse of humanity and the curse of history.

What is peace for Israel? It means that Israel lives in the region with her Arab neighbors, in security and safety. To such logic, I say yes. It means that Israel lives within her borders, secure against any aggression. To such logic, I say yes. It means that Israel obtains all kinds of guarantees that ensure those two factors. To this demand, I say yes. More than that: we declare that we accept all the international guarantees you envisage and accept. We declare that we accept all the guarantees you want from the two superpowers or from either of them, or from the Big Five, or some of them.

Once again, I declare clearly and unequivocally that we agree to any guarantees you accept because, in return, we shall obtain the same guarantees.

In short, then, when we ask: what is peace for Israel, the answer would be: it is that Israel live within her borders with her Arab neighbors, in safety and security within the framework of all the guarantees she accepts and which are offered to the other party. But how can this be achieved? How can we reach this conclusion which would lead us to permanent peace based on justice?

There are facts that should be faced with all courage and clarity. There are Arab territories which Israel has occupied by armed forces. We insist on complete withdrawal; from these territories, including Arab Jerusalem.

I have come to Jerusalem, as the City of Peace, which will always remain as a living embodiment of coexistence among believers of the three religions. It is inadmissable that anyone should conceive the special status of the City of Jerusalem within the framework of annexation or expansionism, but it should be a free and open city for all believers.

Above all, the city should not be severed from those who have made it their abode for centuries. Instead of awakening the prejudices of the Crusaders, we should revive the spirit of Omar ibn el-Khattab and Saladdin, namely the spirit of tolerance and respect for rights. The holy shrines of Islam and Christianity are not only places of worship, but a living testimony of our uninterrupted presence here politically, spiritually and intellectually. Let us make no mistake about the importance and reverence we Christians and Muslims attach to Jerusalem.

Let me tell you, without the slightest hesitation, that I did not come to you under this dome to make a request that your troops evacuate the occupied territories. Complete withdrawal from the Arab territories occupied in 1967 is a logical and undisputed fact. Nobody should plead for that. Any talk about permanent peace based on justice, and any move to ensure our coexistence in peace and security in this part of the world, would become meaningless, while you occupy Arab territories by force of arms. For there is no peace that could be in consonance with, or be built on, the occupation of the land of others. Otherwise, it would not be a serious peace.

Yes, this is a foregone conclusion which is not open to discussion or debate—if intentions are sincere and if endeavours to establish a just and durable peace for ours and the generations to come are genuine.

As for the Palestinians' cause, nobody could deny that it is the crux of the entire problem. Nobody in the world could accept, today, slogans propagated here in Israel, ignoring the existence of the Palestinian People, and questioning their whereabouts. The cause of the Palestinian People, and their legitimate rights are no longer ignored or denied today by anybody. Rather, nobody who has the ability of judgement can deny or ignore it.

It is an acknowledged fact received by the world community, both in the East and in the West, with support and recognition in international documents and official statements. It is of no use to anybody to turn deaf ears to its resounding voice which is being heard day and night, or to overlook its historical reality. Even the United States, your first ally which is absolutely committed to safeguard Israel's security and existence, and which offered and still offers Israel every moral, material and military support—I say—even the United States has opted to face up to reality and facts, and admit that the Palestinian People are entitled to legitimate rights and that the Palestinian problem is the core and essence of the conflict and that, so long as it continues to be unresolved, the conflict will continue to aggravate, reaching new dimensions. In all sincerity, I tell you that there can be no peace without the Palestinians. It is a grave error of unpredictable consequences to overlook or brush aside this cause.

I shall not indulge in the past events since the Balfour Declaration sixty years ago. You are well acquainted with the relevant facts. If you have found the legal and moral justification to set up a national home on a land that did not all belong to you, it is incumbent upon you to show, once again [*sic*] a state on their land. When some extremists ask the Palestinians to give up this sublime objective, this, in fact, means asking them to renounce their identity and every hope for the future.

I hail the Israeli voices that called for the recognition of the Palestinian People's rights to achieve and safeguard peace. Here I tell you, ladies and gentlemen, that it is no use to refrain from recognizing the Palestinian People and their rights to statehood and rights of return.

We, the Arabs, have faced this experience before, with you and with the reality of Israeli existence. The struggle took us from war to war, from victims to more victims, until you and we have today reached the edge of a horrifying abyss and a terrifying disaster, unless together we seize the opportunity today of a durable peace based on justice.

You have to face reality bravely as I have done. There can never be any solution to a problem by evading it or turning a deaf ear to it. Peace cannot last if attempts are made to impose fantasy concepts on which the world has turned its back and announced its unanimous call for the respect of rights and facts. There is no need to enter a vicious circle as to Palestinian rights. It is useless to create obstacles. Otherwise the march of peace will be impeded or peace will be blown up.

As I have told you, there is no happiness to the detriment of others. Direct confrontation and straight-forwardness are the short-cut and the most successful way to reach a clear objective. Direct confrontation concerning the Palestinian problem, and tackling it in one single language with a view to achieving a durable and just peace, lie in the establishment of their state. With all the guarantees you demand, there should be no fear of a newlyborn state that needs the assistance of all countries of the world. When the bells of peace ring, there will be no hands to beat the drums of war. Even if they existed, they would be soundless.

Conceive with me a peace agreement in Geneva that we would herald to a world thirsty for peace, a peace agreement based on the following points:

First: ending the Israeli occupation of the Arab territories occupied in 1967.

Second: achievement of the fundamental rights of the Palestinian People and their right to self-determination, including the right to establish their own state.

Third: the right of all states in the area to live in peace within their boundaries, which will be secure and guaranteed through procedures to be agreed upon, which provide appropriate security to international boundaries, in addition to appropriate international guarantees.

Fourth: Commitment of all states in the region to administer the relations among them in accordance with the objectives and principles concerning the non-resort to force and the solution of differences among them by peaceful means.

Fifth: ending the state of belligerency in the region.

Ladies and Gentlemen, peace is not the mere endorsement of written lines; rather, it is a rewriting of history. Peace is not a game of calling for peace to defend certain whims or hide certain ambitions. Peace is a giant struggle against all and every ambition and whim. Perhaps the examples taken from ancient and modern history teach us all that missiles, warships and nuclear weapons cannot establish security. Rather, they destroy what peace and security build. For the sake of our peoples, and for the sake of the civilizations made by man, we have to defend man everywhere against the rule of the force of arms, so that we may endow the rule of humanity with all the power of the values and principles that promote the sublime position of Mankind.

Allow me to address my call from this rostrum to the People of Israel. I address myself with true and sincere words to every man, woman and child in Israel.

From the Egyptian People who bless this sacred mission of peace, I convey to you the message of peace, the message of the Egyptian People who do not know fanaticism, and whose sons, Muslims, Christians, and Jews, live together in a spirit of cordiality, love and tolerance. This is Egypt whose people have entrusted me with that sacred message, the message of security, safety and peace. To every man, woman and child in Israel, I say: encourage your leadership to struggle for peace, instead of strongholds and hideouts defended by destructive rockets. Introduce to the entire world the image of the new man in this area, so that he might set an example to the man of our age, the man of peace everywhere.

Be the heralds to your sons. Tell them that the past wars were the last of wars and the end of sorrows. Tell them that we are in for a new beginning to a new life—the life of love, prosperity, freedom and peace.

You, bewailing mother; you, widowed wife; you, the son who lost a brother or a father; you, all victims of wars—fill the earth and space with recitals of peace. Fill bosoms and hearts with the aspirations of peace. Turn the song into a reality that blossoms and lives. Make hope a code of conduct and endeavour. The will of peoples is part of the will of God.

Ladies and Gentlemen, before I came to this place, with every beat of my heart and with every sentiment, I prayed to God Almighty, while performing the Qurban Bayram prayers, and while visiting the Holy Sepulchre, to give me strength and to confirm my belief that this visit may achieve the objectives I look forward to, for a happy present and happier future.

I have chosen to set aside all precedents and traditions known by warring countries, in spite of the fact that occupation of the Arab territories is still there. Rather, the declaration of my readiness to proceed to Israel came as a great surprise that stirred many feelings and astounded many minds. Some opinions even doubted its intent. Despite that, the decision was inspired by all the clarity and purity of belief, and with all the true expression of my People's will and intentions.

And I have chosen this difficult road which is considered, in the opinion of many, the most difficult road. I have chosen to come to you with an open heart and an open mind. I have chosen to give this great impetus to all international efforts exerted for peace. I have chosen to present to you, and in your own home, the realities devoid of any schemes or whims, not to manoeuvre or to win a round, but for us to win together, the most dangerous of rounds and battles in modern history—the battle of permanent peace based on justice.

It is not my battle alone, nor is it the battle of the leadership of Israel alone. It is the battle of all and every citizen in all our territories whose right it is to live in peace. It is the commitment of conscience and responsibility in the hearts of millions.

When I put forward this initiative, many asked what it is that I conceived as possible to achieve during this visit, and what my expectations were. And, as I answered the questioners, I announce before you that I have not thought of carrying out this initiative from the concept of what could be achieved during this visit, but I have come here to deliver a message. I have delivered this message, and may God be my witness.

I repeat with Zachariah, *"Love right and justice."*

I quote the following verses from the holy Koran:

"We believe in God and in what has been revealed to us and what was revealed to Abraham, Ismail, Isaac, Jacob, and the tribes and in the books given to Moses, Jesus, and the prophets from their Lord. We make no distinction between one and another among them and to God we submit."

Source: Lukacs, 136–46.

3. THE CAMP DAVID ACCORDS, 17 SEPTEMBER 1978

A FRAMEWORK FOR PEACE IN THE MIDDLE EAST

Muhammad Anwar al-Sadat, President of the Arab Republic of Egypt, and Menachem Begin, Prime Minister of Israel, met with Jimmy Carter, President of the United States of America, at Camp David from September 5 to September 17, 1978, and have agreed on the following framework for peace in the Middle East. They invite other parties to the Arab-Israel conflict to adhere to it.

Preamble

The search for peace in the Middle East must be guided by the following:

——The agreed basis for a peaceful settlement of the conflict between Israel and its neighbors is United Nations Security Council Resolution 242, in all its parts.

——After four wars during 30 years, despite intensive human efforts, the Middle East, which is the cradle of civilization and the birthplace of three great religions, does not yet enjoy the blessings of peace. The people of the Middle East yearn for peace so that the vast human and natural resources of the region can be turned to the pursuits of peace and so that this area can become a model for coexistence and cooperation among nations.

——The historic initiative of President Sadat in visiting Jerusalem and the reception accorded to him by the parliament, government and people of Israel, and the reciprocal visit of Prime Minister Begin to Ismailia, the peace proposals made by both leaders, as well as the warm reception of these missions by the peoples of both countries, have created an unprecedented opportunity for peace which must not be lost if this generation and future generations are to be spared the tragedies of war.

——The provisions of the Charter of the United Nations and the other accepted norms of international law and legitimacy now provide accepted standards for the conduct of relations among all states.

——To achieve a relationship of peace, in the spirit of Article 2 of the United Nations Charter, future negotiations between Israel and any neighbor prepared to negotiate peace and security with it are necessary for the purpose of carrying out all the provisions and principles of Resolutions 242 and 338.

——Peace requires respect for the sovereignty, territorial integrity and political independence of every state in the area and their right to live in peace within secure and recognized boundaries free from threats or acts of force. Progress toward that goal can accelerate movement toward a new era of reconciliation in the Middle East marked by cooperation in promoting economic development, in maintaining stability and in assuring security.

—Security is enhanced by a relationship of peace and by cooperation between nations which enjoy normal relations. In addition, under the terms of peace treaties, the parties can, on the basis of reciprocity, agree to special security arrangements such as demilitarized zones, limited armaments areas, early warning stations, the presence of international forces, liaison, agreed measures for monitoring and other arrangements that they agree are useful.

Framework

Taking these factors into account, the parties are determined to reach a just, comprehensive, and durable settlement of the Middle East conflict through the conclusion of peace treaties based on Security Council Resolutions 242 and 338 in all their parts. Their purpose is to achieve peace and good neighborly relations. They recognize that for peace to endure, it must involve all those who have been most deeply affected by the conflict. They therefore agree that this framework, as appropriate, is intended by them to constitute a basis for peace not only between Egypt and Israel, but also between Israel and each of its other neighbors which is prepared to negotiate peace with Israel on this basis. With that objective in mind, they have agreed to proceed as follows:

A. West Bank and Gaza

1. Egypt, Israel, Jordan and the representatives of the Palestinian people should participate in negotiations on the resolution of the Palestinian problem in all its aspects. To achieve that objective, negotiations relating to the West Bank and Gaza should proceed in three stages:

(a) Egypt and Israel agree that, in order to ensure a peaceful and orderly transfer of authority, and taking into account the security concerns of all the parties, there should be transitional arrangements for the West Bank and Gaza for a period not exceeding five years. In order to provide full autonomy to the inhabitants, under these arrangements the Israeli military government and its civilian administration will be withdrawn as soon as a self-governing authority has been freely elected by the inhabitants of these areas to replace the existing military government. To negotiate the details of a transitional arrangement, Jordan will be invited to join the negotiations on the basis of this framework. These new arrangements should give due consideration both to the principle of self-government by the inhabitants of these territories and to the legitimate security concerns of the parties involved.

(b) Egypt, Israel, and Jordan will agree on the modalities for establishing the elected self-governing authority in the West Bank and Gaza. The delegations of Egypt and Jordan may include Palestinians from the West Bank and Gaza or other Palestinians as mutually agreed. The parties will negotiate an agreement which will define the powers and responsibilities of the self-governing authority to be exercised in the West Bank and Gaza. A withdrawal of Israeli armed forces will take place and there will be a redeployment of the remaining Israeli forces into specified security locations. The agreement will also include arrangements for assuring internal and external security and public order. A strong local police force will be established, which may include Jordanian citizens. In addition, Israeli and Jordanian forces will participate in joint patrols and in the manning of control posts to assure the security of the borders.

(c) When the self-governing authority (administrative council) in the West Bank and Gaza is established and inaugurated, the transitional period of five years will begin. As soon as possible, but not later than the third year after the beginning of the transitional period, negotiations will take place to determine the final status of the West Bank and Gaza and its relationship with its neighbors and to conclude a peace treaty between Israel and Jordan by the end of the transitional period. These negotiations will be conducted among Egypt, Israel, Jordan and the elected representatives of the inhabitants of the West Bank and Gaza. Two separate but related committees will be convened, one committee, consisting of representatives of the four parties which will negotiate and agree on the final status of the West Bank and Gaza, and its relationship with its neighbors, and the second committee, consisting of representatives of Israel and representatives of Jordan to be joined by the elected representatives of the inhabitants of the West Bank and Gaza, to negotiate the peace treaty between Israel and Jordan, taking into account the agreement reached in the final status of the West Bank and Gaza. The negotiations shall be based on all the provisions and principles of UN Security Council Resolution 242. The negotiations will resolve, among other matters, the location of the boundaries and the nature of the security arrangements. The solution from the negotiations must also recognize the legitimate right of the Palestinian people and their just requirements. In this way, the Palestinians will participate in the determination of their own future through:

(1) The negotiations among Egypt, Israel, Jordan and the representatives of the inhabitants of the West Bank and Gaza to agree on the final status of the West Bank and Gaza and other outstanding issues by the end of the transitional period.

(2) Submitting their agreements to a vote by the elected representatives of the inhabitants of the West Bank and Gaza.

(3) Providing for the elected representatives of the inhabitants of the West Bank and Gaza to decide how they shall govern themselves consistent with the provisions of their agreement.

(4) Participating as stated above in the work of the committee negotiating the peace treaty between Israel and Jordan.

2. All necessary measures will be taken and provisions made to assure the security of Israel and its neighbors during the transitional period and beyond. To assist in providing such security, a strong local police force will be constituted by the self-governing authority. It will be composed of inhabitants of the West Bank and Gaza. The police will maintain liaison on internal security matters with the designated Israeli, Jordanian, and Egyptian officers.

3. During the transitional period, representatives of Egypt, Israel, Jordan, and the self-governing authority will constitute a continuing committee to decide by agreement on the modalities of admission of persons displaced from the West Bank and Gaza in 1967, together with necessary measures to prevent disruption and disorder. Other matters of common concern may also be dealt with by this committee.

4. Egypt and Israel will work with each other and with other interested parties to establish agreed procedures for a prompt, just and permanent implementation of the resolution of the refugee problem.

B. Egypt-Israel

1. Egypt and Israel undertake not to resort to the threat or the use of force to settle disputes. Any disputes shall be settled by peaceful means in accordance with the provisions of Article 33 of the Charter of the United Nations.

2. In order to achieve peace between them, the parties agree to negotiate in good faith with a goal of concluding within three months from the signing of the Framework a peace treaty between them, while inviting the other parties to the conflict to proceed simultaneously to negotiate and conclude similar peace treaties with a view to achieving a comprehensive peace in the area. The Framework for the Conclusion of a Peace Treaty between Egypt and Israel will govern the peace negotiations between them. The parties will agree on the modalities and the timetable for the implementation of their obligations under the treaty.

C. Associated Principles

1. Egypt and Israel state that the principles and provisions described below should apply to peace treaties between Israel and each of its neighbors—Egypt, Jordan, Syria and Lebanon.

2. Signatories shall establish among themselves relationships normal to

states at peace with one another. To this end, they should undertake to abide by all the provisions of the Charter of the United Nations. Steps to be taken in this respect include:

(a) full recognition;

(b) abolishing economic boycotts;

(c) guaranteeing that under their jurisdiction the citizens of the other parties shall enjoy the protection of the due process of law.

3. Signatories should explore possibilities for economic development in the context of final peace treaties, with the objective of contributing to the atmosphere of peace, cooperation and friendship which is their common goal.

4. Claims commissions may be established for the mutual settlement of all financial claims.

5. The United States shall be invited to participate in the talks on matters related to the modalities of the implementation of the agreements and working out the timetable for the carrying out of the obligations of the parties.

6. The United Nations Security Council shall be requested to endorse the peace treaties and ensure that their provisions shall not be violated. The permanent members of the Security Council shall be requested to underwrite the peace treaties and ensure respect for the provisions. They shall be requested to conform their policies and actions with the undertaking contained in this Framework.

For the Government of Israel: [signed] *Menachem Begin*

For the Government of the Arab Republic of Egypt:
[signed] *Mohamed Anwar El Sadat*

Witnessed by: [signed] *Jimmy Carter*
President of the United States of America

A FRAMEWORK FOR THE CONCLUSION OF A PEACE TREATY BETWEEN EGYPT AND ISRAEL

In order to achieve peace between them, Israel and Egypt agree to negotiate in good faith with a goal of concluding within three months of the signing of this framework a peace treaty between them:

It is agreed that:

The site of the negotiations will be under a United Nations flag at a location or locations to be mutually agreed.

All of the principles of UN Resolution 242 will apply in this resolution of the dispute between Israel and Egypt.

Unless otherwise mutually agreed, terms of the peace treaty will be implemented between two and three years after the peace treaty is signed.

The following matters are agreed between the parties:

(a) the full exercise of Egyptian sovereignty up to the internationally recognized border between Egypt and mandated Palestine;

(b) the withdrawal of Israeli armed forces from the Sinai;

(c) the use of airfields left by the Israelis near al-Arish, Rafah, Ras en-Naqb, and Sharm el-Sheikh for civilian purposes only, including possible commercial use only by all nations;

(d) the right of free passage by ships of Israel through the Gulf of Suez and the Suez Canal on the basis of the Constantinople Convention of 1888 applying to all nations; the Strait of Tiran and Gulf of Aqaba are international waterways to be open to all nations for unimpeded and nonsuspendable freedom of navigation and overflight;

(e) the construction of a highway between the Sinai and Jordan near Eilat with guaranteed free and peaceful passage by Egypt and Jordan; and

(f) the stationing of military forces listed below.

Stationing of Forces

A. No more than one division (mechanized or infantry) of Egyptian armed forces will be stationed within an area lying approximately 50 km. (30 miles) east of the Gulf of Suez and the Suez Canal.

B. Only United Nations forces and civil police equipped with light weapons to perform normal police functions will be stationed within an area lying west of the international border and the Gulf of Aqaba, varying in width from 20 km. (12 miles) to 40 km. (24 miles).

C. In the area within 3 km. (1.8 miles) east of the international border there will be Israeli limited military forces not to exceed four infantry battalions and United Nations observers.

D. Border patrol units not to exceed three battalions will supplement the civil police in maintaining order in the area not included above.

The exact demarcation of the above areas will be as decided during the peace negotiations.

Early warning stations may exist to insure compliance with the terms of the agreement.

United Nations forces will be stationed: (a) in part of the area in the Sinai lying within about 20 km. of the Mediterranean Sea and adjacent to the international border, and (b) in the Sharm el-Sheikh area to insure freedom of passage through the Strait of Tiran; and these forces will not be removed unless such removal is approved by the Security Council of the United Nations with a unanimous vote of the five permanent members.

After a peace treaty is signed, and after the interim withdrawal is complete, normal relations will be established between Egypt and Israel, including full recognition, including diplomatic, economic and cultural relations; termination of economic boycotts and barriers to the free movement of goods and people; and mutual protection of citizens by the due process of law.

Interim Withdrawal

Between three months and nine months after the signing of the peace treaty, all Israeli forces will withdraw east of a line extending from a point east of El-Arish to Ras Muhammad, the exact location of this line to be determined by mutual agreement.

For the Government of the Arab Republic of Egypt:
A. Sadat

For the Government of Israel:
M. Begin

Witnessed by: *Jimmy Carter*
President of the United States of America

LETTER FROM ISRAELI PRIME MINISTER MENACHEM BEGIN TO PRESIDENT JIMMY CARTER, 17 SEPTEMBER 1978

Dear Mr. President:
I have the honor to inform you that during two weeks after my return home I will submit a motion before Israel's Parliament (the Knesset) to decide on the following question:

If during the negotiations to conclude a peace treaty between Israel and Egypt all outstanding issues are agreed upon, "are you in favor of the removal of the Israeli settlers from the northern and southern Sinai areas or are you in favor of keeping the aforementioned settlers in those areas?"

The vote, Mr. President, on this issue will be completely free from the usual Parliamentary Party discipline to the effect that although the coalition is being now supported by 70 members out of 120, every member of the Knesset, as I believe, both on the Government and the Opposition benches will be enabled to vote in accordance with his own conscience.

Sincerely yours,
Menachem Begin

LETTER FROM PRESIDENT JIMMY CARTER TO EGYPTIAN PRESIDENT ANWAR EL SADAT, 22 SEPTEMBER 1978

Dear Mr. President:
I transmit herewith a copy of a letter to me from Prime Minister Begin

setting forth how he proposes to present the issue of the Sinai settlements to the Knesset for the latter's decision.

In this connection, I understand from your letter that Knesset approval to withdraw all Israeli settlers from Sinai according to a timetable within the period specified for the implementation of the peace treaty is a prerequisite to any negotiations on a peace treaty between Egypt and Israel.

Sincerely,

Jimmy Carter

Enclosure:
Letter from Prime Minister Begin

LETTER FROM EGYPTIAN PRESIDENT ANWAR EL SADAT TO PRESIDENT JIMMY CARTER, 17 SEPTEMBER 1978

Dear Mr. President:

In connection with the "Framework for a Settlement in Sinai" to be signed tonight, I would like to reaffirm the position of the Arab Republic of Egypt with respect to the settlements:

1. All Israeli settlers must be withdrawn from Sinai according to a timetable within the period specified for the implementation of the peace treaty.

2. Agreement by the Israeli Government and its constitutional institutions to this basic principle is therefore a prerequisite to starting peace negotiations for concluding a peace treaty.

3. If Israel fails to meet this commitment, the "Framework" shall be void and invalid.

Sincerely,

Mohamed Anwar El Sadat

LETTER FROM PRESIDENT JIMMY CARTER TO ISRAELI PRIME MINISTER MENACHEM BEGIN, 22 SEPTEMBER 1978

Dear Mr. Prime Minister:

I have received your letter of September 17, 1978, describing how you intend to place the question of the future of Israeli settlements in Sinai before the Knesset for its decision.

Enclosed is a copy of President Sadat's letter to me on this subject.

Sincerely,

Jimmy Carter

Enclosure:
Letter from President Sadat

LETTER FROM EGYPTIAN PRESIDENT ANWAR EL SADAT TO PRESIDENT JIMMY CARTER, 17 SEPTEMBER 1978

Dear Mr. President:
I am writing you to reaffirm the position of the Arab Republic of Egypt with respect to Jerusalem:

1. Arab Jerusalem is an integral part of the West Bank. Legal and historical Arab rights in the City must be respected and restored.
2. Arab Jerusalem should be under Arab sovereignty.
3. The Palestinian inhabitants of Arab Jerusalem are entitled to exercise their legitimate national rights, being part of the Palestinian People in the West Bank.
4. Relevant Security Council Resolutions, particularly Resolutions 242 and 267, must be applied with regard to Jerusalem. All the measures taken by Israel to alter the status of the City are null and void and should be rescinded.
5. All peoples must have free access to the City and enjoy the free exercise of worship and the right to visit and transit to the holy places without distinction or discrimination.
6. The holy places of each faith may be placed under the administration and control of their representatives.
7. Essential functions in the City should be undivided and a joint municipal council composed of an equal number of Arab and Israeli members can supervise the carrying out of these functions. In this way, the City shall be undivided.

Sincerely,

Mohamed Anwar El Sadat

LETTER FROM ISRAELI PRIME MINISTER MENACHEM BEGIN TO PRESIDENT JIMMY CARTER, 17 SEPTEMBER 1978

Dear Mr. President:
I have the honor to inform you, Mr. President, that on 28 June 1967—Israel's Parliament (The Knesset) promulgated and adopted a law to the effect: "the Government is empowered by a decree to apply the law, the jurisdiction and administration of the State to any part of Eretz Israel (land of Israel—Palestine), as stated in that decree."

On the basis of this law, the Government of Israel decreed in July 1967 that Jerusalem is one city indivisible, the Capital of the State of Israel.

Sincerely,

Menachem Begin

LETTER FROM PRESIDENT JIMMY CARTER TO EGYPTIAN PRESIDENT ANWAR EL SADAT, 22 SEPTEMBER 1978

Dear Mr. President:

I have received your letter of September 17, 1978, setting forth the Egyptian position on Jerusalem. I am transmitting a copy of that letter to Prime Minister Begin for his information.

The position of the United States on Jerusalem remains as stated by Ambassador Goldberg in the United Nations General Assembly on July 14, 1967, and subsequently by Ambassador Yost in the United Nations Security Council on July 1, 1969.

Sincerely,

Jimmy Carter

LETTER FROM EGYPTIAN PRESIDENT ANWAR EL SADAT TO PRESIDENT JIMMY CARTER, 17 SEPTEMBER 1978

Dear Mr. President:

In connection with the "Framework for Peace in the Middle East," I am writing you this letter to inform you of the position of the Arab Republic of Egypt, with respect to the implementation of the comprehensive settlement.

To ensure the implementation of the provisions related to the West Bank and Gaza and in order to safeguard the legitimate rights of the Palestinian people, Egypt will be prepared to assume the Arab role emanating from these provisions, following consultations with Jordan and the representatives of the Palestinian people.

Sincerely,

Mohamed Anwar El Sadat

LETTER FROM PRESIDENT JIMMY CARTER TO ISRAELI PRIME MINISTER MENACHEM BEGIN, 22 SEPTEMBER 1978

Dear Mr. Prime Minister:

I hereby acknowledge that you have informed me as follows:

A) In each paragraph of the Agreed Framework Document the expressions "Palestinians" or "Palestinian People" are being and will be construed and understood by you as "Palestinian Arabs." B) In each paragraph in which the expression "West Bank" appears, it is being, and will be, understood by the Government of Israel as Judea and Samaria.

Sincerely,

Jimmy Carter

LETTER FROM SECRETARY OF DEFENSE HAROLD BROWN TO ISRAELI DEFENSE MINISTER EZER WEIZMAN, ACCOMPANYING THE DOCUMENTS AGREED TO AT CAMP DAVID, RELEASED 29 SEPTEMBER 1978

September 28, 1978

Dear Mr. Minister:

The US understands that, in connection with carrying out the agreements reached at Camp David, Israel intends to build two military airbases at appropriate sites in the Negev to replace the airbases at Eitam and Etzion which will be evacuated by Israel in accordance with the peace treaty to be concluded between Egypt and Israel. We also understand the special urgency and priority which Israel attaches to preparing the new bases in light of its conviction that it cannot safely leave the Sinai airbases until the new ones are operational.

I suggest that our two governments consult on the scope and costs of the two new airbases as well as on related forms of assistance which the United States might appropriately provide in light of the special problems which may be presented by carrying out such a project on an urgent basis. The President is prepared to seek the necessary Congressional approvals for such assistance as may be agreed upon by the US side as a result of such consultations.

Harold Brown

Sources: Quandt, *Camp David*, 376–87; MFA.

4. TREATY OF PEACE BETWEEN THE ARAB REPUBLIC OF EGYPT AND THE STATE OF ISRAEL, 26 MARCH 1979

The Government of the Arab Republic of Egypt and the Government of the State of Israel;

PREAMBLE

Convinced of the urgent necessity of the establishment of a just, comprehensive and lasting peace in the Middle East in accordance with Security Council Resolutions 242 and 338;
Reaffirming their adherence to the "Framework for Peace in the Middle East Agreed at Camp David," dated September 17, 1978;
Noting that the aforementioned Framework as appropriate is intended to constitute a basis for peace not only between Egypt and Israel but also between Israel and each of its other Arab neighbors which is prepared to negotiate peace with it on this basis;
Desiring to bring to an end the state of war between them and to establish a peace in which every state in the area can live in security;
Convinced that the conclusion of a Treaty of Peace between Egypt and Israel is an important step in the search for comprehensive peace in the area and for the attainment of the settlement of the Arab-Israeli conflict in all its aspects;
Inviting the other Arab parties to this dispute to join the peace process with Israel guided by and based on the principles of the aforementioned Framework;
Desiring as well to develop friendly relations and cooperation between themselves in accordance with the United Nations Charter and the principles of international law governing international relations in times of peace;
Agree to the following provisions in the free exercise of their sovereignty, in order to implement the "Framework for the Conclusion of a Peace Treaty Between Egypt and Israel":

ARTICLE I

1. The state of war between the Parties will be terminated and peace will be established between them upon the exchange of instruments of ratification of this Treaty.
2. Israel will withdraw all its armed forces and civilians from the Sinai behind the international boundary between Egypt and mandated Palestine, as provided in the annexed protocol (Annex I [not reprinted]), and Egypt will resume the exercise of its full sovereignty over the Sinai.
3. Upon completion of the interim withdrawal provided for in Annex I, the

parties will establish normal and friendly relations, in accordance with Article III (3).

ARTICLE II

The permanent boundary between Egypt and Israel is the recognized international boundary between Egypt and the former mandated territory of Palestine, as shown on the map at Annex II [not reprinted], without prejudice to the issue of the status of the Gaza Strip. The Parties recognize this boundary as inviolable. Each will respect the territorial integrity of the other, including their territorial waters and airspace.

ARTICLE III

1. The Parties will apply between them the provisions of the Charter of the United Nations and the principles of international law governing relations among states in times of peace. In particular:

a. They recognize and will respect each other's sovereignty, territorial integrity and political independence;

b. They recognize and will respect each other's right to live in peace within their secure and recognized boundaries;

c. They will refrain from the threat or use of force, directly or indirectly, against each other and will settle all disputes between them by peaceful means.

2. Each Party undertakes to ensure that acts or threats of belligerency, hostility, or violence do not originate from and are not committed from within its territory, or by any forces subject to its control or by any other forces stationed on its territory, against the population, citizens or property of the other Party. Each Party also undertakes to refrain from organizing, instigating, inciting, assisting or participating in acts or threats of belligerency, hostility, subversion or violence against the other Party, anywhere, and undertakes to ensure that perpetrators of such acts are brought to justice.

3. The Parties agree that the normal relationship established between them will include full recognition, diplomatic, economic and cultural relations, termination of economic boycotts and discriminatory barriers to the free movement of people and goods, and will guarantee the mutual enjoyment by citizens of the due process of law. The process by which they undertake to achieve such a relationship parallel to the implementation of other provisions of this Treaty is set out in the annexed protocol (Annex III [not reprinted]).

ARTICLE IV

1. In order to provide maximum security for both Parties on the basis of reciprocity, agreed security arrangements will be established including

limited force zones in Egyptian and Israeli territory, and United Nations forces and observers, described in detail as to nature and timing in Annex I, and other security arrangements the Parties may agree upon.
2. The Parties agree to the stationing of United Nations personnel in areas described in Annex I. The Parties agree not to request withdrawal of the United Nations personnel and that these personnel will not be removed unless such removal is approved by the Security Council of the United Nations, with the affirmative vote of the five Permanent Members, unless the Parties otherwise agree.
3. A Joint Commission will be established to facilitate the implementation of the Treaty, as provided for in Annex I.
4. The security arrangements provided for in paragraphs 1 and 2 of this Article may at the request of either party be reviewed and amended by mutual agreement of the Parties.

ARTICLE V

1. Ships of Israel, and cargoes destined for or coming from Israel, shall enjoy the right of free passage through the Suez Canal and its approaches through the Gulf of Suez and the Mediterranean Sea on the basis of the Constantinople Convention of 1888, applying to all nations. Israeli nationals, vessels and cargoes, as well as persons, vessels and cargoes destined for or coming from Israel, shall be accorded non-discriminatory treatment in all matters connected with usage of the canal.
2. The Parties consider the Strait of Tiran and the Gulf of Aqaba to be international waterways open to all nations for unimpeded and non-suspendable freedom of navigation and overflight. The parties will respect each other's right to navigation and overflight for access to either country through the Strait of Tiran and the Gulf of Aqaba.

ARTICLE VI

1. This Treaty does not affect and shall not be interpreted as affecting in any way the rights and obligations of the Parties under the Charter of the United Nations.
2. The Parties undertake to fulfill in good faith their obligations under this Treaty, without regard to action or inaction of any other party and independently of any instrument external to this Treaty.
3. They further undertake to take all the necessary measures for the application in their relations of the provisions of the multilateral conventions to which they are parties, including the submission of appropriate notification to the Secretary General of the United Nations and other depositaries of such conventions.
4. The Parties undertake not to enter into any obligations in conflict with this Treaty.

5. Subject to Article 103 of the United Nations Charter, in the event of a conflict between the obligation of the Parties under the present Treaty and any of their other obligations, the obligations under this Treaty will be binding and implemented.

ARTICLE VII

1. Disputes arising out of the application or interpretation of this Treaty shall be resolved by negotiations.
2. Any such disputes which cannot be settled by negotiations shall be resolved by conciliation or submitted to arbitration.

ARTICLE VIII

The Parties agree to establish a claims commission for the mutual settlement of all financial claims.

ARTICLE IX

1. This Treaty shall enter into force upon exchange of instruments of ratification.
2. This Treaty supersedes the Agreement between Egypt and Israel of September, 1975.
3. All protocols, annexes, and maps attached to this Treaty shall be regarded as an integral part hereof.
4. The Treaty shall be communicated to the Secretary General of the United Nations for registration in accordance with the provisions of Article 102 of the Charter of the United Nations.

Done at Washington, DC, this 26th day of March, 1979, in triplicate in the English, Arabic and Hebrew languages, each text being equally authentic. In case of any divergence of interpretation, the English text shall prevail.

For the Government of the Arab Republic of Egypt:
A. Sadat

For the Government of Israel: *M. Begin*

Witnessed by: *Jimmy Carter*
President of the United States of America

Sources: Quandt, *Camp David*, 397–401; MFA.

5. THE REAGAN PEACE PLAN AND "TALKING POINTS," 1 AND 8 SEPTEMBER 1982

THE REAGAN PEACE PLAN, 1 SEPTEMBER 1982

Today has been a day that should make all of us proud. It marked the end of the successful evacuation of the PLO from Beirut, Lebanon. This peaceful step could never have been taken without the good offices of the United States and, especially, the truly heroic work of a great American diplomat, Phillip Habib. Thanks to his efforts, I am happy to announce that the US Marine contingent helping to supervise the evacuation has accomplished its mission.

Our young men should be out of Lebanon within two weeks. They, too, have served the cause of peace with distinction and we can all be very proud of them.

But the situation in Lebanon is only part of the overall problem of the conflict in the Middle East. So, over the past weeks, while events in Beirut dominated the front page, America was engaged in a quiet behind-the-scenes effort to lay the groundwork for a broader peace in the region. For once, there were no premature leaks as US diplomatic missions travelled to mid-East capitals and I met here at home with a wide range of experts to map out an American peace initiative for the long-suffering peoples of the Middle East, Arab and Israeli alike.

It seemed to me that, with the agreement in Lebanon, we had an opportunity for a more far-reaching peace effort in the region—and I was determined to seize the moment. In the words of the Scripture, the time had come to "Follow after the things which make for peace."

Tonight, I want to report to you on the steps we have taken, and the prospects they can open up for a just and lasting peace in the Middle East.

America has long been committed to bringing peace to this troubled region. For more than a generation, successive US Administrations have endeavored to develop a fair and workable process that could lead to a true and lasting Arab-Israeli peace. Our involvement in the search for mid-East peace is not a matter of preference, it is a moral imperative. The strategic importance of the region to the US is well known.

But our policy is motivated by more than strategic interests. We also have an irreversible commitment to the survival and territorial integrity of friendly states. Nor can we ignore the fact that the well-being of much of the world's economy is tied to stability in the strife-torn Middle East. Finally, our traditional humanitarian concerns dictate a continuing effort to peacefully resolve conflicts.

When our Administration assumed office in January 1981, I decided that the general framework for our Middle East policy should follow the broad guidelines laid down by my predecessors.

There were two basic issues we had to address. First, there was the strategic threat to the region posed by the Soviet Union and its surrogates, best demonstrated by the brutal war in Afghanistan; and, second, the peace process between Israel and its Arab neighbors. With regard to the Soviet threat, we have strengthened our efforts to develop with our friends and allies a joint policy to deter the Soviets and their surrogates from further expansion in the region, and, if necessary, to defend against it. With respect to the Arab-Israeli conflict, we have embraced the Camp David framework as the only way to proceed. We have also recognized, however, that solving the Arab-Israeli conflict, in and of itself, cannot assure peace throughout a region as vast and troubled as the Middle East.

Our first objective under the Camp David process was to ensure the successful fulfillment of the Egyptian-Israeli peace treaty. This was achieved with the peaceful return of the Sinai to Egypt in April 1982. To accomplish this, we worked hard with our Egyptian and Israeli friends, and eventually with other friendly countries, to create the multinational force which now operates in the Sinai.

Throughout this period of difficult and time-consuming negotiations, we never lost sight of the next step of Camp David: autonomy talks to pave the way for permitting the Palestinian people to exercise their legitimate rights. However, owing to the tragic assassination of President Sadat and other crises in the area, it was not until January 1982 that we were able to make a major effort to renew these talks. Secretary of State Haig and Ambassador Fairbanks made three visits to Israel and Egypt this year to pursue the autonomy talks. Considerable progress was made in developing the basic outline of an American approach which was to be presented to Egypt and Israel after April.

The successful completion of Israel's withdrawal from Sinai and the courage shown on this occasion by Prime Minister Begin and President Mubarak in living up to their agreements convinced me the time had come for a new American policy to try to bridge the remaining differences between Egypt and Israel on the autonomy process. So, in May, I called for specific measures and a timetable for consultations with the governments of Egypt and Israel on the next steps in the peace process. However, before this effort could be launched, the conflict in Lebanon preempted our efforts. The autonomy talks were basically put on hold while we sought to untangle the parties in Lebanon and still the guns of war.

The Lebanon war, tragic as it was, has left us with a new opportunity for Middle East peace. We must seize it now and bring peace to this troubled area so vital to world stability while there is still time. It was with this strong conviction that over a month ago, before the present negotiations in Beirut had been completed, I directed Secretary of State Shultz to again review our policy and to consult a wide range of outstanding Americans on the best ways to strengthen chances for peace in the Middle East. We have consulted with many officials who were historically involved in the process, with members of Congress, and with individuals from the private sector, and I have held extensive consultations with my own advisors on the principles I will outline to you tonight.

The evacuation of the PLO from Beirut is now complete. And we can now help the Lebanese to rebuild their war-torn country. We owe it to ourselves, and to posterity, to move quickly to build upon this achievement. A stable and revived Lebanon is essential to all our hopes for peace in the region. The people of Lebanon deserve the best efforts of the international community to turn the nightmares of the past several years into a new dawn of hope.

But the opportunities for peace in the Middle East do not begin and end in Lebanon. As we help Lebanon rebuild, we must also move to resolve the root causes of conflict between Arabs and Israelis.

The war in Lebanon has demonstrated many things, but two consequences are key to the peace process:

First, the military losses of the PLO have not diminished the yearning of the Palestinian people for a just solution of their claims; and second, while Israel's military successes in Lebanon have demonstrated that its armed forces are second to none in the region, they alone cannot bring just and lasting peace to Israel and her neighbors.

The question now is how to reconcile Israel's legitimate security concerns with the legitimate rights of the Palestinians. And that answer can only come at the negotiating table. Each party must recognize that the outcome must be acceptable to all and that true peace will require compromises by all.

So, tonight, I am calling for a fresh start. This is the moment for all those directly concerned to get involved—or lend their support—to a workable basis for peace. The Camp David Agreement remains the foundation of our policy. Its language provides all parties with the leeway they need for successful negotiations.

I call on Israel to make clear that the security for which she yearns can only be achieved through genuine peace, a peace requiring magnanimity, vision and courage.

I call on the Palestinian people to recognize that their own political aspirations are inextricably bound to recognition of Israel's right to a secure future.

And I call on the Arab States to accept the reality of Israel—and the reality that peace and justice can be gained only through hard, fair, direct negotiations.

In making these calls upon others, I recognize that the United States has a special responsibility. No other nation is in a position to deal with the key parties to the conflict on the basis of trust and reliability.

The time has come for a new realism on the part of all the peoples of the Middle East. The state of Israel is an accomplished fact; it deserves unchallenged legitimacy within the community of nations. But Israel's legitimacy has thus far been recognized by too few countries, and has been denied by every Arab State except Egypt. Israel exists; it has a right to exist in peace behind secure and defensible borders, and it has a right to demand of its neighbors that they recognize those facts.

I have personally followed and supported Israel's heroic struggle for survival ever since the founding of the state of Israel 34 years ago. In the pre-1967 borders, Israel was barely 10 miles wide at its narrowest point. The bulk of Israel's population lived within artillery range of hostile Arab armies. I am not about to ask Israel to live that way again.

The war in Lebanon has demonstrated another reality in the region. The departure of the Palestinians from Beirut dramatizes more than ever the homelessness of the Palestinian people. Palestinians feel strongly that their cause is more than a question of refugees. I agree. The Camp David Agreement recognized that fact when it spoke of the legitimate rights of the Palestinian people and their just requirements. For peace to endure, it must involve all those who have been most deeply affected by the conflict. Only through the process of negotiation can all the nations of the Middle East achieve a secure peace.

These then are our general goals. What are the specific new American positions, and why are we taking them?

In the Camp David talks thus far, both Israel and Egypt have felt free to express openly their views as to what the outcome should be. Understandably, their views have differed on many points.

The United States has thus far sought to play the role of mediator; we have avoided public comment on the key issues. We have always recognized—and continue to recognize—that only the voluntary agreement of those parties most involved in the conflict can provide an enduring solution. But it has become evident to me that some clearer sense of America's position on the key issues is necessary to encourage wider support for the peace process.

First, as outlined in the Camp David accords, there must be a period of time during which the Palestinian inhabitants of the West Bank and Gaza will have full autonomy over their own affairs. Due consideration must be given to the principle of self-government by the inhabitants of the territories and to the legitimate security concerns of the parties involved.

The purpose of the five-year period of transition which would begin after free elections for a self-governing Palestinian authority is to prove to the Palestinians that they can run their own affairs, and that such Palestinian autonomy poses no threat to Israel's security.

The United States will not support the use of any additional land for the purpose of settlements during the transition period. Indeed, the immediate adoption of a settlement freeze by Israel, more than any other action, could create the confidence needed for wider participation in these talks. Further settlement activity is in no way necessary for the security of Israel and only diminishes the confidence of the Arabs that a final outcome can be freely and fairly negotiated.

I want to make the American position clearly understood: the purpose of this transition period is the peaceful and orderly transfer of domestic authority from Israel to the Palestinian inhabitants of the West Bank and Gaza. At the same time, such a transfer must not interfere with Israel's security requirements.

Beyond the transition period, as we look to the future of the West Bank and Gaza, it is clear to me that peace cannot be achieved by the formation of an independent Palestinian State in those territories. Nor is it achievable on the basis of Israeli sovereignty or permanent control over the West Bank and Gaza.

So the United States will not support the establishment of an independent Palestinian State in the West Bank and Gaza, and we will not support annexation or permanent control by Israel.

There is, however, another way to peace. The final status of these lands must, of course, be reached through the give-and-take of negotiations. But it is the firm view of the United States that self-government by the Palestinians of the West Bank and Gaza in association with Jordan offers the best chance for a durable, just and lasting peace.

We base our approach squarely on the principle that the Arab-Israeli conflict should be resolved through negotiations involving an exchange of territory for peace. This exchange is enshrined in United Nations Security Council Resolution 242, which is, in turn, incorporated in all its parts in the Camp David Agreements. UN Resolution 242 remains wholly valid as the foundation stone of America's Middle East peace effort.

It is the United States' position that—in return for peace—the withdrawal provision of Resolution 242 applies to all fronts, including the West Bank and Gaza.

When the border is negotiated between Jordan and Israel, our view on the extent to which Israel would be asked to give up territory will be heavily affected by the extent of true peace and normalization and the security arrangements offered in return.

Finally, we remain convinced that Jerusalem must remain undivided, but its final status should be decided through negotiations.

In the course of the negotiations to come, the United States will support positions that seem to us fair and reasonable compromises, and likely to promote a sound agreement. We will also put forward our own detailed proposals when we believe they can be helpful. And, make no mistake, the United States will oppose any proposal—from any party and at any point in the negotiating process—that threatens the security of Israel. America's commitment to the security of Israel is iron-clad. And I might add, so is mine.

During the past few days, our ambassadors in Israel, Egypt, Jordan, and Saudi Arabia have presented to their host governments the proposals in full detail that I have outlined here tonight.

I am convinced that these proposals can bring justice, bring security, and bring durability to an Arab-Israeli peace.

The United States will stand by these principles with total dedication.

They are fully consistent with Israel's security requirements and the aspirations of the Palestinians. We will work hard to broaden participation at the peace table as envisaged by the Camp David accords. And I fervently hope that the Palestinians and Jordan, with the support of their Arab colleagues, will accept this opportunity.

Tragic turmoil in the Middle East runs back to the dawn of history. In our modern day, conflict after conflict has taken its brutal toll there. In an age of nuclear challenge and economic interdependence, such conflicts are a threat to all the people of the world, not just the Middle East itself. It is time for us all—in the Middle East and around the world—to call a halt to conflict, hatred and prejudice; it is time for us all to launch a common effort for reconstruction, peace and progress.

It has often been said—and regrettably too often been true—that the story of the search for peace and justice in the Middle East is a tragedy of opportunities missed.

In the aftermath of the settlement in Lebanon we now face an opportunity for a broader peace. This time we must not let it slip from our grasp. We must look beyond the difficulties and obstacles of the present and move with fairness and resolve toward a brighter future. We owe it to ourselves—and to posterity—to do no less. For if we miss this chance to make a fresh start, we may look back on this moment from some later vantage point and realize how much that failure cost us all.

These, then, are the principles upon which America policy towards the Arab-Israeli conflict will be based. I have made a personal commitment to see that they endure and, God willing, that they will come to be seen by all reasonable, compassionate people as fair, achievable, and in the interests of all who wish to see peace in the Middle East.

Tonight, on the eve of what can be a dawning of new hope for the people of the troubled Middle East—and for all the world's people who dream of a just and peaceful future—I ask you, my fellow Americans, for your support and your prayers in this great undertaking.

"TALKING POINTS" SENT TO PRIME MINISTER BEGIN BY PRESIDENT REAGAN, WASHINGTON, DC, 8 SEPTEMBER 1982

General Principles

A. We will maintain our commitment to Camp David.

B. We will maintain our commitment to the conditions we require for recognition of and negotiation with the PLO.

C. We can offer guarantees on the position we adopt in negotiations. We will not be able, however, to guarantee in advance the results of these negotiations.

Transitional Measures

A. Our position is that the objective of the transitional period is the peaceful and orderly transfer of authority from Israel to the Palestinian inhabitants.

B. We will support:

• The decision of full autonomy as giving the Palestinian inhabitants real authority over themselves, the land and its resources, subject to fair safeguards on water.

• Economic, commercial, social and cultural ties between the West Bank, Gaza and Jordan.

• Participation by the Palestinian inhabitants of East Jerusalem in the election of the West Bank–Gaza authority.

• Real settlement freeze.

• Progressive Palestinian responsibility for internal security based on capability and performance.

C. We will oppose:

• Dismantlement of the existing settlements.

• Provisions which represent a legitimate threat to Israel's security, reasonably defined.

• Isolation of the West Bank and Gaza from Israel.

• Measures which accord either the Palestinians or the Israelis generally recognized sovereign rights with the exception of external security, which must remain in Israel's hands during the transitional period.

Final Status Issues

A. UNSC Resolution 242.

It is our position that Resolution 242 applies to the West Bank and Gaza and requires Israeli withdrawal in return for peace. Negotiations must determine the borders. The US position in these negotiations on the extent and nature of the withdrawal will be significantly influenced by the extent and nature of the peace and security arrangements offered in return.

B. Israeli Sovereignty.

It is our belief that the Palestinian problem cannot be resolved (through) Israeli sovereignty or control over the West Bank and Gaza. Accordingly, we will not support such a solution.

C. Palestinian State.

The preference we will pursue in the final status negotiation is association of the West Bank and Gaza with Jordan. We will not support the formation of a Palestinian State in those negotiations. There is no foundation of political support in Israel or the United States for such a solution. The outcome, however, must be determined by negotiations.

D. Self-Determination.

In the Middle East context the term self-determination has been identified exclusively with the formation of a Palestinian State. We will not support this definition of self-determination. We believe that the Palestinians must take the leading role in determining their own future and fully support the provision in Camp David providing for the elected representatives of the inhabitants of the West Bank and Gaza to decide how they shall govern themselves consistent with the provision of their agreement in the final status negotiations.

E. Jerusalem.

We will fully support the position that the status of Jerusalem must be determined through negotiations.

F. Settlements

The status of Israeli settlements must be determined in the course of the final status negotiations. We will not support their continuation as extraterritorial outposts.

Additional Talking Points

1. Approach to Hussein

The President has approached Hussein to determine the extent to which he may be interested in participating.

- King Hussein has received the same US positions as you.
- Hussein considers our proposals serious and gives them serious attention.
- Hussein understands that Camp David is the only base that we will accept for negotiations.
- We are also discussing these proposals with the Saudis.

2. Public Commitment

Whatever the support from these or other Arab States, this is what the President has concluded must be done.

The President is convinced his positions are fair and balanced and fully protective of Israel's security. Beyond that they offer the practical opportunity of eventually achieving the peace treaties Israel must have with its neighbors.

He will be making a speech announcing these positions, probably within a week.

3. Next Procedural Steps

Should the response to the President's proposal be positive, the US would take immediate steps to relaunch the autonomy negotiations with the broadest possible participation as envisaged under the Camp David agreements.

We also contemplate an early visit by Secretary Shultz in the area.

Should there not be a positive response, the President, as he has said in his letter to you, will nonetheless stand by his position with proper dedication.

Source: Lukacs, 72–80.

6. THE ISRAEL-LEBANON AGREEMENT, 17 MAY 1983*

The government of the Republic of Lebanon and the government of the State of Israel, . . .

Having agreed to declare the termination of the state of war between them,

Desiring to ensure lasting security for both their states and to avoid threats and the use of force between them,

Desiring to establish their mutual relations in the manner provided for in this agreement, . . .

Have agreed to the following provisions:

ARTICLE 1

1. The parties agree and undertake to respect the sovereignty, political independence and territorial integrity of each other. They consider the existing international boundary between Lebanon and Israel inviolable.
2. The parties confirm that the state of war between Lebanon and Israel has been terminated and no longer exists.
3. Taking into account the provisions of paragraphs 1 and 2, Israel undertakes to withdraw all its armed forces from Lebanon in accordance with the annex of the present agreement.

ARTICLE 2

The parties, being guided by the principles of the Charter of the United Nations and of international law, undertake to settle their disputes by peaceful means in such a manner as to promote international peace and security and justice.

ARTICLE 3

In order to provide maximum security for Lebanon and Israel, the parties agree to establish and implement security arrangements, including the creation of a security region, as provided for in the annex of the present agreement.

ARTICLE 4

1. The territory of each party will not be used as a base for hostile or terrorist activity against the other party, its territory, or its people.
2. Each party will prevent the existence or organization of irregular forces, armed bands, organizations, bases, offices or infrastructure, the aims and

*Excerpts

purposes of which include incursions or any act of terrorism into the territory of the other party, or any other activity aimed at threatening or endangering the security of the other party and safety of its people. To this end, all agreements and arrangements enabling the presence and functioning on the territory of either party of elements hostile to the other party are null and void.

3. Without prejudice to the inherent right of self-defense in accordance with international law, each party will refrain:

A. From organizing, instigating, assisting, or participating in threats or acts of belligerency, subversion, or incitement or any aggression directed against the other party, its population or property, both within its territory and originating therefrom, or in the territory of the other party.

B. From using the territory of the other party for conducting a military attack against the territory of a third state.

C. From intervening in the internal or external affairs of the other party.

4. Each party undertakes to ensure that preventive action and due proceedings will be taken against persons or organizations perpetrating acts in violation of this article.

ARTICLE 5

Consistent with the termination of the state of war and within the framework of their constitutional provisions, the parties will abstain from any form of hostile propaganda against each other.

ARTICLE 6

Each party will prevent entry into, deployment in, or passage through its territory, its air space and, subject to the right of innocent passage in accordance with international law, its territorial sea, by military forces, armament, or military equipment of any state hostile to the other party.

ARTICLE 7

Except as provided in the present agreement, nothing will preclude the deployment on Lebanese territory of international forces requested and accepted by the government of Lebanon to assist in maintaining its authority. New contributors to such forces shall be selected from among states having diplomatic relations with both parties to the present agreement.

ARTICLE 8

1. A. Upon entry into force of the present agreement, a Joint Liaison Committee will be established by the parties, in which the United States of America will be a participant, and will commence its functions. . . .

B. The Joint Liaison Committee will address itself on a continuing basis to the development of mutual relations between Lebanon and Israel, *inter alia* the regulation of the movement of goods, products and persons, communications, etc. . . .
2. During the six-month period after the withdrawal of all Israeli armed forces from Lebanon in accordance with Article 1 of the present agreement and the simultaneous restoration of Lebanese government authority along the international boundary between Lebanon and Israel, and in the light of the termination of the state of war, the parties shall initiate, within the Joint Liaison Committee, *bona fide* negotiations in order to conclude agreements on the movement of goods, products and persons and their implementation on a nondiscriminatory basis. . . .

ANNEX: SECURITY ARRANGEMENTS

A. A security region [in southern Lebanon] in which the government of Lebanon undertakes to implement the security arrangements agreed upon in this annex is hereby established. . . .

The Lebanese authorities will enforce special security measures aimed at detecting and preventing hostile activities as well as the introduction into or movement through the security region of unauthorized armed men or military equipment. . . .

B. Lebanese Police . . . may be stationed in the security region without restrictions as to their numbers. These forces and elements will be equipped only with personal and light automatic weapons. . . .

C. Two Lebanese Army brigades may be stationed in the security region. One will be the Lebanese Army territorial brigade. . . . The other will be a regular Lebanese Army brigade. . . .

D. The existing local units will be integrated as such into the Lebanese Army, in conformity with Lebanese Army regulations. . . .

Source: Laqueur and Rubin, 469–71. Entire text of the Agreement is in Colin Legum et al., eds., *Middle East Contemporary Survey*, vol. 7 (1982–83), New York and London: Holmes and Meier, 1985, pp. 690–97, 758–60.

7. THE HUSSEIN-PERES AGREEMENT (THE LONDON DOCUMENT), 11 APRIL 1987

(Accord between the Government of Jordan, which has confirmed it to the Government of the United States, and the Foreign Minister of Israel, pending the approval of the Government of Israel. Parts "A" and "B," which will be made public upon agreement of the parties, will be treated as proposals of the United States to which Jordan and Israel have agreed. Part "C" is to be treated with great confidentiality, as commitments to the United States from the Government of Jordan to be transmitted to the Government of Israel.)

A THREE-PART UNDERSTANDING BETWEEN JORDAN AND ISRAEL

A. Invitation by the UN secretary general: The UN secretary general will send invitations to the five permanent members of the Security Council and to the parties involved in the Israeli-Arab conflict to negotiate an agreement by peaceful means based on UN Resolutions 242 and 338 with the purpose of attaining comprehensive peace in the region and security for the countries in the area, and granting the Palestinian people their legitimate rights.

B. Decisions of the international conference: The participants in the conference agree that the purpose of the negotiations is to attain by peaceful means an agreement about all the aspects of the Palestinian problem. The conference invites the sides to set up regional bilateral committees to negotiate bilateral issues.

C. Nature of the agreement between Jordan and Israel: Israel and Jordan agree that: 1) the international conference will not impose a solution and will not veto any agreement reached by the sides; 2) the negotiations will be conducted in bilateral committees in a direct manner; 3) the Palestinian issue will be discussed in a meeting of the Jordanian, Palestinian and Israeli delegations; 4) the representatives of the Palestinians will be included in the Jordanian-Palestinian delegation; 5) participation in the conference will be based on acceptance of UN Resolutions 242 and 338 by the sides and the renunciation of violence and terror; 6) each committee will conduct negotiations independently; 7) other issues will be resolved through mutual agreement between Jordan and Israel.

This document of understanding is pending approval of the incumbent governments of Israel and Jordan. The content of this document will be presented and proposed to the United States.

Source: Quandt, *The Middle East*, 475–76

8. US-USSR LETTER OF INVITATION TO THE PEACE TALKS IN MADRID, 18 OCTOBER 1991

After extensive consultations with Arab states, Israel, and the Palestinians, the United States and the Soviet Union believe that an historic opportunity exists to advance the prospects for genuine peace throughout the region. The United States and the Soviet Union are prepared to assist the parties to achieve a just, lasting and comprehensive peace settlement, through direct negotiations along two tracks, between Israel and the Arab states, and between Israel and the Palestinians, based on United Nations Security Council Resolutions 242 and 338. The objective of this process is real peace.

Toward that end, the president of the US and the president of the USSR invite you to a peace conference, which their countries will co-sponsor, followed immediately by direct negotiations. The conference will be convened in Madrid on 30 October 1991.

President Bush and President Gorbachev request your acceptance of this invitation no later than 6 P.M. Washington time, 23 October 1991, in order to ensure proper organization and preparation of the conference.

Direct bilateral negotiations will begin four days after the opening of the conference. Those parties who wish to attend multilateral negotiations will convene two weeks after the opening of the conference to organize those negotiations. The co-sponsors believe that those negotiations should focus on region-wide issues such as arms control and regional security, water, refugee issues, environment, economic development, and other subjects of mutual interest.

The co-sponsors will chair the conference which will be held at ministerial level. Governments to be invited include Israel, Syria, Lebanon and Jordan. Palestinians will be invited and attend as part of a joint Jordanian-Palestinian delegation. Egypt will be invited to the conference as a participant. The European Community will be a participant in the conference, alongside the United States and the Soviet Union and will be represented by its presidency. The Gulf Cooperation Council will be invited to send its secretary-general to the conference as an observer, and GCC member states will be invited to participate in organizing the negotiations on multilateral issues. The United Nations will be invited to send an observer, representing the secretary-general.

The conference will have no power to impose solutions on the parties or veto agreements reached by them. It will have no authority to make decisions for the parties and no ability to vote on issues or results. The conference can reconvene only with the consent of all the parties.

With respect to negotiations between Israel and Palestinians who are part of the joint Jordanian-Palestinian delegation, negotiations will be conducted in phases, beginning with talks on interim self-government arrangements. These talks will be conducted with the objective of reaching agreement within one year. Once agreed the interim self-government arrangements will last for a period of five years. Beginning the third year of the period of interim self-government arrangements, negotiations will take place on permanent status. These permanent status negotiations, and the negotiations between Israel and the Arab states, will take place on the basis of Resolutions 242 and 338.

It is understood that the co-sponsors are committed to making this process succeed. It is their intention to convene the conference and negotiations with those parties who agree to attend.

The co-sponsors believe that this process offers the promise of ending decades of confrontation and conflict and the hope of a lasting peace. Thus, the co-sponsors hope that the parties will approach these negotiations in a spirit of good will and mutual respect. In this way, the peace process can begin to break down the mutual suspicions and mistrust that perpetuate the conflict and allow the parties to begin to resolve their differences. Indeed, only through such a process can real peace and reconciliation among the Arab states, Israel and the Palestinians be achieved. And only through this process can the peoples of the Middle East attain the peace and security they richly deserve.

Sources: IPS, Document A.1, 3–4; MFA.

9. US LETTER OF ASSURANCES TO THE PALESTINIANS, 18 OCTOBER 1991

The Palestinian decision to attend a peace conference to launch direct negotiations with Israel represents an important step in the search for a comprehensive, just and lasting peace in the region. The United States has long believed that Palestinian participation is critical to the success of our efforts.

In the context of the process on which we are embarking, we want to respond to your request for certain assurances related to this process.

These assurances constitute US understandings and intentions concerning the conference and ensuing negotiations. These assurances are consistent with United States policy and do not undermine or contradict United Nations Security Council Resolutions 242 and 338. Moreover, there will be no assurances provided to one party that are not known to all the others. By this we can foster a sense of confidence and minimize chances for misunderstandings.

As President Bush stated in his March 6, 1991 address to Congress, the United States continues to believe firmly that a comprehensive peace must be grounded in United Nations Security Council Resolutions 242 and 338 and the principle of territory for peace. Such an outcome must also provide for security and recognition for all states in the region, including Israel, and for legitimate political rights for the Palestinian people. Anything else, the President noted, would fail the twin tests of fairness and security.

The process we are trying to create offers Palestinians a way to achieve these objectives. The United States believes that there should be an end to the Israeli occupation which can occur only through genuine and meaningful negotiations. The United States also believes that this process should create a new relationship of mutuality where Palestinians and Israelis can respect one another's security, identity, and political rights. We believe Palestinians should gain control over political, economic and other decisions that affect their lives and fate.

Direct bilateral negotiations will begin four days after the opening of the conference; those parties who wish to attend multilateral negotiations will convene two weeks after the opening of the conference to organize those negotiations. In this regard, the United States will support Palestinian involvement in any bilateral or multilateral negotiations on refugees and in all multilateral negotiations. The conference and the negotiations that follow will be based on UN Security Council Resolutions 242 and 338.

The process will proceed along two tracks through direct negotiations between Israel and Arab states and Israel and Palestinians. The United States is determined to achieve a comprehensive settlement of the Arab-Israeli conflict and will do its utmost to ensure that the process moves forward along both tracks toward this end.

In pursuit of a comprehensive settlement, all the negotiations should proceed as quickly as possible toward agreement. For its part, the United States will work for serious negotiations and will also seek to avoid prolongation and stalling by any party.

The conference will be co-sponsored by the United States and the Soviet Union. The European Community will be participant in the conference alongside the United States and the Soviet Union and be represented by its Presidency. The conference can reconvene only with the consent of all the parties.

With regard to the role of the United Nations, the UN Secretary General will send a representative to the conference as an observer. The co-sponsors will keep the Secretary General apprised of the process of the negotiations. Agreements reached between the parties will be registered with the UN Secretariat and reported to the Security Council, and the parties will seek the Council's endorsement of such agreements. Since it is in the interest of all parties for this process to succeed, while this process is actively ongoing, the United States will not support a competing or parallel process in the United Nations Security Council.

The United States does not seek to determine who speaks for Palestinians in this process. We are seeking to launch a political negotiating process that directly involves Palestinians and offers a pathway for achieving the legitimate political rights of the Palestinian people and for participation in the determination of their future. We believe that a joint Jordanian-Palestinian delegation offers the most promising pathway toward this end.

Only Palestinians can choose their delegation members, which are not subject to veto from anyone. The United States understands that members of the delegation will be Palestinians from the territories who agree to negotiations on two tracks, in phases, and who are willing to live in peace with Israel. No party can be forced to sit with anyone it does not want to sit with.

Palestinians will be free to announce their component of the joint delegation and to make a statement during the opening of the conference. They may also raise any issue pertaining to the substance of the negotiations during the negotiations.

The United States understands how much importance Palestinians attach to the question of east Jerusalem. Thus, we want to assure you that nothing Palestinians do in choosing their delegation members in this phase of the process will affect their claim to east Jerusalem, or be prejudicial or precedential to the outcome of negotiations. It remains the firm position of the United States that Jerusalem must never again be a divided city and that its final status should be decided by negotiations. Thus, we do not recognize Israel's annexation of east Jerusalem or the extension of its municipal boundaries, and we encourage all sides to avoid unilateral acts that would exacerbate local tensions or make negotiations more difficult or preempt their final outcome. It is also the United States position that a Palestinian resident in Jordan with ties to a prominent Jerusalem family would be eligible to join the Jordanian side of the delegation.

Furthermore, it is also the United States position that Palestinians of east Jerusalem should be able to participate by voting in the elections for an interim self-governing authority. The United States further believes that Palestinians from east Jerusalem and Palestinians outside the occupied territories who meet the three criteria should be able to participate in the negotiations on final status. And, the United States supports the right of Palestinians to bring any issue, including east Jerusalem, to the table.

Because the issues at stake are so complex and the emotions so deep, the United States has long maintained that a transitional period is required to break down the walls of suspicion and mistrust and lay the basis for sustainable negotiations on the final status of the occupied territories. The purpose of negotiations on transitional arrangements is to effect the peaceful and orderly transfer of authority from Israel to Palestinians. Palestinians need to achieve rapid control over political, economic, and other decisions that affect their lives and to adjust to a new situation in which Palestinians exercise authority in the West Bank and Gaza. For its part, the United States will strive from the outset and encourage all parties to adopt steps that can create an environment of confidence and mutual trust, including respect for human rights.

As you are aware with respect to negotiations between Israel and Palestinians, negotiations will be conducted in phases, beginning with talks on interim self-government arrangements. These talks will be conducted with the objective of reaching agreement within one year. Once agreed, the interim self-government arrangements will last for a period of five years. Beginning the third year of the period of interim self-government arrangements, negotiations will take place on permanent status. It is the aim of the United States that permanent status negotiations will be concluded by the end of the transitional period.

It has long been our position that only direct negotiations based on UN Security Council Resolutions 242 and 338 can produce a real peace. No one can dictate the outcome in advance. The United States understands that Palestinians must be free, in opening statements at the conference and in the negotiations that follow, to raise any issue of importance to them. Thus, Palestinians are free to argue for whatever outcome they believe best meets their requirements. The United States will accept any outcome agreed by the parties. In this regard and consistent with longstanding US policies, confederation is not excluded as a possible outcome of negotiations in final status.

The United States has long believed that no party should take unilateral actions that seek to predetermine issues that can only be resolved through negotiations. In this regard the United States has opposed and will continue to oppose settlement activity in the territories occupied in 1967, which remains an obstacle to peace.

The United States will act as an honest broker in trying to resolve the Arab-Israeli conflict. It is our intention, together with the Soviet Union, to play the role of a driving force in this process to help the parties move forward toward a comprehensive peace. Any party will have access to the co-sponsors at any time. The United States is prepared to participate in all stages of the negotiations, with the consent of the parties to each negotiation.

These are the assurances that the United States is providing concerning the implementation of the initiative we have discussed. We are persuaded that we have a real opportunity to accomplish something very important in the peace process. And we are prepared to work hard together with you in the period ahead to build on the progress we have made. There will be difficult challenges for all parties. But with Palestinians' continued commitment and creativity, we have a real chance of moving to a peace conference and to negotiations and then on toward the broader peace that we all seek.

Source: IPS, Document A.2, 5–8.

10. US LETTER OF ASSURANCES TO ISRAEL, 18 OCTOBER 1991

Israel's decision to attend a peace conference on the Middle East in order to launch direct and bilateral negotiation for peace is an important step that brings Israel closer to the peace and security it so aspires to. Now, it is time for all the sides to take decisions, in order to enable a rapid motion towards a Conference and negotiations. And indeed, only through direct negotiations can real peace and security be achieved.

In the context of the process on which we are embarking, we want to respond to your request for certain assurances related to this process. These assurances constitute the United States understanding and intentions concerning the Conference and the negotiations.

We have made it clear from the beginning that the United States will be ready to supply assurances which fit with our policy and which are not weakening or contradicting the framework we created for the convening of the peace process. We also declared that no assurances will be provided to one party that are not known to all the others.

This process of negotiation is based on the special relations between our two countries which are based on common values and interests and on respect for democracy. Since the creation of the State of Israel the United States has understood that the challenges which Israel faces are tied to the essence of its existence. During quite a long period Israel has been living in a region where its neighbors refused to recognize its existence and tried to destroy it. Therefore, the key for promoting peace has always been the recognition of Israel's security needs and the need for close cooperation between our two countries in order to fulfill these needs.

We assure you that our commitment to Israel's security remains unaltered. Anyone who tries to drive a wedge between us in an attempt to damage this commitment cannot understand the deep ties between our two countries and the character of our commitment to Israel's security, including the commitment to preserve its qualitative advantage. We want to emphasize once again our stand that Israel has the right to secure and defensible borders that should be agreed upon in direct negotiations and that will be acceptable to its neighbors. The United States believes that the aim of this process is a just and lasting peace that will be achieved through talks based on UN Resolutions 242 and 338 including signing peace agreements with full diplomatic relations between Israel and its neighbors.

You and the other parties have informed us that there were various interpretations of Security Council Resolution 242 and they will be presented during the negotiations. In accordance with the United States traditional policy, we do not support the creation of an independent Palestinian State. Neither do we support the continuation of the Israeli rule or annexation of the Occupied Territories.

The Conference will have no power to impose solutions on the parties or to veto the agreements achieved by it. It will not have the power to take decisions nor the right of veto on questions or conclusions. The conference can be reconvened only by agreement of all the parties.

Direct bilateral negotiations will begin 4 days after the opening of the Conference. Those parties who wish to attend multilateral negotiations will convene two weeks after the opening of the Conference to organize those negotiations. The United States supports the participation and the organization of those multilateral negotiations. We believe that the debates should focus on general regional issues such as water, environment, arms control and regional security, economic development, the question of refugees and other issues.

The United States is committed to obtain a comprehensive peace settlement of the Israeli-Arab conflict and will do its utmost to ensure that the process moves forward along both tracks to this end. The United States hopes to enlarge the scope of peace and to include in it other states in the region.

The United States does not support linkage between the various negotiations for achievement of a comprehensive settlement.

The United States believes that no party in the process can be forced to sit with anyone it does not want to sit with. No surprises should occur concerning the nature of the representation in the Conference or in the negotiations. The United States believes that the Palestinians will be represented in a common Jordanian-Palestinian delegation. Palestinian residents of the West Bank and Gaza who agree to the two tracks concept and to negotiation by phases, and who are willing to live in peace with Israel will take part in the delegation and the negotiations on interim arrangements.

Moreover—it is not the United States aim to bring the PLO into the process or to make Israel enter a dialogue or negotiation with the PLO. The United States will act as an honest broker in trying to solve the Israeli-Arab conflict.

The United States believes that a transitional period is required to break down the walls of suspicion and mistrust and lay the basis for negotiation on the final status.

In context of the negotiation between Israel and the Palestinians, the negotiations will be conducted in phases, beginning with talks on interim-arrangements for self-government that will last five years. These talks will be conducted with the objective of reaching agreement within one year. Beginning the third year of the period of interim-arrangements, negotiations will take place on a permanent settlement. In the light of our special relations with Israel, the United States agrees to consult Israel and to take its stands into consideration on the question of the peace process. At the same time the United States reserves their right to declare their traditional stands whenever needed.

You expressed a special concern about the Golan Heights. In this context, the United States continues to stand behind the assurance given by President Ford to Prime Minister Rabin on September 1, 1975, whereby the United States will support the stand that a comprehensive settlement with Syria, concerning a peace treaty, must enforce Israel's security before any attack directed from the Golan Heights.

The United States continues to support the idea that a just and lasting peace must be accepted by the two parties. The United States has not yet elaborated a definite stand on the issue of borders. When it has to do so, it will pay great attention to the Israeli stand whereby any arrangement with Syria should be based on Israel's continued presence on the Golan Heights. In this context, the United States is ready to propose American guarantees for border security arrangements agreed upon between Israel and Syria, according to our constitutional process.

In the context of Lebanon and in accordance with the United States traditional policy, we believe that Israel has the right to security along its northern border. Moreover—the United States remains committed to the withdrawal of all the foreign forces from Lebanon as well as the dismantling of militias.

We continue to see the peace treaty between Israel and Egypt and the ties between them, as the cornerstone of our policy in the region and to support the fulfillment of the peace accords between Israel and Egypt and of its related agreements.

These are the assurances that the United States is providing concerning the implementation of the initiative we have discussed. Through common work, based on the mutual trust that has always characterized our relations, Israel and the United States can advance towards the peace that was denied to Israel for a long period.

Source: IPS, Document A.3, 9–11

11. PRESENTATION OF THE NEW GOVERNMENT, ADDRESS TO THE KNESSET BY PRIME MINISTER YITZHAK RABIN, 13 JULY 1992*

. . . [T]his Government is determined to expend all the energy, to take any path, to do everything necessary, possible, and more, for the sake of national and personal security, to achieve peace and prevent war, to do away with unemployment, for the sake of immigration and absorption, for economic growth, to strengthen the foundations of democracy and the rule of law, to ensure equality for all citizens, and to protect human rights. We are going to change the national order of priorities.

. . . Despite possible differences of opinion among the members of the coalition, which have come from various parts of the political spectrum, the new Government is united by the sense permeating the people of Israel that this is a propitious hour, a time of great possibilities and opportunities that we shall do our utmost not to lose or squander. . . .

. . . [I]n the last decade of the twentieth century, the atlases, history and geography books no longer present an up-to-date picture of the world. Walls of enmity have fallen, borders have disappeared, powers have crumbled and ideologies collapsed, states have been born, states have died and also, the gates of emigration have been flung open. And it is our duty, to ourselves and to our children, to see the new world as it is now—to discern its dangers, explore its prospects, and do everything possible so that the State of Israel will fit into this world whose face is changing. No longer are we necessarily "A people that dwells alone," and no longer is it true that "the whole world is against us." We must overcome the sense of isolation that has held us in its thrall for almost half a century. We must join the international movement toward peace, reconciliation, and cooperation that is spreading over the entire globe these days—lest we be the last to remain, all alone, in the station.

The new Government has accordingly made it a prime goal to promote the making of peace and take vigorous steps that will lead to the conclusion of the Arab-Israeli conflict. We shall do so based on the recognition by the Arab countries, and the Palestinians, that Israel is a sovereign state with a right to live in peace and security. We believe wholeheartedly that peace is possible, that it is imperative, and that it will ensue. "I shall believe in the future," wrote the poet Shaul Tchernihovsky. "Even if it is far off, the day will come when peace and blessings are borne from nation to nation"—and I want to believe that that day is not far off.

The Government will propose to the Arab states and the Palestinians the continuation of the peace talks based upon the framework forged at the Madrid Conference. As a first step toward a permanent solution we shall

*Excerpts

discuss the institution of autonomy in Judea, Samaria, and the Gaza District. We do not intend to lose precious time. The Government's first directive to the negotiating teams will be to step up the talks and hold ongoing discussions between the sides. Within a short time we shall renew the talks in order to diminish the flame of enmity between the Palestinians and the State of Israel.

As a first step, to illustrate our sincerity and good will, I wish to invite the Jordanian-Palestinian delegation to an informal talk, here in Jerusalem, so that we can hear their views, make ours heard, and create an appropriate atmosphere for neighborly relations.

To you, the Palestinians in the territories, I wish to say from this rostrum—We have been fated to live together on the same patch of land, in the same country. We lead our lives with you, beside you and against you. You have failed in the war against us. One hundred years of your bloodshed and terror against us have brought you only suffering, humiliation, bereavement, and pain. You have lost thousands of your sons and daughters, and you are losing ground all the time. For 44 years now, you have been living under a delusion. Your leaders have led you through lies and deceit. They have missed every opportunity, rejected all the proposals for a settlement, and have taken you from one tragedy to another.

And you, Palestinians in the territories, who live in the wretched poverty of Gaza and Khan Yunis, in the refugee camps of Hebron and Shechem; you who have never known a single day of freedom and joy in your lives—listen to us, if only this once. We offer you the fairest and most viable proposal from our standpoint today—autonomy—self-government—with all its advantages and limitations. You will not get everything you want. Perhaps neither will we. So once and for all, take your destiny in your hands. Don't lose this opportunity that may never return. Take our proposal seriously—to avoid further suffering, and grief; to end the shedding of tears and of blood.

The new Government urges the Palestinians in the territories to give peace a chance—and to cease all violent and terrorist activity for the duration of the negotiations on the subject of autonomy. We are well aware that the Palestinians are not all of a single mold, that there are exceptions and differences among them. But we urge the population, which has been suffering for years, and the perpetrators of the riots in the territories, to foreswear stones and knives and await the results of the talks that may well bring peace to the Middle East. If you reject this proposal, we shall go on talking but treat the territories as though there were no dialogue going on between us. Instead of extending a friendly hand, we will employ every possible means to prevent terror and violence. The choice, in this case, is yours.

We have lost our finest sons and daughters in the struggle over this land and in the war against the Arab armies. My comrades in the Israel Defense Forces, and I myself as a former military man who took part in

Israel's war, lovingly preserve the memory of the fallen and regard ourselves as sharing in the pain of the families whose sleepless nights, year in and year out, are one long Day of Remembrance to them. . . .

. . . [W]e shall continue to fight for our right to live here in peace and tranquility. No knife or stone, no fire-bomb or land-mine will stop us. The Government presented here today sees itself as responsible for the security of every one of Israel's citizens, Jews and Arabs, within the State of Israel, in Judea, in Samaria, and in the Gaza District.

We shall strike hard, without flinching, at terrorists and those who abet them. There will be no compromises in the war against terror. The IDF and the other security forces will prove to the agents of bloodshed that our lives are not for the taking. We shall act to contain the hostile activities as much as possible and maintain the personal security of the inhabitants of Israel and the territories while both upholding the law and guarding the rights of the individual.

. . . [T]he plan to apply self-government to the Palestinians in Judea, Samaria, and Gaza—the autonomy of the Camp David Accords—is an interim settlement for a period of five years. No later than three years after its institution, discussions will begin on the permanent solution. It is only natural that the holding of talks on the subject creates concern among those among us who have chosen to settle in Judea, Samaria, and the Gaza District. I hereby inform you that the Government, by means of the IDF and the other security services, will be responsible for the security and welfare of the residents of Judea, Samaria and the Gaza District. However, at the same time, the Government will refrain from any steps and activities that would disrupt the proper conduct of the peace negotiations.

We see the need to stress that the Government will continue to enhance and strengthen Jewish settlement along the lines of confrontation, due to their importance for security, and in greater Jerusalem.

This Government, like all of its predecessors, believes there is no disagreement in this House concerning Jerusalem as the eternal capital of Israel. United Jerusalem has been and will forever be the capital of the Jewish People, under Israeli sovereignty, a focus of the dreams and longings of every Jew. The Government is firm in its resolve that Jerusalem will not be open to negotiation. The coming years will also be marked by the extension of construction in greater Jerusalem. All Jews, religious and secular, have vowed "If I forget, thee, O Jerusalem, may my right hand wither." This vow unites us all and certainly includes me as a native of Jerusalem. The Government will safeguard freedom of worship for the followers of all religions and all communities in Jerusalem. It will rigorously maintain free access to the Holy Places for all sects and ensure the conduct of a normal and pleasant life for those who visit and reside in the city.

. . . [T]he winds of peace have lately been blowing from Moscow to Washington, from Berlin to Beijing. The voluntary liquidation of weapons of mass destruction and the abrogation of military pacts have lessened the risk of war in the Middle East, as well. And yet this region, with Syria and Jordan, Iraq and Lebanon, is still fraught with danger. Thus when it comes to security, we will concede not a thing. From our standpoint, security takes preference even over peace. A number of countries in our region have recently stepped up their efforts to develop and produce nuclear weapons. According to published information, Iraq was very close to attaining nuclear arms. Fortunately, its nuclear capability was discovered in time and, according to various testimonies, was damaged during and following the Gulf War. The possibility that nuclear weapons will be introduced into the Middle East in the coming years is a very grave and negative development from Israel's standpoint. The Government, from its very outset—and possibly in collaboration with other countries—will address itself to thwarting any possibility that one of Israel's enemies will possess nuclear weapons. Israel has long been prepared to face the threat of nuclear arms. At the same time, this situation requires us to give further thought to the urgent need to end the Arab-Israeli conflict and live in peace with our Arab partners.

. . . [F]rom this moment forward the concept of "Peace process" is no longer relevant. From now on we shall not speak of a "process" but of making peace. In that peace-making we wish to call upon the aid of Egypt, whose late leader, President Anwar Sadat, exhibited such courage and was able to bequeath to his people—and to us—the first peace agreement. The Government will seek further ways of improving neighborly relations and strengthening ties with Egypt and its president, Hosni Mubarak.

I call upon the leaders of the Arab countries to follow the lead of Egypt and its president and take the step that will bring us—and them—peace. I invite the King of Jordan and the Presidents of Syria and Lebanon to this rostrum in Israel's Knesset, here in Jerusalem, for the purpose of talking peace. In the service of peace, I am prepared to travel to Amman, Damascus, and Beirut today, tomorrow. For there is no greater victory than the victory of peace. Wars have their victors and their vanquished, but everyone is a victor in peace.

Sharing with us in the making of peace will also be the United States, whose friendship and special closeness we prize. We shall spare no effort to strengthen and improve the special relationship we have with the one Power in the world. Of course we shall avail ourselves of its advice, but the decisions will be ours alone, of Israel as a sovereign and independent state. We shall also take care to cultivate and strengthen our ties with the European Community. Even if we've not always seen eye to eye and have had our differences with the Europeans, we have no doubt that the road to peace will pass through Europe as well.

We shall strengthen every possible tie with Russia and the other states of the Commonwealth, with China, and with every country that responds to our outstretched hand.

. . . [S]ecurity is not only the tank, the plane, and the missile boat. Security is also, and perhaps above all, the man; the Israeli citizen. Security is a man's education; it is his home, his school, his street and neighborhood, the society that has fostered him. Security is also a man's hope. It is the peace of mind and livelihood of the immigrant from Leningrad, the roof over the head of the immigrant from Gondar in Ethiopia, the factory that employs a demobilized soldier, a young native son. It means merging into our way of life and culture; that, too, is security.

Sources: Laqueur and Rubin, 589–93; entire text in MFA.

12. LETTERS EXCHANGED BETWEEN PLO CHAIRMAN ARAFAT, ISRAELI PRIME MINISTER RABIN, AND NORWEGIAN FOREIGN MINISTER HOLST, TUNIS AND JERUSALEM, 9 SEPTEMBER 1993

LETTER FROM YASSER ARAFAT TO PRIME MINISTER RABIN

September 9, 1993

Yitzhak Rabin
Prime Minister of Israel

Mr. Prime Minister,
The signing of the Declaration of Principles marks a new era in the history of the Middle East. In firm conviction thereof, I would like to confirm the following PLO commitments:

The PLO recognizes the right of the State of Israel to exist in peace and security.

The PLO accepts United Nations Security Council Resolutions 242 and 338.

The PLO commits itself to the Middle East peace process and to a peaceful resolution of the conflict between the two sides and declares that all outstanding issues relating to permanent status will be resolved through negotiations.

The PLO considers that the signing of the Declaration of Principles constitutes a historic event, inaugurating a new epoch of peaceful coexistence, free from violence and all other acts which endanger peace and stability. Accordingly, the PLO renounces the use of terrorism and other acts of violence and will assume responsibility over all PLO elements and personnel in order to assure their compliance, prevent violations and discipline violators.

In view of the promise of a new era and the signing of the Declaration of Principles and based on Palestinian acceptance of Security Council Resolutions 242 and 338, the PLO affirms that those articles of the Palestinian Covenant which deny Israel's right to exist and the provisions of the Covenant which are inconsistent with the commitments of this letter are now inoperative and no longer valid. Consequently, the PLO undertakes to submit to the Palestinian National Council for formal approval the necessary changes in regard to the Palestinian Covenant.

Sincerely,
Yasser Arafat
Chairman
The Palestine Liberation Organization

LETTER FROM YASSER ARAFAT TO NORWEGIAN FOREIGN MINISTER HOLST

September 9, 1993

His Excellency
Johan Jørgen Holst
Foreign Minister of Norway

Dear Minister Holst,
I would like to confirm to you that, upon the signing of the Declaration of Principles, I will include the following positions in my public statements:

In light of the new era marked by the signing of the Declaration of Principles, the PLO encourages and calls upon the Palestinian people in the West Bank and Gaza Strip to take part in the steps leading to the normalization of life, rejecting violence and terrorism, contributing to peace and stability and participating actively in shaping reconstruction, economic development and cooperation.

Sincerely,
Yasser Arafat
Chairman
The Palestine Liberation Organization

LETTER FROM PRIME MINISTER RABIN TO YASSER ARAFAT

September 9, 1993

Yasser Arafat
Chairman
The Palestinian Liberation Organization

Mr. Chairman,
In response to your letter of September 9, 1993, I wish to confirm to you that, in light of the PLO commitments included in your letter, the Government of Israel has decided to recognize the PLO as the representative of the Palestinian people and commence negotiations with the PLO within the Middle East peace process.

Yitzhak Rabin
Prime Minister of Israel

Sources: IPS, Document B.2, 128–29; MFA.

13. DECLARATION OF PRINCIPLES ON INTERIM SELF-GOVERNMENT ARRANGEMENTS, 13 SEPTEMBER 1993

The Government of the State of Israel and the PLO team (in the Jordanian-Palestinian delegation to the Middle East Peace Conference) (the "Palestinian Delegation"), representing the Palestinian people, agree that it is time to put an end to decades of confrontation and conflict, recognize their mutual legitimate and political rights, and strive to live in peaceful coexistence and mutual dignity and security and achieve a just, lasting and comprehensive peace settlement and historic reconciliation through the agreed political process. Accordingly, the two sides agree to the following principles:

ARTICLE I—AIM OF THE NEGOTIATIONS

The aim of the Israeli-Palestinian negotiations within the current Middle East peace process is, among other things, to establish a Palestinian Interim Self-Government Authority, the elected Council (the "Council"), for the Palestinian people in the West Bank and the Gaza Strip, for a transitional period not exceeding five years, leading to a permanent settlement based on Security Council Resolutions 242 and 338.

It is understood that the interim arrangements are an integral part of the whole peace process and that the negotiations on the permanent status will lead to the implementation of Security Council Resolutions 242 and 338.

ARTICLE II—FRAMEWORK FOR THE INTERIM PERIOD

The agreed framework for the interim period is set forth in this Declaration of Principles.

ARTICLE III—ELECTIONS

1. In order that the Palestinian people in the West Bank and Gaza Strip may govern themselves according to democratic principles, direct, free and general political elections will be held for the Council under agreed supervision and international observation, while the Palestinian police will ensure public order.
2. An agreement will be concluded on the exact mode and conditions of the elections in accordance with the protocol attached as Annex I [not reprinted], with the goal of holding the elections not later than nine months after the entry into force of this Declaration of Principles.

3. These elections will constitute a significant interim preparatory step toward the realization of the legitimate rights of the Palestinian people and their just requirements.

ARTICLE IV—JURISDICTION

Jurisdiction of the Council will cover West Bank and Gaza Strip territory, except for issues that will be negotiated in the permanent status negotiations. The two sides view the West Bank and the Gaza Strip as a single territorial unit, whose integrity will be preserved during the interim period.

ARTICLE V—TRANSITIONAL PERIOD AND PERMANENT STATUS NEGOTIATIONS

1. The five-year transitional period will begin upon the withdrawal from the Gaza Strip and Jericho area.
2. Permanent status negotiations will commence as soon as possible, but not later than the beginning of the third year of the interim period, between the Government of Israel and the Palestinian people representatives.
3. It is understood that these negotiations shall cover remaining issues, including: Jerusalem, refugees, settlements, security arrangements, borders, relations and cooperation with other neighbors, and other issues of common interest.
4. The two parties agree that the outcome of the permanent status negotiations should not be prejudiced or preempted by agreements reached for the interim period.

ARTICLE VI—PREPARATORY TRANSFER OF POWERS AND RESPONSIBILITIES

1. Upon the entry into force of this Declaration of Principles and the withdrawal from the Gaza Strip and the Jericho area, a transfer of authority from the Israeli military government and its Civil Administration to the authorised Palestinians for this task, as detailed herein, will commence. This transfer of authority will be of a preparatory nature until the inauguration of the Council.
2. Immediately after the entry into force of this Declaration of Principles and the withdrawal from the Gaza Strip and Jericho area, with the view to promoting economic development in the West Bank and Gaza Strip, authority will be transferred to the Palestinians in the following spheres: education and culture, health, social welfare, direct taxation, and tourism. The Palestinian side will commence in building the Palestinian police

force, as agreed upon. Pending the inauguration of the Council, the two parties may negotiate the transfer of additional powers and responsibilities, as agreed upon.

ARTICLE VII—INTERIM AGREEMENT

1. The Israeli and Palestinian delegations will negotiate an agreement on the interim period (the "Interim Agreement").
2. The Interim Agreement shall specify, among other things, the structure of the Council, the number of its members, and the transfer of powers and responsibilities from the Israeli military government and its Civil Administration to the Council. The Interim Agreement shall also specify the Council's executive authority, legislative authority in accordance with Article IX below, and the independent Palestinian judicial organs.
3. The Interim Agreement shall include arrangements, to be implemented upon the inauguration of the Council, for the assumption by the Council of all of the powers and responsibilities transferred previously in accordance with Article VI above.
4. In order to enable the Council to promote economic growth, upon its inauguration, the Council will establish, among other things, a Palestinian Electricity Authority, a Gaza Sea Port Authority, a Palestinian Development Bank, a Palestinian Export Promotion Board, a Palestinian Environmental Authority, a Palestinian Land Authority and a Palestinian Water Administration Authority, and any other authorities agreed upon, in accordance with the Interim Agreement that will specify their powers and responsibilities.
5. After the inauguration of the Council, the Civil Administration will be dissolved, and the Israeli military government will be withdrawn.

ARTICLE VIII—PUBLIC ORDER AND SECURITY

In order to guarantee public order and internal security for the Palestinians of the West Bank and the Gaza Strip, the Council will establish a strong police force, while Israel will continue to carry the responsibility for defending against external threats, as well as the responsibility for overall security of Israelis for the purpose of safeguarding their internal security and public order.

ARTICLE IX—LAWS AND MILITARY ORDERS

1. The Council will be empowered to legislate, in accordance with the Interim Agreement, within all authorities transferred to it.
2. Both parties will review jointly laws and military orders presently in force in remaining spheres.

ARTICLE X—JOINT ISRAELI-PALESTINIAN LIAISON COMMITTEE

In order to provide for a smooth implementation of this Declaration of Principles and any subsequent agreements pertaining to the interim period, upon the entry into force of this Declaration of Principles, a Joint Israeli-Palestinian Liaison Committee will be established in order to deal with issues requiring coordination, other issues of common interest, and disputes.

ARTICLE XI—ISRAELI-PALESTINIAN COOPERATION IN ECONOMIC FIELDS

Recognizing the mutual benefit of cooperation in promoting the development of the West Bank, the Gaza Strip and Israel, upon the entry into force of this Declaration of Principles, an Israeli-Palestinian Economic Cooperation Committee will be established in order to develop and implement in a cooperative manner the programs identified in the protocols attached as Annex III and Annex IV [neither reprinted].

ARTICLE XII—LIAISON AND COOPERATION WITH JORDAN AND EGYPT

The two parties will invite the Governments of Jordan and Egypt to participate in establishing further liaison and cooperation arrangements between the Government of Israel and the Palestinian representatives, on the one hand, and the Governments of Jordan and Egypt, on the other hand, to promote cooperation between them. These arrangements will include the constitution of a Continuing Committee that will decide by agreement on the modalities of admission of persons displaced from the West Bank and Gaza Strip in 1967, together with necessary measures to prevent disruption and disorder.

Other matters of common concern will be dealt with by this Committee.

ARTICLE XIII—REDEPLOYMENT OF ISRAELI FORCES

1. After the entry into force of this Declaration of Principles, and not later than the eve of elections for the Council, a redeployment of Israeli military forces in the West Bank and the Gaza Strip will take place, in addition to withdrawal of Israeli forces carried out in accordance with Article XIV.
2. In redeploying its military forces, Israel will be guided by the principle that its military forces should be redeployed outside populated areas.
3. Further redeployments to specified locations will be gradually implemented commensurate with the assumption of responsibility for public

order and internal security by the Palestinian police force pursuant to Article VIII above.

ARTICLE XIV—ISRAELI WITHDRAWAL FROM THE GAZA STRIP AND JERICHO AREA

Israel will withdraw from the Gaza Strip and Jericho area, as detailed in the protocol attached as Annex II [not reprinted].

ARTICLE XV—RESOLUTION OF DISPUTES

1. Disputes arising out of the application or interpretation of this Declaration of Principles, or any subsequent agreements pertaining to the interim period, shall be resolved by negotiations through the Joint Liaison Committee to be established pursuant to Article X above.
2. Disputes which cannot be settled by negotiations may be resolved by a mechanism of conciliation to be agreed upon by the parties.
3. The parties may agree to submit to arbitration disputes relating to the interim period, which cannot be settled through conciliation. To this end, upon the agreement of both parties, the parties will establish an Arbitration Committee.

ARTICLE XVI—ISRAELI-PALESTINIAN COOPERATION CONCERNING REGIONAL PROGRAMS

Both parties view the multilateral working groups as an appropriate instrument for promoting a "Marshall Plan," the regional programs and other programs, including special programs for the West Bank and Gaza Strip, as indicated in the protocol attached as Annex IV [not reprinted].

ARTICLE XVII—MISCELLANEOUS PROVISIONS

1. This Declaration of Principles will enter into force one month after its signing.
2. All protocols annexed to this Declaration of Principles and Agreed Minutes pertaining thereto shall be regarded as an integral part hereof.

Done at Washington, DC, this thirteenth day of September, 1993.

For the Government of Israel: *Shimon Peres*
For the PLO: *Mahmoud Abbas (Abu Mazen)*

Witnessed By:
The United States of America: *Warren Christopher*
The Russian Federation: *Andrei Zozyrev*

Sources: IPS, Document B.1, 117–27; MFA.

14. TREATY OF PEACE BETWEEN THE STATE OF ISRAEL AND THE HASHEMITE KINGDOM OF JORDAN, 26 OCTOBER 1994

PREAMBLE

The Government of the State of Israel and the Government of the Hashemite Kingdom of Jordan:
Bearing in mind the Washington Declaration, signed by them on 25th July, 1994, and which they are both committed to honour;
Aiming at the achievement of a just, lasting and comprehensive peace in the Middle East based an Security Council resolutions 242 and 338 in all their aspects;
Bearing in mind the importance of maintaining and strengthening peace based on freedom, equality, justice and respect for fundamental human rights, thereby overcoming psychological barriers and promoting human dignity;
Reaffirming their faith in the purposes and principles of the Charter of the United Nations and recognising their right and obligation to live in peace with each other as well as with all states, within secure and recognised boundaries;
Desiring to develop friendly relations and co-operation between them in accordance with the principles of international law governing international relations in time of peace;
Desiring as well to ensure lasting security for both their States and in particular to avoid threats and the use of force between them;
Bearing in mind that in their Washington Declaration of 25th July, 1994, they declared the termination of the state of belligerency between them;
Deciding to establish peace between them in accordance with this Treaty of Peace;
Have agreed as follows:

ARTICLE 1—ESTABLISHMENT OF PEACE

Peace is hereby established between the State of Israel and the Hashemite Kingdom of Jordan (the "Parties") effective from the exchange of the instruments of ratification of this Treaty.

ARTICLE 2—GENERAL PRINCIPLES

The Parties will apply between them the provisions of the Charter of the United Nations and the principles of international law governing relations among states in times of peace. In particular:
1. They recognise and will respect each other's sovereignty, territorial integrity and political independence;

2. They recognise and will respect each other's right to live in peace within secure and recognised boundaries;
3. They will develop good neighbourly relations of co-operation between them to ensure lasting security, will refrain from the threat or use of force against each other and will settle all disputes between them by peaceful means;
4. They respect and recognise the sovereignty, territorial integrity and political independence of every state in the region;
5. They respect and recognise the pivotal role of human development and dignity in regional and bilateral relationships;
6. They further believe that within their control, involuntary movements of persons in such a way as to adversely prejudice the security of either Party should not be permitted.

ARTICLE 3—INTERNATIONAL BOUNDARY

1. The international boundary between Israel and Jordan is delimited with reference to the boundary definition under the Mandate as is shown in Annex I (a), on the mapping materials attached thereto and co-ordinates specified therein [Annex I not reprinted].
2. The boundary, as set out in Annex I (a), is the permanent, secure and recognised international boundary between Israel and Jordan, without prejudice to the status of any territories that came under Israeli military government control in 1967.
3. The parties recognise the international boundary, as well as each other's territory, territorial waters and airspace, as inviolable, and will respect and comply with them.
4. The demarcation of the boundary will take place as set forth in Appendix (I) to Annex I (a) and will be concluded not later than nine months after the signing of the Treaty.
5. It is agreed that where the boundary follows a river, in the event of natural changes in the course of the flow of the river as described in Annex I (a), the boundary shall follow the new course of the flow. In the event of any other changes the boundary shall not be affected unless otherwise agreed.
6. Immediately upon the exchange of the instruments of ratification of this Treaty, each Party will deploy on its side of the international boundary as defined in Annex I (a).
7. The Parties shall, upon the signature of the Treaty, enter into negotiations to conclude, within 9 months, an agreement on the delimitation of their maritime boundary in the Gulf of Aqaba.
8. Taking into account the special circumstances of the Naharayim / Baqura area, which is under Jordanian sovereignty, with Israeli private ownership rights, the Parties agreed to apply the provisions set out in Annex I (b).

9. With respect to the Zofar/Al-Ghamr area, the provisions set out in Annex I (c) will apply.

ARTICLE 4—SECURITY

1. a. Both Parties, acknowledging that mutual understanding and co-operation in security-related matters will form a significant part of their relations and will further enhance the security of the region, take upon themselves to base their security relations on mutual trust, advancement of joint interests and co-operation, and to aim towards a regional framework of partnership in peace.

b. Towards that goal the Parties recognise the achievements of the European Community and European Union in the development of the Conference on Security and Co-operation in Europe (CSCE) and commit themselves to the creation, in the Middle East, of a CSCME (Conference on Security and Co-operation in the Middle East).

This commitment entails the adoption of regional models of security successfully implemented in the post World War era (along the lines of the Helsinki process) culminating in a regional zone of security and stability.

2. The obligations referred to in this Article are without prejudice to the inherent right of self-defence in accordance with the United Nations Charter.

3. The Parties undertake, in accordance with the provisions of this Article, the following:

a. to refrain from the threat or use of force or weapons, conventional, non-conventional or of any other kind, against each other, or of other actions or activities that adversely affect the security of the other Party;

b. to refrain from organising, instigating, inciting, assisting or participating in acts or threats of belligerency, hostility, subversion or violence against the other Party;

c. to take necessary and effective measures to ensure that acts or threats of belligerency, hostility, subversion or violence against the other Party do not originate from, and are not committed within, through or over their territory (hereinafter the term "territory" includes the airspace and territorial waters).

4. Consistent with the era of peace and with the efforts to build regional security and to avoid and prevent aggression and violence, the Parties further agree to refrain from the following:

a. joining or in any way assisting, promoting or co-operating with any coalition, organisation or alliance with a military or security character with a third party, the objectives or activities of which include launching aggression or other acts of military hostility against the other Party, in contravention of the provisions of the present Treaty.

b. allowing the entry, stationing and operating on their territory, or through it, of military forces, personnel or materiel of a third party, in circumstances which may adversely prejudice the security of the other Party.

5. Both Parties will take necessary and effective measures, and will co-operate in combating terrorism of all kinds. The Parties undertake:

a. to take necessary and effective measures to prevent acts of terrorism, subversion or violence from being carried out from their territory or through it and to take necessary and effective measures to combat such activities and all their perpetrators.

b. without prejudice to the basic rights of freedom of expression and association, to take necessary and effective measures to prevent the entry, presence and co-operation in their territory of any group or organisation, and their infrastructure, which threatens the security of the other Party by the use of or incitement to the use of, violent means.

c. to co-operate in preventing and combating cross-boundary infiltrations.

6. Any question as to the implementation of this Article will be dealt with through a mechanism of consultations which will include a liaison system, verification, supervision, and where necessary, other mechanisms, and higher level consultation. The details of the mechanism of consultations will be contained in an agreement to be concluded by the Parties within 3 months of the exchange of the instruments of ratification of this Treaty.

7. The Parties undertake to work as a matter of priority, and as soon as possible in the context of the Multilateral Working Group on Arms Control and Regional Security, and jointly, towards the following:

a. the creation in the Middle East of a region free from hostile alliances and coalitions;

b. the creation of a Middle East free from weapons of mass destruction, both conventional and non-conventional, in the context of a comprehensive, lasting and stable peace, characterised by the renunciation of the use of force, reconciliation and goodwill.

ARTICLE 5—DIPLOMATIC AND OTHER BILATERAL RELATIONS

1. The Parties agree to establish full diplomatic and consular relations and to exchange resident ambassadors within one month of the exchange of the instruments of ratification of this Treaty.

2. The Parties agree that the normal relationship between them will further include economic and cultural relations.

ARTICLE 6—WATER

With the view to achieving a comprehensive and lasting settlement of all the water problems between them:

1. The Parties agree mutually to recognise the rightful allocations of both of them in Jordan River and Yarmouk River waters and Araba/Arava ground water in accordance with the agreed acceptable principles, quantities and quality as set out in Annex II [not reprinted], which shall be fully respected and complied with.
2. The Parties, recognising the necessity to find a practical, just and agreed solution to their water problems and with the view that the subject of water can form the basis for the advancement of co-operation between them, jointly undertake to ensure that the management and development of their water resources do not, in any way, harm the water resources of the other Party.
3. The Parties recognise that their water resources are not sufficient to meet their needs. More water should be supplied for their use through various methods, including projects of regional and international co-operation.
4. In light of paragraph 3 of this Article, with the understanding that co-operation in water-related subjects would be to the benefit of both Parties, and will help alleviate their water shortages, and that water issues along their entire boundary must be dealt with in their totality, including the possibility of trans-boundary water transfers, the Parties agree to search for ways to alleviate water shortages and to co-operate in the following fields:

a. development of existing and new water resources, increasing the water availability including co-operation on a regional basis as appropriate, and minimising wastage of water resources through the chain of their uses;

b. prevention of contamination of water resources;

c. mutual assistance in the alleviation of water shortages;

d. transfer of information and joint research and development in water-related subjects, and review of the potentials for enhancement of water resources development and use.

5. The implementation of both Parties' undertakings under this Article is detailed in Annex II [not reprinted].

ARTICLE 7—ECONOMIC RELATIONS

1. Viewing economic development and prosperity as pillars of peace, security and harmonious relations between states, peoples and individual human beings, the Parties, taking note of understandings reached between them, affirm their mutual desire to promote economic co-operation between them, as well as within the framework of wider regional economic co-operation.
2. In order to accomplish this goal, the Parties agree to the following:

a. to remove all discriminatory barriers to normal economic relations, to terminate economic boycotts directed at each other, and to co-operate in terminating boycotts against either Party by third parties;

b. recognising that the principle of free and unimpeded flow of goods and services should guide their relations, the Parties will enter into negotiations with a view to concluding agreements on economic co-operation, including trade and the establishment of a free trade area, investment, banking, industrial co-operation and labour, for the purpose of promoting beneficial economic relations, based on principles to be agreed upon, as well as on human development considerations on a regional basis. These negotiations will be concluded no later than 6 months from the exchange of the instruments of ratification of this Treaty.

c. to co-operate bilaterally, as well as in multilateral forums, towards the promotion of their respective economies and of their neighbourly economic relations with other regional parties.

ARTICLE 8—REFUGEES AND DISPLACED PERSONS

1. Recognising the massive human problems caused to both Parties by the conflict in the Middle East, as well as the contribution made by them towards the alleviation of human suffering, the Parties will seek to further alleviate those problems arising on a bilateral level.

2. Recognising that the above human problems caused by the conflict in the Middle East cannot be fully resolved on the bilateral level, the Parties will seek to resolve them in appropriate forums, in accordance with international law, including the following:

a. in the case of displaced persons, in a quadripartite committee together with Egypt and the Palestinians:

b. in the case of refugees,

(i) in the framework of the Multilateral Working Group on Refugees;

(ii) in negotiations, in a framework to be agreed, bilateral or otherwise, in conjunction with and at the same time as the permanent status negotiations pertaining to the territories referred to in Article 3 of this Treaty;

c. through the implementation of agreed United Nations programmes and other agreed international economic programmes concerning refugees and displaced persons, including assistance to their settlement.

ARTICLE 9—PLACES OF HISTORICAL AND RELIGIOUS SIGNIFICANCE

1. Each party will provide freedom of access to places of religious and historical significance.

2. In this regard, in accordance with the Washington Declaration, Israel respects the present special role of the Hashemite Kingdom of Jordan in Muslim Holy shrines in Jerusalem. When negotiations on the permanent status will take place, Israel will give high priority to the Jordanian historic role in these shrines.

3. The Parties will act together to promote interfaith relations among the three monotheistic religions, with the aim of working towards religious understanding, moral commitment, freedom of religious worship, and tolerance and peace.

ARTICLE 10—CULTURAL AND SCIENTIFIC EXCHANGES

The Parties, wishing to remove biases developed through periods of conflict, recognise the desirability of cultural and scientific exchanges in all fields, and agree to establish normal cultural relations between them. Thus, they shall, as soon as possible and not later than 9 months from the exchange of the instruments of ratification of this Treaty, conclude the negotiations on cultural and scientific agreements.

ARTICLE 11—MUTUAL UNDERSTANDING AND GOOD NEIGHBOURLY RELATIONS

1. The Parties will seek to foster mutual understanding and tolerance based on shared historic values, and accordingly undertake:

a. to abstain from hostile or discriminatory propaganda against each other, and to take all possible legal and administrative measures to prevent the dissemination of such propaganda by any organisation or individual present in the territory of either Party;

b. as soon as possible, and not later than 3 months from the exchange of the instruments of ratification of this Treaty, to repeal all adverse or discriminatory references and expressions of hostility in their respective legislation;

c. to refrain in all government publications from any such references or expressions;

d. to ensure mutual enjoyment by each other's citizens of due process of law within their respective legal systems and before their courts.

2. Paragraph 1 (a) of this Article is without prejudice to the right to freedom of expression as contained in the International Covenant on Civil and Political Rights.

3. A joint committee shall be formed to examine incidents where one Party claims there has been a violation of this Article.

ARTICLE 12—COMBATING CRIME AND DRUGS

The Parties will co-operate in combating crime, with an emphasis on smuggling, and will take all necessary measures to combat and prevent such activities as the production of, as well as the trafficking in illicit drugs, and will bring to trial perpetrators of such acts. In this regard, they take note of the understandings reached between them in the above spheres, in accordance with Annex III [not reprinted] and undertake to conclude all relevant agreements not later than 9 months from the date of the exchange of the instruments of ratification of this Treaty.

ARTICLE 13—TRANSPORTATION AND ROADS

Taking note of the progress already made in the area of transportation, the Parties recognise the mutuality of interest in good neighbourly relations in the area of transportation and agree to the following means to promote relations between them in this sphere:
1. Each party will permit the free movement of nationals and vehicles of the other into and within its territory according to the general rules applicable to nationals and vehicles of other states. Neither party will impose discriminatory taxes or restrictions on the free movement of persons and vehicles from its territory to the territory of the other.
2. The Parties will open and maintain roads and border-crossings between their countries and will consider further road and rail links between them.
3. The Parties will continue their negotiations concerning mutual transportation agreements in the above and other areas, such as joint projects, traffic safety, transport standards and norms, licensing of vehicles, land passages, shipment of goods and cargo, and meteorology, to be concluded not later than 6 months from the exchange of the instruments of ratification of this Treaty.
4. The Parties agree to continue their negotiations for a highway to be constructed and maintained between Egypt, Israel and Jordan near Eilat.

ARTICLE 14—FREEDOM OF NAVIGATION AND ACCESS TO PORTS

1. Without prejudice to the provisions of paragraph 3, each Party recognises the right of the vessels of the other Party to innocent passage through its territorial waters in accordance with the rules of international law.
2. Each Party will grant normal access to its ports for vessels and cargoes of the other, as well as vessels and cargoes destined for or coming from the other Party. Such access will be granted on the same conditions as generally applicable to vessels and cargoes of other nations.
3. The Parties consider the Strait of Tiran and the Gulf of Aqaba to be international waterways open to all nations for unimpeded and non-suspendable freedom of navigation and overflight. The Parties will respect each other's right to navigation and overflight for access to either Party through the Strait of Tiran and the Gulf of Aqaba.

ARTICLE 15—CIVIL AVIATION

1. The Parties recognise as applicable to each other the rights, privileges and obligations provided for by the multilateral aviation agreements to which they are both party, particularly by the 1944 Convention on Interna-

tional Civil Aviation (The Chicago Convention) and the 1944 International Air Services Transit Agreement.
2. Any declaration of national emergency by a Party under Article 89 of the Chicago Convention will not be applied to the other Party on a discriminatory basis.
3. The Parties take note of the negotiations on the international air corridor to be opened between them in accordance with the Washington Declaration. In addition, the Parties shall, upon ratification of this Treaty, enter into negotiations for the purpose of concluding a Civil Aviation Agreement. All the above negotiations are to be concluded not later than 6 months from the exchange of the instruments of ratification of this Treaty.

ARTICLE 16—POSTS AND TELECOMMUNICATIONS

The Parties take note of the opening between them, in accordance with the Washington Declaration, of direct telephone and facsimile lines. Postal links, the negotiations on which having been concluded, will be activated upon the signature of this Treaty. The Parties further agree that normal wireless and cable communications and television relay services by cable, radio and satellite, will be established between them, in accordance with all relevant international conventions and regulations. The negotiations on these subjects will be concluded not later than 9 months from the exchange of the instruments of ratification of this Treaty.

ARTICLE 17—TOURISM

The Parties affirm their mutual desire to promote co-operation between them in the field of tourism. In order to accomplish this goal, the Parties—taking note of the understandings reached between them concerning tourism—agree to negotiate, as soon as possible, and to conclude not later than 3 months from the exchange of the instruments of ratification of this Treaty, an agreement to facilitate and encourage mutual tourism and tourism from third countries.

ARTICLE 18—ENVIRONMENT

The Parties will co-operate in matters relating to the environment, a sphere to which they attach great importance, including conservation of nature and prevention of pollution, as set forth in Annex IV [not reprinted]. They will negotiate an agreement on the above, to be concluded not later than 6 months from the exchange of the instruments of ratification of this Treaty.

ARTICLE 19—ENERGY

1. The Parties will co-operate in the development of energy resources, including the development of energy-related projects such as the utilisation of solar energy.

2. The Parties, having concluded their negotiations on the interconnecting of their electric grids in the Eilat-Aqaba area, will implement the interconnecting upon the signature of this Treaty. The Parties view this step as a part of a wider binational and regional concept. They agree to continue their negotiations as soon as possible to widen the scope of their interconnected grids.
3. The Parties will conclude the relevant agreements in the field of energy within 6 months from the date of exchange of the instruments of ratification of this Treaty.

ARTICLE 20—RIFT VALLEY DEVELOPMENT

The Parties attach great importance to the integrated development of the Jordan Rift Valley area, including joint projects in the economic, environmental, energy-related and tourism fields. Taking note of the Terms of Reference developed in the framework of the Trilateral Israel-Jordan-US Economic Committee towards the Jordan Rift Valley Development Master Plan, they will vigorously continue their efforts towards the completion of planning and towards implementation.

ARTICLE 21—HEALTH

The Parties will co-operate in the area of health and shall negotiate with a view to the conclusion of an agreement within 9 months of the exchange of instruments of ratification of this Treaty.

ARTICLE 22—AGRICULTURE

The Parties will co-operate in the areas of agriculture, including veterinary services, plant protection, biotechnology and marketing, and shall negotiate with a view to the conclusion of an agreement within 6 months from the date of the exchange of instruments of ratification of this Treaty.

ARTICLE 23—AQABA AND EILAT

The Parties agree to enter into negotiations, as soon as possible, and not later than one month from the exchange of the instruments of ratification of this Treaty, on arrangements that would enable the joint development of the towns of Aqaba and Eilat with regard to such matters, inter alia, as joint tourism development, joint customs, free trade zone, co-operation in aviation, prevention of pollution, maritime matters, police, customs and health co-operation. The Parties will conclude all relevant agreements within 9 months from the exchange of instruments of ratification of the Treaty.

ARTICLE 24—CLAIMS

The Parties agree to establish a claims commission for the mutual settlement of all financial claims.

ARTICLE 25—RIGHTS AND OBLIGATIONS

1. This Treaty does not affect and shall not be interpreted as affecting, in any way, the rights and obligations of the Parties under the Charter of the United Nations.
2. The Parties undertake to fulfil in good faith their obligations under this Treaty, without regard to action or inaction of any other party and independently of any instrument inconsistent with this Treaty. For the purposes of this paragraph each Party represents to the other that in its opinion and interpretation there is no inconsistency between their existing treaty obligations and this Treaty.
3. They further undertake to take all the necessary measures for the application in their relations of the provisions of the multilateral conventions to which they are parties, including the submission of appropriate notification to the Secretary General of the United Nations and other depositories of such conventions.
4. Both Parties will also take all the necessary steps to abolish all pejorative references to the other Party, in multilateral conventions to which they are parties, to the extent that such references exist.
5. The Parties undertake not to enter into any obligation in conflict with this Treaty.
6. Subject to Article 103 of the United Nations Charter, in the event of a conflict between the obligations of the Parties under the present Treaty and any of their other obligations, the obligations under this Treaty will be binding and implemented.

ARTICLE 26—LEGISLATION

Within 3 months of the exchange of ratifications of this Treaty the Parties undertake to enact any legislation necessary in order to implement the Treaty, and to terminate any international commitments and to repeal any legislation that is inconsistent with the Treaty.

ARTICLE 27—RATIFICATION

1. This Treaty shall be ratified by both Parties in conformity with their respective national procedures. It shall enter into force on the exchange of instruments of ratification.
2. The Annexes, Appendices, and other attachments to this Treaty shall be considered integral parts thereof.

ARTICLE 28—INTERIM MEASURES

The Parties will apply, in certain spheres, to be agreed upon, interim measures pending the conclusion of the relevant agreements in accordance with this Treaty, as stipulated in Annex V [not reprinted].

ARTICLE 29—SETTLEMENT OF DISPUTES

1. Disputes arising out of the application or interpretation of this Treaty shall be resolved by negotiations.
2. Any such disputes which cannot be settled by negotiations shall be resolved by conciliation or submitted to arbitration.

ARTICLE 30—REGISTRATION

This Treaty shall be transmitted to the Secretary General of the United Nations for registration in accordance with the provisions of Article 102 of the Charter of the United Nations.

Done at the Arava/Araba Crossing Point this day Heshvan 21st, 5775, Jumada Al-Ula 21st, 1415 which corresponds to 26th October, 1994 in the Hebrew, English and Arabic languages, all texts being equally authentic. In case of divergence of interpretation the English text shall prevail.

For the State of Israel:	*Yitzhak Rabin,* Prime Minister
For the Hashemite Kingdom of Jordan:	
	Abdul Salam Majali, Prime Minister
Witnessed by:	*William J. Clinton,* President of the United States of America

Sources: Laqueur and Rubin, 665–74; MFA.

15. REMARKS BY HIS MAJESTY KING HUSSEIN AT THE FUNERAL FOR ISRAELI PRIME MINISTER YITZHAK RABIN, JERUSALEM, 6 NOVEMBER 1995

Mrs. Leah Rabin, my friends, I had never thought that the moment would come like this when I would grieve the loss of a brother, a colleague and a friend, a man, a soldier, who met us on the opposite side of a divide, whom we respected, as he respected us, a man I came to know because I realized, as he did, that we had to cross over the divide, establish a dialogue, get to know each other, and strive to leave for those who follow us a legacy that is worthy of them. And so we did. And so we became brethren and friends.

I have never been used to standing except with you next to me, speaking of peace, speaking of our dreams and hopes for generations to come that must live in peace, enjoy human dignity, come together, work together to build a better future, which is our right.

Never in all my thoughts would it occur to me that my first visit to Jerusalem in response to your invitation, the invitation of the speaker of the Knesset, the invitation of the president of Israel, would be on such an occasion. He lived as a soldier. He died as a soldier for peace. And I believe it is time for all of us to come out openly and to speak our peace, not here today but for all the times to come. We belong to the camp for peace. We believe in peace. We believe that our one God wishes us to live in peace and wish his peace upon us. For these are his teachings to all the followers of the three great monotheistic religions, the children of Abraham.

Let us not keep silent. Let our voices rise high to speak of our commitment to peace for all times to come. And let us tell those who live in darkness, who are the enemies of life and true faith and religion and the teachings of our one God, this is where we stand. This is our camp. Maybe God will bless you with the realization that you must join in, and we pray that he will. But otherwise we are not ashamed. Nor are we afraid. Nor are we anything but determined to fulfill the legacy for which my friend fell, as did my grandfather in this very city when I was with him and but a young boy.

He was a man of courage, a man of vision, and he was endowed with one of the greatest virtues any man can have. He was endowed with humility. He felt with those around him. And in a position of responsibility, he placed himself, as I do and have done, often in the place of the other partner, to achieve a worthy goal. And we achieve peace, an honorable peace and a lasting peace.

He had courage, he had vision, and he had a commitment to peace. And standing here, I commit before you, before my people in Jordan, before the world, myself to continue to do my utmost to ensure that we leave a similar legacy. And when my time comes, I hope it will be like my grandfather's and like Yitzhak Rabin's.

May your spirit rise high and may it sense what the people of Jordan, my family, the people of Israel, and decent people throughout the world feel today. So many live and so many inevitably die. This is the will of God. This is the way of all. But those who are fortunate and lucky in life, those who are great, are those who leave something behind. And you are such a man, my friend.

The faces in my country, amongst the majority of our people, in our armed forces, and people who once were your enemies, are somber today and their hearts are heavy. Let us hope and pray that God will give us all guidance, each in his respective position, to do what he can for the better future that Yitzhak Rabin sought with determination and courage.

As long as I live, I will be proud to have known him, to have worked with him, as a brother and as a friend and as a man. And the relationship of friendship that we had is something unique, and I am proud of that. On behalf of the people of Jordan, my larger Jordanian family, my Hashemite family, all those who belong to the camp for peace, to all those who belong to the camp of peace, our deepest sympathies, our deepest condolences, as we share together this moment of remembrance and commitment, to continue our struggle for the future of generations to come, as did Yitzhak Rabin, and to fulfill his legacy.

Thank you.

Source: Jordan Information Bureau, Washington, DC.

16. NOTE FOR THE RECORD (RE: HEBRON), 15 JANUARY 1997

Prime Minister Benjamin Netanyahu and *Rayyis* (President) Yasir Arafat met on 15 January 1997 in the presence of the US Special Middle East Coordinator, Dennis Ross. They requested him to prepare this Note for the Record to summarize what they agreed upon at their meeting.

MUTUAL UNDERTAKINGS

The two leaders agreed that the Oslo peace process must move forward to succeed. Both parties to the Interim Agreement have concerns and obligations. Accordingly, the two leaders reaffirmed their commitment to implement the Interim Agreement on the basis of reciprocity and, in this context, conveyed the following undertakings to each other:

ISRAELI RESPONSIBILITIES

The Israeli side reaffirms its commitments to the following measures and principles in accordance with the Interim Agreement:

Issues for Implementation

1 *Further Redeployment Phases*
The first phase of further redeployments will be carried out during the first week of March.
2 *Prisoner Release Issues*
Prisoner release issues will be dealt with in accordance with the Interim Agreement's provisions and procedures, including Annex VII.

Issues for Negotiation

3 *Outstanding Interim Agreement Issues*
Negotiations on the following outstanding issues from the Interim Agreement will be immediately resumed. Negotiations on these issues will be conducted in parallel:

1 Safe Passage
2 Gaza Airport
3 Gaza port
4 Passages
5 Economic, financial, civilian and security issues
6 People-to-people

4 *Permanent Status Negotiations*
Permanent status negotiations will be resumed within two months after implementation of the Hebron Protocol.

PALESTINIAN RESPONSIBILITIES

The Palestinian side reaffirms its commitments to the following measures and principles in accordance with the Interim Agreement:

1 *Complete the process of revising the Palestinian National Charter*

2 *Fighting terror and preventing violence*

   1 Strengthening security cooperation

   2 Preventing incitement and hostile propaganda, as specified in Article XXII of the Interim Agreement

   3 Combat systematically and effectively terrorist organizations and infrastructure

   4 Apprehension, prosecution and punishment of terrorists

   5 Requests for transfer of suspects and defendants will be acted upon in accordance with Article II(7)(f) of Annex IV to the Interim Agreement

   6 Confiscation of illegal firearms

3 *Size of Palestinian Police will be pursuant to the Interim Agreement.*

4 *Exercise of Palestinian governmental activity,* and location of Palestinian governmental offices, will be as specified in the Interim Agreement.

The aforementioned commitments will be dealt with immediately and in parallel.

OTHER ISSUES

Either party is free to raise other issues not specified above related to implementation of the Interim Agreement and obligations of both sides arising from the Interim Agreement.

Prepared by Ambassador Dennis Ross at the request of Prime Minister Benjamin Netanyahu and Rayyis Yasser Arafat.

Sources: *JPS* 26:3 (Spring 1997), 138–39; MFA.

BIBLIOGRAPHY

PRIMARY AND AUTOBIOGRAPHICAL SOURCES

Abbas, Mahmoud [Abu Mazen], *Through Secret Channels: The Road to Oslo: Senior PLO Leader Abu Mazen's Revealing Story of the Negotiations with Israel,* Concord, MA: Paul [Reading: Garnet], 1995.

[Abd al-Shafi, Haydar,] "Interview with Haydar 'Abd al-Shafi," *Journal of Palestine Studies* (hereafter *JPS*) 25:1 (Autumn 1995), 76–85.

[Abu-Sharif, Bassam] *Best of Enemies: The Memoirs of Bassam Abu-Sharif and Uzi Mahnaimi,* Boston: Little, Brown, 1995.

al-Tal, Abdallah, "The Jordanian-Israeli Negotiations," in *Israel in the Middle East: Documents and Readings on Society, Politics and Foreign Relations, 1948–Present,* eds. Itamar Rabinovich and Jehuda Reinharz, New York and Oxford: Oxford University Press, 1984, 71–73.

Avnery, Uri, *My Friend, the Enemy,* Westport, CT: Lawrence Hill, 1986.

The Beirut Massacre: The Complete Kahan Commission Report, New York: Karz-Cohl Publishers, 1983.

Ben-Gurion, David, *Min ha-Yoman* [From Ben-Gurion's Diary, The War of Independence], eds. G. Rivlin and E. Orren, Tel Aviv: Misrad ha-Bitachon, 1986.

———, *My Talks with Arab Leaders,* transl. Misha Louvish and Aryeh Rubinstein, ed. M. Louvish, Jerusalem: Keter, 1972.

Caradon, Lord, Arthur J. Goldberg, Mohammed H. El-Zayyat, and Abba Eban, *UN Security Council Resolution 242: A Case Study in Diplomatic Ambiguity,* introduction by Joseph J. Sisco, Washington, DC: Institute for the Study of Diplomacy, Edmund A. Walsh School of Foreign Service, Georgetown University, 1981.

Carter, Jimmy, *The Blood of Abraham: Insights into the Middle East,* Lafayetteville: University of Arkansas Press, 1993.

———, *Keeping Faith: Memoirs of a President,* New York: Bantam, 1982.

Dayan, Moshe, *Breakthrough: A Personal Account of the Egypt-Israel Peace Negotiations,* London: Weidenfeld and Nicolson, 1981.

Eytan, Walter, *The First Ten Years: A Diplomatic History of Israel,* New York: Simon and Schuster, 1958.

Habib, Philip, *Diplomacy and the Search for Peace in the Middle East,* Georgetown: Institute for the Study of Diplomacy, 1985.

Indyk, Martin, The Jimmy Carter Lecture, Moshe Dayan Center for Middle Eastern and African Studies, Tel Aviv University, 16 May 1995.

Institute for Palestine Studies, *The Palestinian-Israeli Peace Agreement: A Documentary Record,* 2nd edition, Washington, DC: Institute for Palestine Studies, 1994.

Israel Ministry of Foreign Affairs, Information Division, *The Middle East Peace Process: An Overview,* Jerusalem: Israel Ministry of Foreign Affairs (MFA), December 1995.

Israel State Archives, *Documents on the Foreign Policy of Israel,* vol. III—*Armistice Negotiations with the Arab States, December 1948–July 1949,* ed. Yemima Rosenthal, Jerusalem: 1983.

———, *Documents on the Foreign Policy of Israel,* vol. IV (May-December 1949), ed. Yemima Rosenthal, Jerusalem: 1986.

———, *Documents on the Foreign Policy of Israel,* vol. V (1950), ed. Yehoshua Freundlich, Jerusalem: 1988.

Israeli, Raphael, ed., *PLO in Lebanon: Selected Documents,* London: Weidenfeld and Nicolson, 1983.

Kamil, Muhammad Ibrahim, *The Camp David Accords: A Testimony,* New York: KPI, 1986.

Kissinger, Henry, *White House Years,* Boston: Little, Brown, 1979.

———, *Years of Upheaval,* Boston: Little, Brown, 1982.

Laqueur, Walter, and Barry Rubin, eds., *The Israel-Arab Reader: A Documentary History of the Middle East Conflict,* 5th rev. and updated ed., New York: Penguin, 1995.

Lukacs, Yehuda, ed., *The Israeli-Palestinian Conflict: A Documentary Record, 1967–1990,* Cambridge and New York: Cambridge University Press, 1992.

"The Madrid Peace Conference (Special Document File)," *JPS* 21:2 (Winter 1992), 117–49.

McDonald, James G., *My Mission in Israel, 1948–1951,* New York: Simon and Schuster, 1951.

Medzini, Meron, ed., *Israel's Foreign Relations: Selected Documents, 1947–1974,* vol. II, Jerusalem: Ministry of Foreign Affairs, 1976.

Muasher, Marwan, "Jordanian Attitudes to the Peace Process," lecture by the Ambassador of Jordan to Israel, Tel Aviv University: Moshe Dayan Center for Middle Eastern and African Studies, 12 June 1995.

"The Peace Process (Special Document File)," *JPS* 21:3 (Spring 1992), 126–46.

Peres, Shimon, *The New Middle East,* New York: Henry Holt, 1993.

———, address to the Fifth Session of the Trilateral Talks, Dead Sea Spa Hotel, Jordan, 20 July 1994, MFA.

Quandt, William B., *Camp David: Peacemaking and Politics,* Washington, DC: The Brookings Institution, 1986.

Rabie, Mohamed, *US-PLO Dialogue: Secret Diplomacy and Conflict Resolution,* foreword by Harold H. Saunders, Gainesville, FL: University Press of Florida, 1995.

Rabin, Yitzhak, *The Rabin Memoirs* [trans. Dov Goldstein], expanded edition with afterword by Yoram Peri, Berkeley: University of California Press, 1996.

Rabinovich, Itamar and Jehuda Reinharz, eds., *Israel in the Middle East: Documents and Readings on Society, Politics and Foreign Relations, 1948–Present,* New York and Oxford: Oxford University Press, 1984.

Rafael, Gideon, *Destination Peace: Three Decades of Israeli Foreign Policy: A Personal Memoir,* New York: Stein and Day, 1981.

Riad, Mahmoud, *The Struggle for Peace in the Middle East,* London and New York: Quartet Books, 1981.

Rubinstein, Elyakim, "The Israel-Jordan Peace Treaty" (Hebrew), lecture to Middle East course, Israel Ministry of Foreign Affairs, 26 February 1995.

———, remarks, Israel-Jordan Peace Talks (Ein Avrona), 18 July 1994, MFA.

el-Sadat, Anwar, *In Search of Identity: An Autobiography,* New York: Harper and Row, 1978.

[Said, Edward W.], "Symbols vs. Substance: A Year after the Declaration of Principles, an Interview with Edward Said," *JPS* 24:2 (Winter 1995), 60–72.

[Shaath, Nabil,] "The Oslo Agreement: An Interview with Nabil Shaath" (9 September 1993), *JPS* 23:1 (Autumn 1993), 5–13.

Sharef, Zeev, "Negotiations with King Abdullah and the Formation of a Governmental Structure," in *Israel in the Middle East: Documents and Readings on Society, Politics and Foreign Relations, 1948–Present,* eds. Itamar Rabinovich and Jehuda Reinharz, New York and Oxford: Oxford University Press, 1984, 32–36.

Siilasvuo, Ensio, *In the Service of Peace in the Middle East, 1967–1979,* London and New York: Hurst and St. Martin's, 1992.

United States, Department of State, *Foreign Relations of the United States: Diplomatic Papers 1949,* vol. VI, Washington, DC: 1977.

Weizman, Ezer, *The Battle for Peace,* New York: Bantam, 1981.

PRESS

The Christian Science Monitor

The Gazette (Montreal)

The Guardian (London)

Jerusalem Post International Edition (JPI)

New York Times (NYT)

Washington Post

SECONDARY SOURCES—BOOKS

Ajami, Fouad, *The Arab Predicament,* rev. ed., Cambridge: Cambridge University Press, 1992.

Antonius, George, *The Arab Awakening,* 2nd ed. London: Hamish Hamilton, 1946.

Aruri, Naseer, ed., *Middle East Crucible: Studies on the Arab-Israeli War of October, 1973,* Wilmette, IL: Medina Press, 1975.

———, *The Obstruction of Peace: The US, Israel and the Palestinians,* Monroe, ME: Common Courage Press, 1995.

Barakat, Halim, ed., *Toward a Viable Lebanon,* Washington, DC: Georgetown University, Center for Contemporary Arab Studies, 1988.

Bar-Joseph, Uri, *The Best of Enemies: Israel and Transjordan in the War of 1948,* London: Frank Cass, 1987.

Bar-On, Mordechai, *The Gates of Gaza: Israel's Road to Suez and Back, 1955–1957,* transl. Ruth Rossing, New York: St. Martin's, 1994.

Bar-Siman-Tov, Yaacov, *Israel and the Peace Process, 1977–1982: In Search of Legitimacy for Peace,* Albany: State University of New York Press, 1994.

Bauer, Yehuda, *From Diplomacy to Resistance: A History of Jewish Palestine, 1939–1945,* transl. Alton M. Winters, Philadelphia: Jewish Publication Society, 1970.

Benvenisti, Meron, *Intimate Enemies: Jews and Arabs in a Shared Land,* foreword by Thomas L. Friedman, Berkeley: University of California Press, 1995.

Ben-Zvi, Abraham, *Between Lausanne and Geneva: International Conferences and the Arab-Israeli Conflict,* Tel Aviv: Tel Aviv University, Jaffee Center for Strategic Studies (Study No. 13) and Boulder, CO: Westview Press, 1989.

Berger, Earl, *The Covenant and the Sword,* Toronto: University of Toronto Press, 1965.

Black, Ian, *Zionism and the Arabs, 1936–1939,* unpublished Ph.D. dissertation, University of London, 1978.

Brynen, Rex, *Sanctuary and Survival: The PLO in Lebanon,* Boulder, CO: Westview Press, 1990.

Caplan, Neil, *Futile Diplomacy, vol. I—Early Arab-Zionist Negotiation Attempts, 1913–1931,* London: Frank Cass, 1983.

———, *Futile Diplomacy, vol. II—Arab-Zionist Negotiations and the End of the Mandate,* London: Frank Cass, 1986.

———, *Futile Diplomacy, vol. III—The United Nations, the Great Powers, and Middle East Peacemaking, 1948–1954,* London: Frank Cass, 1997.

———, *Futile Diplomacy, vol. IV—Operation Alpha and the Failure of Anglo-American Coercive Diplomacy in the Arab-Israeli Conflict, 1954–1956,* London: Frank Cass, 1997.

———, *The Lausanne Conference, 1949: A Case Study in Middle East Peacemaking,* Tel Aviv: Moshe Dayan Center for Middle Eastern and African Studies (Occasional Papers, No. 113), 1993.

———, *Palestine Jewry and the Arab Question, 1917–1925,* London: Frank Cass, 1978.

Cobban, Helena, *The Palestine Liberation Organization: People, Power and Politics,* London: Cambridge University Press, 1984.

Cohen, Michael J., *Palestine and the Great Powers, 1945–1948,* Princeton: Princeton University Press, 1982.

Cohen, Raymond, *Culture and Conflict in Egyptian-Israeli Relations: A Dialogue of the Deaf,* Bloomington and Indianapolis: Indiana University Press, 1990.

Collings, Deirdre, ed., *Peace For Lebanon? From War to Reconstruction,* Boulder, CO, and London: Lynne Rienner, 1994.

Cordesman, Anthony H., *Perilous Prospects: The Peace Process and the Arab-Israeli Military Balance,* Boulder, CO: Westview Press, 1996.

Davis, M. Thomas, *40 KM into Lebanon,* Washington, DC: National Defense University Press, 1987.

Dawn, C. Ernest, *From Ottomanism to Arabism: Essays on the Origins of Arab Nationalism,* Urbana and Chicago: University of Illinois Press, 1973.

Eisenberg, Laura Zittrain, *My Enemy's Enemy: Lebanon in the Early Zionist Imagination, 1900–1948,* Detroit: Wayne State University Press, 1994.

Elpeleg, Zvi, *The Grand Mufti: Haj Amin al-Hussaini, Founder of the Palestinian National Movement,* transl. David Harvey, ed. Shmuel Himelstein, London: Frank Cass, 1993.

Evron, Yair, *War and Intervention in Lebanon: The Israeli-Syrian Deterrence Dialogue,* Baltimore: Johns Hopkins University Press, 1987.

Feste, Karen A., *Plans for Peace: Negotiation and the Arab-Israeli Conflict,* New York: Praeger, 1991.

Fischhoff, Baruch, Kenneth Kotovsky, Hussain Tuma, and Jacobo Bielak, eds., *A Two-State Solution in the Middle East: Prospects and Possibilities,* Pittsburgh: Carnegie Mellon University Press, 1993.

Fisk, Robert, *Pity the Nation: Lebanon at War,* London: Deutsch, 1990.

Flapan, Simha, ed., *When Enemies Dare to Talk: An Israeli-Palestinian Debate (5/6 September 1978),* London: Croom Helm, 1979.

Forsythe, David P., *United Nations Peacemaking: The Conciliation Commission for Palestine,* Baltimore and London: Johns Hopkins University Press, 1972.

Frankel, Glenn, *Beyond the Promised Land: Jews and Arabs on the Hard Road to a New Israel,* New York: Simon and Schuster / Touchstone Books, 1996.

Freedman, Robert O., ed., *The Intifada: Its Impact on Israel, the Arab World, and the Superpowers,* Gainesville: University Presses of Florida, 1991.

Friedlander, Melvin A., *Sadat and Begin: The Domestic Politics of Peacemaking,* Boulder, CO: Westview Press, 1983.

Friedman, Isaiah, *The Question of Palestine, 1914–1918: British-Jewish-Arab Relations,* New York: Schocken, 1973.

Fromkin, David, *A Peace to End All Peace: The Fall of the Ottoman Empire and the Creation of the Modern Middle East,* New York: Avon, 1989.

Gabriel, Richard A., *Operation Peace for Galilee,* New York: Hill and Wang, 1984.

Garfinkle, Adam, *Israel and Jordan in the Shadow of War: Functional Ties and Futile Diplomacy in a Small Place,* New York: St. Martin's, 1992.

Gelber, Yoav, *Jewish-Transjordanian Relations, 1921–1948,* London: Frank Cass, 1997.

Gilmour, David, *Lebanon: The Fractured Country,* New York: St. Martin's, 1984.

Gordon, David C., *The Republic of Lebanon: Nation in Jeopardy,* Boulder, CO: Westview Press, 1983.

Gromoll, Robert H., *The May 17 Accord: Studies of Diplomacy and Negotiations on Troop Withdrawals from Lebanon,* Pittsburgh: Graduate School of Public and International Affairs, Pew Charitable Trusts, 1987.

Haass, Richard N., *Conflicts Unending: The United States and Regional Disputes,* New Haven and London: Yale University Press, 1990.

Haim, Sylvia G., ed., *Arab Nationalism: An Anthology,* Berkeley and Los Angeles: University of California Press, 1962.

Haley, P. Edward, and Lewis W. Snider, eds., *Lebanon in Crisis,* New York: Syracuse University Press, 1979.

Hareven, Shulamith, *The Vocabulary of Peace: Life, Culture and Politics in the Middle East,* San Francisco: Mercury House, 1995.

Harkabi, Yehoshafat, *Israel's Fateful Hour,* New York: Harper and Row, 1988.

———, *The Palestinian Covenant and Its Meaning,* London: Valentine Mitchell, 1979.

Harris, William, *Faces of Lebanon: Sects, Wars and Global Extensions,* Princeton: Marcus Wiener, 1997.

Heikal, Mohamed, *Cutting the Lion's Tail: Suez through Egyptian Eyes,* London: Deutsch, 1957.

———, *The Road to Ramadan,* New York: Ballantine Books, 1975.

———, *Secret Channels: The Inside Story of Arab-Israeli Peace Negotiations,* London: HarperCollins, 1996.

Hertzberg, Arthur, ed., *The Zionist Idea: A Historical Analysis and Reader,* New York: Meridian, 1960 (Atheneum reprint, 1982).

Herzog, Chaim, *The Arab-Israeli Wars,* New York: Random House, 1982.

———, *The War of Atonement: October 1973,* Boston: Little, Brown, 1975.

Hof, Frederic C., *Galilee Divided: The Israel-Lebanon Frontier, 1916–1984,* Boulder, CO: Westview Press, 1985.

Hollis, Rosemary, and Nadim Shehadi, eds., *Lebanon on Hold: Implications for Middle East Peace,* London: Royal Institute of International Affairs, 1996.

Horowitz, David, ed. and the Jerusalem Report staff, *Shalom Friend: The Life and Legacy of Yitzhak Rabin,* New York: New Market Press, 1996.

Hunter, F. Robert, *The Palestinian Uprising: A War by Other Means,* 2nd ed., Berkeley: University of California Press, 1993.

Hurewitz, J. C., *The Struggle for Palestine,* New York: Norton, 1950.

Kass, Ilana, and Bard O'Neill, *The Deadly Embrace: The Impact of Israeli and Palestin-*

ian Rejectionism on the Peace Process, Lanham, MD: University Press of America, 1997.

Kedourie, Elie, *In the Anglo-Arab Labyrinth, The McMahon-Husayn Correspondence and Its Interpretations, 1914–1939,* Cambridge: Cambridge University Press, 1976.

Khalidi, Rashid, *Under Siege: PLO Decisionmaking during the 1982 War,* New York: Columbia University Press, 1986.

Khalidi, Rashid, et al., eds., *The Origins of Arab Nationalism,* New York: Columbia University Press, 1993.

Khalidi, Walid, *Conflict and Violence in Lebanon: Confrontation in the Middle East,* Cambridge: Center for International Studies, Harvard University, 1979.

———, ed., *From Haven to Conquest: Readings in Zionism and the Palestine Problem until 1948,* Washington, DC: Institute for Palestine Studies, 1971 (reprint 1987).

Khouri, Fred J., *The Arab-Israeli Dilemma,* 3rd ed., Syracuse: Syracuse University Press, 1985.

Kimche, David, *The Last Option: After Nasser, Arafat, and Saddam Hussein, The Quest for Peace in the Middle East,* New York: Scribner's Sons, 1991.

Kimmerling, Baruch, and Joel S. Migdal, *Palestinians: The Making of a People,* New York: Free Press, 1993.

Klieman, Aharon S., *Israel and the World after 40 Years,* Washington, DC: Pergamon-Brassey's International Defense Publishers, 1990.

———, *Israel, Jordan, Palestine: The Search for a Durable Peace,* Beverly Hills, CA: Sage Publications [The Washington Papers/83, published for the Center for Strategic and International Studies, Georgetown University], 1981.

———, *Statecraft in the Dark: Israel's Practice of Quiet Diplomacy,* Jerusalem: Jerusalem Post and Boulder, CO: Westview Press, for Jaffee Center for Strategic Studies, Tel Aviv University, 1988.

Kyle, Keith, *Suez 1956,* New York: St. Martin's, 1991.

Laqueur, Walter, *A History of Zionism,* New York: Schocken, 1972.

———, *Confrontation: The Middle East and World Politics,* New York: Quadrangle Books, 1974.

Legum, Colin, Haim Shaked, and Daniel Dishon, eds., *Middle East Contemporary Survey,* vol. VII, 1982–1983, New York and London: Holmes and Meier [Shiloah Center for Middle East and North African Studies, Tel Aviv University], 1985.

Lesch, Ann Mosely, *Arab Politics in Palestine, 1917–1939: The Frustration of a National Movement,* Ithaca and London: Cornell University Press, 1979.

Louis, Wm. Roger, and Roger Owen, eds., *Suez 1956: The Crisis and Its Consequences,* Oxford: Oxford Universityi Press, 1989.

Louis, Wm. Roger, and Robert W. Stookey, eds., *The End of the Palestine Mandate,* Austin: University of Texas Press, 1986.

Lustick, Ian, *For the Land and the Lord: Jewish Fundamentalism in Israel,* New York: Council on Foreign Relations, 1988.

———, *Israel and Jordan: The Implications of an Adversarial Partnership,* Berkeley: Institute of International Studies, University of California, 1978.

Mahler, Gregory S., ed., *Israel after Begin,* Albany: State University of New York Press, 1990.

Makovsky, David, *Making Peace with the PLO: The Rabin Government's Road to the Oslo Accord,* Boulder, CO: Westview Press, 1996.

Mandel, Neville J., *The Arabs and Zionism before World War I,* Berkeley: University of California Press, 1976.

Mattar, Philip, *The Mufti of Jerusalem: al-Hajj Amin al-Husayni and the Palestinian National Movement,* New York: Columbia University Press, 1988 [rev. ed. 1992].

McDermott, Anthony, and Kjell Skjelsbaek, eds., *The Mutlinational Force in Beirut, 1982–1984,* Miami: Florida International University Press, 1991.

McDowall, David, *The Palestinians: The Road to Nationhood,* Concord: Paul, 1995.

Melman, Yossi, and Dan Raviv, *Beyond the Uprising: Israelis, Jordanians, and Palestinians,* New York: Greenwood Press, 1989.

Miller, Aaron David, *The PLO and the Politics of Survival,* New York: Praeger [The Washington Papers/99, published for the Center for Strategic and International Studies, Georgetown University], 1983.

Morris, Benny, *The Birth of the Palestinian Refugee Problem, 1947–1949,* London: Cambridge University Press, 1987.

Nasrallah, Fida, *Prospects for Lebanon: The Questions of South Lebanon,* London: Centre for Lebanese Studies, 1992.

Nevo, Joseph, *King Abdallah and Palestine: A Territorial Ambition,* New York: St. Martin's, 1997.

Norton, Augustus Richard, *Amal and the Shi'a: Struggle for the Soul of Lebanon,* Austin: University of Texas, 1987.

Oren, Michael B., *Origins of the Second Arab-Israel War: Egypt, Israel and the Great Powers, 1952–56,* London: Frank Cass, 1992.

Pappé, Ilan, *The Making of the Arab-Israeli Conflict, 1947–1951,* London and New York: I. B. Tauris, 1992.

Parker, Richard B., *The Politics of Miscalculation in the Middle East,* Bloomington: Indiana University Press, 1993.

———, *The Six Day War: A Retrospective,* Gainesville: University Presses of Florida, 1996.

Peters, Joel, *Pathways to Peace: The Multilateral Arab-Israeli Peace Talks,* Washington, DC: The Brookings Institution, 1996.

Porath, Yehoshua, *The Emergence of the Palestinian Arab National Movement, 1918–1929,* London: Frank Cass, 1974.

———, *The Palestinian Arab National Movement, 1929–1939: From Riots to Rebellion,* London: Frank Cass, 1977.

Quandt, William B., *Decade of Decisions: American Policy toward the Arab-Israeli Conflict, 1967–1976,* Berkeley: University of California Press, 1977.

———, ed., *The Middle East: Ten Years after Camp David,* Washington, DC: The Brookings Institution, 1988.

———, *Peace Process: American Diplomacy and the Arab-Israeli Conflict since 1967,* Washington, DC: The Brookings Institution, 1993.

Quandt, William B., Fuad Jabber, and Ann Mosely Lesch, *The Politics of Palestinian Nationalism,* Berkeley: University of California Press, 1973.

Rabinovich, Itamar, *The Road Not Taken: Early Arab-Israeli Negotiations,* New York and Oxford: Oxford University Press, 1991.

———, *The War for Lebanon, 1970–1983,* Ithaca: Cornell University Press, 1984.

Randal, Jonathan C., *Going All the Way: Christian Warlords, Israeli Adventurers and the War in Lebanon,* New York: Vintage Books, 1983.

Rubin, Barry, *The Arab States and the Palestine Conflict,* Syracuse: Syracuse University Press, 1981.

Rubin, Barry, and Laura Blum, *The May 1983 Agreement over Lebanon,* Baltimore: Foreign Policy Institute, Johns Hopkins University, Pew Charitable Trusts, 1988.

Rubin, Barry, Joseph Ginat, and Moshe Ma'oz, eds., *From War to Peace: Arab-Israel Relations, 1973–1993,* New York: New York University Press, 1995.

Rubin, Jeffrey Z., ed., *Dynamics of Third Party Intervention,* New York: Praeger, 1981.

Rubinstein, Alvin Z., ed., *The Arab-Israeli Conflict: Perspectives,* 2nd ed., New York: Praeger, 1991.

Sachar, Howard M., *A History of Israel from the Rise of Zionism to Our Time,* 2nd ed., New York: Knopf, 1996.

Said, Edward, *Peace and Its Discontents: Essays on Palestine in the Middle East Peace Process,* preface by Christopher Hitchens, New York: Vintage, 1995.

Salibi, Kamal, *A House of Many Mansions: The History of Lebanon Reconsidered,* Berkeley: University of California Press, 1988.

Sanders, Ronald, *The High Walls of Jerusalem: A History of the Balfour Declaration and the Birth of the British Mandate for Palestine,* New York: Holt, Rinehart and Winston, 1983.

Satloff, Robert B., *From Abdullah to Hussein: Jordan in Transition,* New York and Oxford: Oxford University Press, 1994.

Saunders, Harold H., *The Other Walls: The Arab-Israeli Peace Process in a Global Perspective,* rev. ed., Princeton: Princeton University Press, 1991.

Schiff, Ze'ev, and Ehud Ya'ari, *Intifada: The Palestinian Uprising—Israel's Third Front,* New York: Simon and Schuster, 1990.

———, *Israel's Lebanon War,* New York: Simon and Schuster, 1984.

Seale, Patrick, *Asad: The Struggle for the Middle East,* Berkeley: University of California Press, 1989.

Sheehan, E. R. F., *The Arabs, Israelis and Kissinger: A Secret History of American Diplomacy in the Middle East,* New York: Reader's Digest Press, 1976.

Shlaim, Avi, *Collusion across the Jordan: King Abdullah, the Zionist Movement, and the Partition of Palestine,* Oxford: Clarendon Press, 1988.

Sicker, Martin, *Between Hashemites and Zionists: The Struggle for Palestine, 1908–1988,* New York and London: Holmes and Meier, 1989.

Spiegel, Steven L., ed., *The Arab-Israeli Search for Peace,* Boulder, CO, and London: Lynne Rienner, 1992.

———, *The Other Arab-Israeli Conflict: Making America's Middle East Policy, from Truman to Reagan,* Chicago: University of Chicago Press, 1985.

Sprinzak, Ehud, *The Ascendance of Israel's Radical Right,* New York: Oxford University Press, 1991.

Stein, Janice Gross, ed., *Getting to the Table: The Processes of International Prenegotiation,* Baltimore: Johns Hopkins University Press, 1989.

Stein, Kenneth W., *The Land Question in Palestine, 1917–1939,* Chapel Hill: University of North Carolina Press, 1984.

Stein, Kenneth W., and Samuel W. Lewis (with Sheryl J. Brown), *Making Peace among Arabs and Israelis: Lessons from Fifty Years of Negotiating Experience,* Washington, DC: United States Institute of Peace, October 1991.

Stein, Leonard, *The Balfour Declaration,* London: Vallentine Mitchell, 1961.

Stoessinger, John G., *Why Nations Go to War,* New York: St. Martin's, 1978.

Suleiman, Michael W., ed., *US Policy on Palestine from Wilson to Clinton,* Normal, IL: Association of Arab-American University Graduates, Inc. (AAUG), 1995.

Sykes, Christopher, *Crossroads to Israel, 1917–1948,* Bloomington: Indiana University Press, 1965.

Tanter, Raymond, *Who's at the Helm? Lessons of Lebanon,* Boulder, CO: Westview Press, 1990.
Telhami, Shibley, *Power and Leadership in International Bargaining: The Path to the Camp David Accords,* New York and Oxford: Columbia University Press, 1990.
Tessler, Mark, *A History of the Israeli-Palestinian Conflict,* Bloomington: Indiana University Press, 1994.
Touval, Saadia, *The Peace Brokers: Mediators in the Arab-Israeli Conflict, 1948–1979,* Princeton: Princeton University Press, 1982.
Vital, David, *The Origins of Zionism,* Oxford: Oxford University Press, 1975.
———, *Zionism: The Crucial Phase,* Oxford: Oxford University Press, 1987.
———, *Zionism: The Formative Years,* Oxford: Oxford University Press, 1982.
Yaniv, Avner, *Dilemmas of Security: Politics, Strategy, and the Israeli Experience in Lebanon,* Oxford: Oxford University Press, 1987.
Young, Ronald J., *Missed Opportunities for Peace: US Middle East Policy: 1981–1986,* Philadelphia: American Friends Service Committee, 1987.

SECONDARY SOURCES—ARTICLES

Abukhalil, As'as, "Determinants and Characteristics of Syrian Policy in Lebanon," in *Peace for Lebanon? From War to Reconstruction,* ed. Deirdre Collings, Boulder, CO: Lynne Rienner, 1994, 123–36.
Abu-Amr, Ziad, "Hamas: A Historical and Political Background," *JPS* 22:4 (Summer 1993), 5–19.
———, "Palestinian-Israeli Negotiations: A Palestinian Perspective," in *The Arab-Israeli Search for Peace,* ed. Steven L. Spiegel, Boulder, CO, and London: Lynne Rienner, 1992, 27–36.
Alpher, Joseph, "From Wagner to Arafat: Demonology and Survival," *Jerusalem Quarterly* 33 (Fall 1984), 3–13.
———, "Why Israel Should Recognize the PLO and Invite Arafat to Jerusalem," *Moment* (July-August 1988), 10–17.
Amir, Yehuda, "Interpersonal Contact between Arabs and Israelis," *Jerusalem Quarterly* 13 (Fall 1979), 3–17.
Aronoff, Myron J., and Yael S. Aronoff, "A Cultural Approach to Explaining Domestic Influences on Current Israeli Foreign Policy: The Peace Negotiations," *Brown Journal of World Affairs* 3:2 (Summer-Fall 1996), 83–101.
Aruri, Naseer H., "Palestine—How to Redress the Wrongs of Oslo?" *Middle East International* no. 536, 25 October 1996, 18–19.
Avnery, Uri, "Should the Palestinians Change the Charter?" *New Outlook* 23:2 (March 1980), 19–23; and 23:3 (April 1980), 26–31.
Bannerman, M. Graeme, "Arabs and Israelis: Slow Walk toward Peace," *Foreign Affairs* 72:1 (1992–93), 142–57.
Bruck, Connie, "The Wounds of Peace," *New Yorker,* 14 October 1996, 64–91.
Bulliet, Richard W., "The Future of the Islamic Movement: The Israeli-PLO Accord," *Foreign Affairs* 72:5 (November-December 1993), 38–44.
Cahnman, Sam, "Inching toward Peace," *JR,* 28 January 1993, 30–31.
Caplan, Neil, "Faisal Ibn Husain and the Zionists: A Re-examination with Documents," *International History Review* 5:4 (November 1983), 561–614.
———, "Negotiation and the Arab-Israeli Conflict," *Jerusalem Quarterly* 6 (Winter 1978), 3–19.

———, "A Tale of Two Cities: The Rhodes and Lausanne Conferences, 1949," *JPS* 21:3 (Spring 1992), 5–34.

Caplan, Neil, and Ian Black, "Israel and Lebanon: Origins of a Relationship," *Jerusalem Quarterly* 27 (Spring 1983), 48–58.

Carmon, Yigal, "The Story behind the Handshake," *Commentary* (March 1994), 25–29.

Dajani, Burhan, "The September 1993 Israeli-PLO Documents: A Textual Analysis," *JPS* 23:3 (Spring 1994), 5–23.

Deshen, Shlomo, "Applied Anthropology in International Conflict Resolution: The Case of the Israeli Debate on Middle Eastern Peace Settlement Proposals," *Human Organization* 51:2 (Summer 1992), 180–84.

Dishon, Daniel, "Sadat's Arab Adversaries," *Jerusalem Quarterly* 8 (Summer 1978), 3–15.

Eban, Abba, "Camp David: The Unfinished Business," *Foreign Affairs* 57 (Winter 1978–79), 343–54.

———, "Diplomatic Perspectives: Opening Remarks," in *A Two-State Solution in the Middle East: Prospects and Possibilities,* eds. Baruch Fischhoff, Kenneth Kotovsky, Hussain Tuma, and Jacobo Bielak, Pittsburgh: Carnegie Mellon University Press, 1993, 5–13.

Eisenberg, Laura Zittrain, "Desperate Diplomacy: The Zionist-Maronite Treaty of 1946," *Studies in Zionism* 13:2 (Autumn 1992), 147–63.

———, "History Revisited or Revamped? The Roots of Contemporary Israeli Interests in Lebanon," lecture delivered at the Moshe Dayan Center for Middle Eastern and African Studies, Tel Aviv University, 20 October 1993.

———, "Israel's South Lebanon Imbroglio," *Middle East Quarterly* 4:2 (June 1997), 60–69.

———, "Passive Belligerency: Israel and the 1991 Gulf War," *Journal of Strategic Studies* 15:3 (September 1992), 304–29.

Elon, Amos, "Israel and the End of Zionism," *New York Review of Books,* 19 December 1996, 22–30.

———, "The Thinking Men's War," *New York Times Magazine,* 11 May 1997, 40–43.

Elsarraj, Eyad, "Shaping a Culture of Peace," *Palestine-Israel Journal of Politics, Economics and Culture* I:4 (Autumn 1994), 59–61.

Fellman, Gordon, "The Struggle toward a Peace Culture: Rabin's Career, the Assassination, and Paradigm Shift," paper presented at the Association for Israel Studies Annual Conference, Boston, 1–3 June 1996.

Fisher, Roger, "Playing the Wrong Game," in *Dynamics of Third Party Intervention,* ed. Jeffrey Z. Rubin, New York: Praeger, 1981, 95–121.

Gazit, Shlomo, "After the Gulf War: The Arab World and the Peace Process," in *The Arab-Israeli Search for Peace,* ed. Steven L. Spiegel, Boulder, CO, and London: Lynne Rienner, 1992, 17–36.

Gelber, Yoav, "Antecedents of the Jewish-Druze Alliance in Palestine," *Middle Eastern Studies* 28:2 (April 1992), 352–73.

Genkin, Stephanie, "Not Quite Normal," *JR,* 7 September 1995, 22–25.

Gerges, Fawaz A., "Egyptian-Israeli Relations Turn Sour," *Foreign Affairs* 74:3 (May-June 1995), 69–78.

Golan, Galia, "Arab-Israeli Peace Negotiations: An Israeli View," in *The Arab-Israeli Search for Peace,* ed. Steven L. Spiegel, Boulder, CO, and London: Lynne Rienner, 1992, 37–47.

Goodman, Hirsh, "The Mirage of Peace," *JR,* 5 October 1995, 72.
———. "Oslo II: Can It Work?" *JR,* 19 October 1995, 58.
Hareven, Alouph, "Can We Learn to Live Together?" *Jerusalem Quarterly* 14 (Winter 1980), 8–17.
Heller, Mark A., "The Israeli-Palestinian Accord: An Israeli View," *Current History* 93:580 (February 1994), 56–61.
———, "Rabin and Arafat: Alone, Together," *Current History* 94:591 (January 1995), 28–32.
Herzog, Chaim, "Divide the Land, Not the People," *JR,* 10 August 1995, 60.
Horowitz, David, "Beyond the Law," *JR,* 21 September 1995, 26.
Hudson, Michael, "The Clinton Administration and the Middle East: Squandering the Inheritance?" *Current History* 93:580 (February 1994), 49–54.
———, "Lebanon's US Connection in the New World Order," in *Peace for Lebanon? From War to Reconstruction,* ed. Deirdre Collings, Boulder, CO: Lynne Rienner, 1994, 137–48.
———, "The United States' Involvement in Lebanon," in *Toward a Viable Lebanon,* ed. Halim Barakat, Washington, DC: Georgetown University, Center for Contemporary Arab Studies, 1988, 210–31.
Inbar, Efraim, "Great Power Mediation: The USA and the May 1983 Israeli-Lebanese Agreement," *Journal of Peace Research* 28:1 (1 February 1991), 71–84.
Karsh, Efraim, "Peace Not Love: Toward a Comprehensive Arab-Israeli Settlement," *Washington Quarterly* 17:2 (Spring 1994), 143–56.
Keren, Michael, "Israeli Professionals and the Peace Process," *Israel Affairs* 1:1 (Autumn 1994), 149–63.
Khalidi, Muhammad Ali, "A First Visit to Palestine," *JPS* 24:3 (Spring 1995), 74–80.
Khalidi, Rashid, "A Palestinian View of the Accord with Israel," *Current History* 93:580 (February 1994), 62–66.
———, "Problems of Foreign Intervention in Lebanon," *American Arab Affairs* 7 (Winter 1983–84), 24–29.
Klieman, Aharon, "Approaching the Finish Line: The United States in Post-Oslo Peace Making," Ramat Gan: Begin-Sadat Center for Strategic Studies, Bar-Ilan University, 1995 (Security and Policy Studies, No. 22), June 1995.
———, "New Directions in Israel's Foreign Policy," *Israel Affairs* 1:1 (Autumn 1994), 96–117.
Lesch, Ann M., "The Reagan Administration's Policy toward the Palestinians," in *US Policy on Palestine from Wilson to Clinton,* ed. Michael W. Suleiman, Normal, IL: AAUG Press, 1995, 175–93.
Lewis, Samuel W., "Israel: The Peres Era and Its Legacy," *Foreign Affairs* 65:3 (1987), 597–602.
———, "The United States and Israel: Constancy and Change," in *The Middle East: Ten Years after Camp David,* ed. William B. Quandt, Washington, DC: The Brookings Institution, 1988, 217–57.
Mahmood, Zahid, "Sadat and Camp David Reappraised," *JPS* 15:1 (Autumn 1985), 62–87.
Mansour, Camille, "The Palestinian-Israeli Peace Negotiations: An Overview and Assessment," *JPS* 22:3 (Spring 1993), 5–31.
Morris, Benny, "Israel and the Lebanese Phalange: The Birth of a Relationship, 1948–1951." *Studies in Zionism* 5:1 (Spring 1984), 125–44.

———, "The Phalange Connection," *Jerusalem Post Magazine*, 1 July 1983, 7–8.

Muslih, Muhammad, "Arafat's Dilemma," *Current History* 94:591 (January 1995), 23–27.

———, "Towards Coexistence: An Analysis of the Resolutions of the Palestine National Council," *JPS* 19:4 (Summer 1990), 3–29; reprinted in *From War to Peace: Arab-Israeli Relations 1973–1993*, eds. Barry Rubin, Joseph Ginat, and Moshe Ma'oz, New York: New York University Press, 1995, 265–91.

Mylroie, Laurie, "Israel in the Middle East," in *Israel after Begin*, ed. Gregory S. Mahler, Albany: State University of New York Press, 1990, 137–54.

Neff, Donald, "Nixon's Middle East Policy: From Balance to Bias," in *US Policy on Palestine from Wilson to Clinton*, ed. Michael W. Suleiman, Normal, IL: AAUG Press, 1995, 133–62.

Norton, Augustus Richard, "Lebanon after Ta'if: Is the Civil War Over?" *Middle East Journal* 45 (Summer 1991), 457–73.

Oren, Michael, "Secret Egypt-Israel Peace Initiatives Prior to the Suez Campaign," *Middle Eastern Studies* 26:3 (July 1990), 351–70.

Pappé, Ilan, "Moshe Sharett, David Ben-Gurion and the 'Palestine Option,' 1948–1956," *Studies in Zionism* 7:1 (Spring 1986), 77–96.

Peres, Shimon, "A Strategy for Peace in the Middle East," *Foreign Affairs* 58 (Summer 1980), 887–901.

"Psychological Dimensions of the Conflict," *Palestine-Israel Journal of Politics, Economics and Culture* I:4 (Autumn 1994).

Quandt, William B., "Reagan's Lebanon Policy: Trial and Error," *Middle East Journal* 38 (Spring 1984), 237–54.

———, "US Policy toward the Arab-Israeli Conflict," in *The Middle East: Ten Years after Camp David*, ed. William B. Quandt, Washington, DC: The Brookings Institution, 1988, 357–86.

Rabinovich, Itamar, "Seven Wars and One Peace Treaty," in Alvin Z. Rubinstein, ed., *The Arab-Israeli Conflict: Perspectives*, 2nd ed., New York: Praeger, 1991, 34–58.

Rafael, Gideon, "UN Resolution 242: A Common Denominator," in *The Israel-Arab Reader: A Documentary History of the Middle East Conflict*, eds. Walter Laqueur and Barry Rubin, New York: Penguin, 1995, 197–212.

Rothman, Jay, "Negotiation as Consolidation: Prenegotiation in the Israeli-Palestinian Conflict," *Jerusalem Journal of International Relations* 13:1 (1991), 22–43.

Rubenberg, Cheryl A., "The Bush Administration and the Palestinians: A Reassessment," in *US Policy on Palestine from Wilson to Clinton*, ed. Michael W. Suleiman, Normal, IL: AAUG Press, 1995, 195–221.

Sahliyeh, Emile, "Jordan and the Palestinians," in *The Middle East: Ten Years after Camp David*, ed. William B. Quandt, Washington, DC: The Brookings Institution, 1988, 279–318.

Said, Edward W., "The Mirage of Peace," *Nation*, 16 October 1995, 413–20.

———, "Projecting Jerusalem," *JPS* 25:1 (Autumn 1995), 5–14.

Saunders, Harold H., "Reconstituting the Arab-Israeli Peace Process," in *The Middle East: Ten Years after Camp David*, ed. William B. Quandt, Washington, DC: The Brookings Institution, 1988, 413–41.

———, "We Need a Larger Theory of Negotiation: The Importance of Pre-Negotiation Phases," *Negotiation Journal* 1:3 (1985), 249–62.

Schiff, Ze'ev, "The Green Light," *Foreign Policy* 50 (Spring 1983), 73–85.

———, "Lebanon: Motivations and Interests in Israel's Policy," *Middle East Journal* 38:2 (Spring 1984), 220–27.

Schueftan, Dan, "Jordan's 'Israeli Option,'" in *Jordan in the Middle East: The Making of a Pivotal State,* eds. Joseph Nevo and Ilan Pappé, London: Frank Cass, 1994, 254–82.

———, "Jordan's Motivation for a Settlement with Israel," *Jerusalem Quarterly* 44 (Fall 1987), 79–120.

Sela, Avraham, "Transjordan, Israel and the 1948 War: Myth, Historiography and Reality," *Middle Eastern Studies* 28:4 (October 1992), 623–88.

Shaath, Nabeel, "Diplomatic Perspectives: Opening Remarks," in *A Two-State Solution in the Middle East: Prospects and Possibilities,* eds. Baruch Fischhoff, Kenneth Kotovsky, Hussain Tuma, and Jacobo Bielak, Pittsburgh: Carnegie Mellon University Press, 1993, 14–19.

Shaltiel, Eli, "David Ben-Gurion on Partition," *Jerusalem Quarterly* 10 (Winter 1979), 38–59.

Shamir, Shimon, "The Collapse of Project Alpha," in *Suez 1956: The Crisis and Its Consequences,* eds. Wm. Roger Louis and Roger Owen, Oxford: Clarendon Press, 1989, 73–100.

———, "Israeli Views of Egypt and the Peace Process: The Duality of Vision," in *The Middle East: Ten Years after Camp David,* ed. William B. Quandt, Washington, DC: The Brookings Institution, 1988, 187–216.

Shapira, Anita, "The Option on Ghaur al-Kibd: Contacts between Emir Abdallah and the Zionist Executive, 1932–1935," *Studies in Zionism* 2 (Autumn 1980), 239–83.

Shlaim, Avi, "The Oslo Accord," *JPS* 23:3 (Spring 1994), 24–40.

———, "Prelude to the Accord: Likud, Labour, and the Palestinians," *JPS* 23:2 (Winter 1994), 5–19.

Smith, Charles D., "The Invention of a Tradition: The Question of Arab Acceptance of the Zionist Right to Palestine during World War I," *JPS* 22:2 (Winter 1993), 48–61.

Spiegel, Steven L., and David J. Pervin, "Introduction: The Search for Arab-Israeli Peace after the Cold War," in *The Arab-Israeli Search for Peace,* ed. Steven L. Spiegel, Boulder, CO, and London: Lynne Rienner, 1992, 1–13.

Stein, Janice Gross, "Structure, Tactics and Strategies of Mediation: Kissinger and Carter in the Middle East," *Negotiation Journal* 1:4 (October 1985), 331–47.

Stork, Joe, "The Clinton Administration and the Palestine Question," in *US Policy on Palestine from Wilson to Clinton,* ed. Michael W. Suleiman, Normal, IL: AAUG Press, 1995, 223–32.

Susser, Asher, "Jordan, the PLO, and the Palestine Question," in *Jordan in the Middle East: The Making of a Pivotal State,* eds. Joseph Nevo and Ilan Pappé, London: Frank Cass, 1994.

Susser, Leslie, "What Next?!" *JR,* 7 October 1993, 18.

Tamari, Salim, "In League with Zion: Israel's Search for a Native Pillar," *JPS* 12:4 (Summer 1983), 41–56.

Telhami, Shibley, "Israeli Foreign Policy after the Gulf War," in *The Arab-Israeli Search for Peace,* ed. Steven L. Spiegel, Boulder, CO, and London: Lynne Rienner, 1992, 49–61.

Terry, Janice J., "The Carter Administration and the Palestinians," in *US Policy on Palestine from Wilson to Clinton,* ed. Michael W. Suleiman, Normal, IL: AAUG Press, 1995, 163–74.

Yorke, Valerie, "Domestic Politics and the Prospects for an Arab-Israeli Peace," *JPS* 17:4 (Summer 1988), 17–20.

Zak, Moshe, "An International Conference on the Middle East," *Jerusalem Quarterly* 37 (1986), 14–28.

———, "A Survey of Israel's Contacts with Jordan," in *Israel in the Middle East: Documents and Readings on Society, Politics and Foreign Relations, 1948–Present,* eds. Itamar Rabinovich and Jehuda Reinharz, New York and Oxford: Oxford University Press, 1984, 337–42.

———, "Talking to Hussein," *JPI,* w/e 4 May 1985, pp. 10–12 [reprinted from the *Washington Quarterly,* winter 1985].

Zartman, I. William, "The Negotiation Process in the Middle East," in *The Arab-Israeli Search for Peace,* ed. Steven L. Spiegel, Boulder, CO, and London: Lynne Rienner, 1992, 63–70.

Zunes, Stephen, "The Israeli-Jordanian Agreement: Peace or Pax Americana?" *Middle East Policy* 3:4 (April 1995), 57–68.

INDEX

Laura Zittrain Eisenberg
is Visiting Associate Professor in the History Department at Carnegie Mellon University. She is the author of *My Enemy's Enemy: Lebanon in the Early Zionist Imagination, 1900–1948.*

Neil Caplan
teaches in the Humanities Department at Vanier College in Montreal, Canada. His publications include *Palestine Jewry and the Arab Question, 1917–1925, The Lausanne Conference, 1949: A Case Study in Middle East Peacemaking,* and a multi-volume documentary history of the Arab-Israeli conflict, *Futile Diplomacy.*